History Mal...

20th Century Ireland

- ❏ Carson
- ❏ Craig
- ❏ Griffith
- ☑ Collins
- ❏ Cosgrave
- ❏ De Valera
- ❏ Brookeborough
- ❏ O'Neill
- ❏ Lemass
- ❏ MacBride

Author: A. M. Kehoe

 Mentor Publications Ltd., Zion Court, Rathgar, Dublin 6.

© Copyright Mentor Publications Ltd. 1989
All rights reserved.

ISBN 0 947548 03 3

Publishers: Mentor Publications Ltd. Zion Court, Rathgar,
Dublin 6, Republic of Ireland.

History Makers

of

20th Century Ireland

Contents

		Page
1.	Carson	5
2.	Craig	20
3.	Griffith	40
4.	Collins	54
5.	Cosgrave	69
6.	De Valera	96
7.	Brookeborough	135
8.	O'Neill	150
9.	Lemass	162
10.	MacBride	181

Preface

This collection of Irish biographies is intended as a companion volume to the *History Makers of 20th Century Europe.* It answers a need for concise but comprehensive biographical material on Irish political leaders, both North and South. The biographies of Carson, Craig, Griffith and Collins, in particular, provide a comprehensive survey of the events leading to the foundation of both states.

A complete history of the Northern Ireland State is provided through the biographies of Craig, Brookeborough and O'Neill. The history of the Irish State, since its foundation until the mid 1960's, unfolds through the biographies of Cosgrave, de Valera, MacBride and Lemass.

This collection of Irish biographies will assist in the development of a fuller understanding of events, both North and South, and of the political figures behind those events. It will be particularly useful to Leaving Certificate students who require a comprehensive and critical appraisal of developments and personalities within both states of Ireland until 1966.

A. M. Kehoe
Author

1. Carson

Early Influences

Carson, "the uncrowned King of Ulster" at the height of the Ulster Unionist campaign against Home Rule 1912 - 1914, was born Edward Carson in Dublin on 9th February 1854. Upon completion of an Arts degree in Trinity College Dublin, Carson entered upon a career in law which was to span more than half a century. At school and college Carson showed little promise of the brilliance which was to mark his long distinguished career both at the Irish and the English bar and which was to make him one of the outstanding advocates of the period.

Carson joined the Irish Bar in 1877 and first came to public notice in 1881. Gladstone's Second Land Act of 1881, setting up a Land Commission to adjudicate on "fair rents", resulted in half a million "fair rent" cases being taken by young barristers like Carson. Carson's successful advocacy on behalf of tenants led to his being asked by local nationalists and Land League enthusiasts in Waterford to stand for parliament as a "no rent" candidate. Carson declined, but it is worth noting that Carson was considered a radical. His approval of the Liberal government's disestablishment of the Church of Ireland in 1869 almost placed him in the Liberal camp. Gladstone's espousal of Home Rule in 1886 as the "final solution" to the Irish question ended Carson's affiliations with the Liberal Party. The continuing union of Britain and Ireland was to be the "guiding star" of his political life. In the general election in July 1886 which followed the defeat of the First Home Rule Bill, Carson had voted for Liberal Unionists (93 Liberals had voted against the First Home Rule Bill and, under the leadership of Joseph Chamberlain, became Liberal Unionists prepared to support the Conservatives and to keep them in power for an almost unbroken twenty years.) Carson welcomed the return of the Conservatives then firmly committed to the Unionist cause and welcomed Conservative Prime Minister Lord Salisbury's promise to give Ireland "twenty years of resolute government".

Edward Carson (1854 - 1935)

"Coercion Carson"

Among Lord Salisbury's team of officials to provide "resolute government" in Ireland was Chief Secretary Balfour. He soon became known as "Bloody" Balfour for his rigorous enforcement of a new Crimes Act (1887) which allowed for the imposition of martial law in areas of agrarian unrest and which imposed mandatory prison sentences for boycotting or resisting eviction. The Crimes Act was designed to suppress the Plan of Campaign, urged by Nationalist MPs Dillon and O'Brien as a new phase of the land war of the 1880's. Dillon and O'Brien were among 24 Irish MPs to be arrested and tried under the Crimes Act.

The success of Balfour's Coercion policy depended upon the effectiveness of the prosecution of cases taken before the courts. Carson was chosen as Crown Prosecutor a few days after the Crimes Act became law. The first prosecution under the Crimes Act led to the Mitchelstown "massacre" in 1887 when an attempt to arraign MPs Dillon and O'Brien at Mitchelstown District Court in September 1887 resulted in riots and in the deaths of three supporters of the Plan of Campaign. Undeterred, Carson, who quickly earned the nicknames "Coercion Carson" and "Castle bloodhound", had warrants issued for the arrest and remand in custody of the members of parliament, Dillon and O'Brien. His reputation as a successful Crown Prosecutor, enabled him, to become, in 1889 at thirty-five years, the youngest QC in the country. Carson had reached the top of the legal profession in Ireland. Balfour was to say later "I made Carson and he made me." In July 1892 Carson joined the government as Solicitor-General for Ireland. In the same month he embarked on a political career when he stood for election as Liberal Unionist for Trinity College Dublin. Ironically, the election which brought Carson into parliament also returned the ageing Gladstone and the Liberals to power. The spectre of Home Rule loomed again.

Carson and Irish Unionism

Carson's maiden speech in Parliament was a scathing attack on the Liberal government's attempt to reverse Conservative government policy by repealing the most reprehensible provisions of the Crimes Act and by setting up an Evicted Tenants Commission to consider the claims of tenants evicted by landlords during the Plan of Campaign from 1886. Carson's speech spanning two parliamentary sessions was acclaimed even by Gladstone, the Liberal leader, as the best maiden speech he had ever heard. Carson, however, was unable to prevent the passage of the Second Home Rule bill by the Liberal-dominated House of Commons after more than 200 hours of heated parliamentary debate during the summer of 1893. The Unionists were not unduly dismayed. The increasingly vociferous Ulster Unionists added powerful economic arguments against Home Rule to the racial and religious arguments of Carson and the Irish Unionists. On 8th September 1893 the Second Home Rule bill was rejected by a Conservative dominated House of Lords by 419 votes to 41. Gladstone's resignation in 1894 and death in 1898 in his ninetieth year meant the postponement both of reform of the House of Lords and Home Rule until the Irish Parliamentary Party once again held the balance of power in the House of Commons following two general elections in 1910. Although Carson did not become leader of the Irish Unionist Party at Westminster until 1910, his maiden speech and his unflagging opposition to the Second Home Rule bill in 1893 marked him out as the Irish Unionist MPs most effective spokesman in Parliament.

In 1895 the Conservatives returned to power following a general election caused by the resignation of Gladstone's successor, anti-Home-Ruler Lord Rosebery, who, unlike Gladstone, could not rely upon the votes of the Irish Home Rule MPs. Thus the defeat of the second Home Rule bill ushered in another long period of Conservative Unionist rule. Carson may well have expected a government post in a

Conservative government of which Balfour was government Leader in the House of Commons. (Prime Minister Lord Salisbury's membership of the House of Lords prevented him from leading the government in the House of Commons). Carson's opposition to the Conservative policy of "killing home rule with kindness", in particular its attacks upon landlordism through the Balfour Land Act of 1891 and a further Conservative land act of 1896 which made land purchase an attractive possibility, ensured his exclusion from government. Between 1895 and 1900, when Carson was offered the post of Solicitor-General of England, Carson was one of the most outspoken of government critics. Carson's "rebellion" against government policy in Ireland during the 1890s foreshadowed his Unionist "rebellion" against British government policy from 1910. The leading "Tory rebel" of the 1890's became the leading Unionist "rebel" one decade later.

Exclusion from government enabled Carson to build a successful legal career in England. Carson joined the English Bar in 1893. Within one year he was a member of the senior Bar. Involvement in a series of sensational cases such as the Wilde libel case in 1895, which resulted in the imprisonment and disgrace of fellow Irishman Oscar Wilde, ensured Carson's meteoric rise to the top in the English legal profession. By 1900 Carson was one of the highest earners at the English bar and had achieved a number of legal firsts. In 1889, at thirty-five years, he was the youngest Irish QC. In 1894 he became the first Irish QC to become an English QC and in 1900 he became the first to have successively held the posts of Solicitor-General of Ireland and England. In the same year he received another honour when he was knighted and became Sir Edward Carson.

Carson and Ulster Unionism

Carson was therefore a leading figure in British public life and a leading member of the Conservative Party when he was asked to lead the Irish Unionist Party in 1910. J.C. Beckett, first Professor of Irish History at Queen's University Belfast, states that, even if there had been no "Ulster question", Carson would still have had an important place in the legal and political history of the early twentieth century. Ulster Unionism did not make Carson but Carson can be said to have made Ulster Unionism. Carson was described as "a new force" in politics after making his maiden speech in Parliament in 1893. Ulster Unionism dating from the First Home Rule campaign of 1886 was in fact the new force in British and Irish politics. Parliamentary reform, in particular the Secret Ballot Act of 1872 and the Parliamentary Reform Act of 1884 which gave the vote to householders and trebled the Irish electorate, rendered negligible the electoral influence of Irish Unionists outside the province of Ulster. In the 1885 general election, after which Parnell and 85 Home Rule MPs held the balance between Conservatives and Liberals and forced Gladstone's conversion to Home Rule, Unionists won only 18 of the 103 Irish seats at Westminster. Of those 18, sixteen were from Ulster. Between 1886 and 1914 only two Irish Unionist MPs, one of whom was Carson, were returned from Southern Ireland. Carson knew that the strongest expression of Unionism came from Ulster and that the fate of Irish Unionism lay with Ulster.

Ulster Unionists for their part were happy with Carson's oft-repeated commitment to Unionism. The Conservative government's "devolution" proposals of 1904-1905 were condemned by Unionists as Home Rule by instalments. Opposition was so forceful that Wyndham, Conservative Chief Secretary, was forced to resign although his Catholic Under-Secretary, McDonnell, survived and helped the succeeding Liberal administration to draw up a further equally unacceptable devolution scheme in the Irish Council Bill of 1907. The "devolution crisis" of 1904-1905 prompted Ulster Unionists, shocked by the Conservative government's treachery, to form an Ulster Unionist Council in March 1905 representative of local Unionist associations, the secret militant Protestant organisation, the Orange Order, and Unionist MPs. The Ulster Unionist Council noted with satisfaction Carson's resignation from the post of Chief Secretary offered to him by Conservative P.M. Balfour in the wake of Wyndham's resignation and held by Carson for just one day in 1905. By resigning Carson was registering his opposition to the Conservative government's policies in Ireland during 1904-05. In so doing he won the approval and admiration of the Ulster Unionist Council. As chairman of the Irish Unionist party from 1910 Carson became Vice-president of the Ulster Unionist Council. Although not from Ulster, Carson was accepted without reservation by the Ulster Unionist Council who in their 1910 annual report wrote this of Carson, "Ulster Unionists feel confident that they can place implicit faith in his guidance in the present crisis". Carson, one of the most effective orators in the English-speaking world in the early twentieth century, united British and Irish Unionist opinion behind the Ulster Unionist cause.

The return in 1906 of a Liberal government, independent of all political parties including the Irish party, meant that the much-feared Home Rule crisis did not immediately materialise. The crushing defeat in the 1906 election of the Conservatives, the worst the Conservative Party had ever suffered at the polls, encouraged the Liberals to confront the issue which was the biggest obstacle to effective Liberal rule, viz. the veto exercised by a Conservative-dominated House of Lords on Liberal legislation. When the House of Lords broke with tradition and rejected Chancellor of the Exchequer Lloyd George's People's Budget in 1909, Prime Minister Asquith called a general election in 1910 on the constitutional issue of statutory limitation of the powers of the House of Lords. The results of two general elections in 1910 freed the Liberals from the constraints of a hostile House of Lords but made the Liberal Party the prisoner of the Irish Parliamentary party. As in 1886, when 86 Irish MPs held the balance of power between British Liberals and Conservatives, 83 Irish MPs held the balance between Liberals and Conservatives after 1910. Before the January election P.M. Asquith in an effort to win the considerable Irish vote in Britain, as well as the support of Redmond and the Irish Nationalists, stated publicly Liberal willingness to "set up in Ireland a system of full self-government in regard to purely Irish affairs."

The Parliament Act of 1911 abolishing the absolute veto of the House of Lords, removed the last constitutional barrier to Home Rule. Under the terms of the Parliament Act 1911 a Home Rule Bill such as that passed by the Commons in 1893 would come into effect with or without House of Lords approval within two years, provided it passed three successive readings during three successive sessions of the House of Commons.

The Unionist Campaign against Home Rule

Carson was determined to use the two years between the introduction and passing of the Third Home Rule Bill to demonstrate the depth of Unionist opposition to Home Rule. As Unionist opposition was strongest in Ulster the Unionist campaign led by Carson centred on Ulster. Even before the Third Home Rule Bill was introduced in April 1912 Carson and the Ulster Unionists were on the attack. The Ulster campaign against the Third Home Rule Bill was launched in spectacular style with a monster meeting on September 23, 1911 at Craigavon, the home of Ulster Unionist James Craig, who became Carson's second-in-command and first Prime Minister of the Northern Ireland state 1921-40.

The impressive turn-out of 50,000 Orange men and Unionists from all over the province was designed to convince Carson, as much as British public opinion, of the sincerity of Ulster Unionists.

For Carson the Craigavon meeting was his introduction to Ulster Unionists. Before his arrival in Ulster he wrote to Craig about his anxiety "to satisfy myself that the people over there really mean to resist". Carson was not disappointed nor did he disappoint Ulster Unionists in his first address to them. Determined to prove that he was a man of action as well as of words, Carson outlined a contingency plan for a provisional government. "We must be prepared the morning Home Rule passes, ourselves to become responsible for the government of the Protestant Province of Ulster." Two days later the Ulster Unionist Council appointed a Commission of five leading Ulster Unionists "to take immediate steps, in consultation with Sir Edward Carson, to frame and submit a Constitution for a Provisional Government of Ulster". This was no abject betrayal of the cause of Irish Unionism which Carson claimed was "the guiding star" of his political life. To Carson, the lawyer, Irish Unionism was his biggest "case" yet. Ulster Unionism was the strongest argument in defence of Irish Unionism. "If Ulster succeeds, Home Rule is dead" Carson asserted with the conviction of one who firmly believed that Home Rule for the rest of Ireland without Ulster was simply unworkable. Carson's strategy in the period 1911-14 was to demonstrate the lengths, including rebellion and separation from the rest of Ireland, to which Ulster was determined to go in order to render Home Rule from a Dublin-based parliament for all of Ireland, unworkable.

Carson and indeed the Conservative Unionist Party in Britain (in 1912 in response to the Third Home Rule Bill of that year the Conservative and Liberal Unionist Parties formally fused into the Conservative Unionist Party) saw nothing wrong in advocating loyalty to the Crown and Empire and in urging disloyalty and rebellion against the lawful government of the Crown. Pro-Union did not mean pro-government. The Conservative Unionist Party considered the recent attack upon the constitutional rights of the House of Lords and the proposed attack upon Empire envisaged in the Third Home Rule Bill as an act of treason which Unionists must resist with every means at their disposal. The resignation of British Conservative leader Balfour in November 1911 led to speculation that Carson, his protégé, might succeed to leadership of the British Conservative Party. Carson declined the leadership in favour of Scots-Canadian Bonar Law whose father was an Ulster Presbyterian minister. In the opinion of A.T.Q. Stewart, Reader in Irish History at Queen's University Belfast, "short of Carson himself" Ulster could not have had a more sympathetic Leader of the Opposition.

Just two days before Liberal P.M. Asquith introduced the third Home Rule Bill in the House of Commons in April 1912 Bonar Law was in Ulster being introduced to the Ulster Unionists. The mass meeting organised to impress Bonar Law in the Show Grounds Balmoral, outside Belfast on April 9, 1912, out-rivalled the Craigavon meeting of September 1911 in splendour and size. Over 100,000 heard Bonar Law proclaim, "you hold the pass, the pass for the Empire". At a British Unionist rally at Bleinheim, the ancestral home of Randolph Churchill, the same year, Bonar Law declared, "I can imagine no length of resistance to which Ulster can go in which I would not be prepared to support them." To desperate Ulster Unionists these utterances denoted British Conservative Party support for their campaign of unconstitutional activity against Home Rule.

Ulster's Solemn League and Covenant

As early as March 1912 Carson wrote, "I have made up my mind to recommend very drastic action in Ulster during this year... this is the critical year". The "drastic action" decided upon, in response to the Third Home Rule Bill under debate in the House of Commons from April 1912, was to organise a series of mass meetings starting in Enniskillen, Co. Fermanagh on September 18th and culminating in a nation-wide signing of Ulster's Solemn League and Covenant on "Ulster Day" Saturday September 28th 1912. Carson and Craig were among the first to sign the Ulster Covenant in Belfast's City Hall condemning Home Rule as "disastrous to the material well-being of Ulster as well as the whole of Ireland... and perilous to the unity of the Empire" and pledging themselves solemnly "to stand by one another in defending for ourselves and our children our cherished position of equal citizenship in the United Kingdom, and in using all means which may be found necessary to defeat the present conspiracy to set up a Home Rule Parliament." Almost half a million people signed the Solemn League and Covenant, 218,206 men and 228,991 women throughout Ulster and 19,162 men and 5,055 women in the rest of Ireland and Britain. Those who signed were given a copy which was frequently hung, adorned by the Orange sash, in a revered position in the home of the signatory as a permanent reminder of Unionist solidarity and resistance. Carson rounded off "Ulster Day" with huge Unionist rallies in Liverpool and Glasgow where British Unionists pledged their support. To Carson the real value of the Solemn League and Covenant was that it pledged the signatories to each other as well as to the Unionist cause. On October 5th 1912 Carson wrote, "we are now bound in solemn covenant each to the other. Let us each prove a worthy covenantor."

The geographical distribution of the Covenantors with Ulster signatories outnumbering Irish Unionist signatories by almost 20 to one, far from uniting the Irish and Ulster Unionists as Carson had hoped, only served to strengthen the case for special consideration for Ulster Unionism. Carson had already made the case for Ulster in September 1911 by urging Unionists to take over "those places we are able to control" and to become "responsible for the government of the Protestant Province of Ulster". Carson was in no position to reject out of hand the Liberal amendment of Agar-Robartes in June 1912 proposing the exclusion of the four most Protestant counties, Antrim, Armagh, Derry and Down. Carson, who opposed partition in principle, suggested exclusion of the nine counties province of Ulster in the hope that this would prove equally unacceptable, and moved such an amendment on New Year's Day 1913. It was, however, combined Liberal and Irish Nationalist opposition to partition, rather than Unionist opposition, which killed all amendments to the Third

Home Rule Bill at this stage. On 16th January 1913 the Third Home Rule Bill was passed by the House of Commons. As predicted, it was rejected by 326 to 69 votes in the House of Lords two weeks later and began the second of its three circuits almost immediately.

The Ulster Volunteer Force

Carson's great fear was that Ulster Unionists would not be taken seriously. In March 1912 he expressed that fear to a friend, "there is a growing feeling that we do not mean business". Carson had been most impressed by the discipline and military bearing of Orangemen and Unionists during parades and demonstrations since the Craigavon meeting in 1911. During 1912 it was pointed out that local Justices of the Peace could authorise drilling and military organisation of Volunteers for the purpose of maintaining the constitution of the United Kingdom. In January 1913, in response to the first passing of the Third Home Rule Bill through the House of Commons, the Ulster Unionist Council decided to unite local detachments of Volunteers into a single military body, the Ulster Volunteer Force, (UVF) to be limited to 100,000 men many of whom had signed the Covenant in their own blood. Although not present at the Ulster Unionist Council meeting which decided to form the UVF (Carson's wife was dying at the time) Carson endorsed the decision declaring that the Covenant would not be abandoned without force. In April 1913, within a few weeks of his wife's death, Carson was back in Belfast declaring, "my one affection left me is my love of Ireland." At the opening of a new drill hall for the Ulster Volunteers in Belfast he assumed total responsibility for the activities of the UVF declaring, "if they (i.e. the government) wish to test the legality of anything we are doing, or have done, do not let them take humble men. I am responsible for everything."

Carson saw the UVF, 90,000 strong at the end of 1913 and commanded by a retired British army officer Lieutenant-General Richardson, as a means of marshalling Unionist and Loyalist anger and directing it against the British government. Carson told the Volunteers, "Our quarrel is with the Government." Above all Carson, who had surprised Loyalists by supporting the Nationalist demand for a Catholic National University in 1908, feared the disintegration of Ulster Unionism into sectarian strife and a religious civil war, which would give the British government the excuse to intervene militarily in order to restore law and order. The expulsion of Catholic workers from the Harland and Wolff shipyards in Belfast in the summer of 1912 was a cause for concern. Carson was quick to dissociate the UVF from sectarian violence and told volunteers "Remember you have no quarrel with individuals. We welcome, aye and we love, every individual Irishman, even though opposed to us". As Tim Healy Nationalist M.P. said, the UVF provided Carson with a "safety valve for the Orangemen".

The campaign against the Liberal government gathered momentum during 1913 as the Third Home Rule Bill was passed for the second time by the House of Commons in July 1913. It was rejected again by the Lords and the Liberals were forced once again to introduce it in the Commons for the third and final time. On September 23rd, the second anniversary of the Craigavon meeting, the Ulster Unionist Council announced publicly the formation of a provisional government of Ulster to take over should the Home Rule Bill become law. Carson became Chairman of a 77 member executive. It was at this time that Carson became resigned to the fact that, as one historian has put it, northern Unionists "would vote against Home Rule for Ireland to the end of time, but they would only fight for the exclusion of Ulster". Carson, in November 1913, admitted, "they (Irish Unionists) are so different from the North of Ireland and do so little to help themselves". In an earlier meeting with Southern Irish Unionists, Carson had asked them "if I win in Ulster am I to refuse the fruits of victory because you have lost?" The question was of far greater significance than the generous negative response of the Southern Unionists. Carson did not feel that he was abandoning fellow-Southern Irish Unionists. The continuation of British rule in Ulster was their only protection.

The decision to form a provisional government and the creation of the Irish Volunteers in November 1913 to oppose the Ulster Volunteers in the event of the UVF preventing Home Rule from being enforced, made the arming of the UVF imperative. In anticipation of the arming of private armies the government had banned completely on December 5th 1913 the importation of arms and ammunition into Ireland. In January 1914 Carson finally gave his consent to a plan to be undertaken by a dare-devil Unionist, Major Crawford, "who in 1890s had conceived a plan to kidnap Gladstone" and whisk him away to an island retreat somewhere in the Pacific. The scheme to buy a large quantity of rifles and ammunition from Britain's enemy Germany and to acquire a ship and run the guns into an Ulster port seemed as foolhardy in early 1914.

"Carson's Army" as the UVF was popularly known, was the first of the Twentieth-Century style private armies, which played such an important role in the rise of fascism during the inter-War years. Although no Hitler or Mussolini, Carson demonstrated between 1911-14 that governments will often yield to the threat of force what they have denied to democratic majorities. For Carson, a leading legal authority, to contemplate illegal activity was indicative of the mood of rebellion sweeping through Unionist circles in both Britain and Ireland. As early as July 1912 Bonar Law, British Conservative leader, condemned the Liberal government as "a Revolutionary Committee which has seized upon despotic power by fraud". Bonar Law however failed to persuade the new King, George V, known to be sympathetic to the Unionist cause, to take the extraordinary step of using the royal prerogative to dismiss the government and force a general election. Notwithstanding this the Conservative leadership was prepared to consider holding up in the House of Lords the Annual Army Bill due in April 1914 and thus to threaten essential supplies to the armed forces just months before the outbreak of World War I. The much-publicised threat to the Army in spring 1914 raised the critical issue of the reaction of a largely pro-Unionist Army officer corps in the event of their being ordered to coerce Unionist Ulster. The so-called "Curragh mutiny" of March 1914 provided the answer.

The "Curragh Mutiny"

The Liberal government for long had been toying with the idea of arresting Carson and suppressing the Ulster Volunteers. Apart from the danger of provoking civil war, the difficulty of securing a conviction against Carson from a jury within Ulster or Britain, was an obvious deterrent. The need, however, to move against Ulster before mass arming of the Ulster Volunteers made such action more difficult, prompted the British War Office to take action. In March 1914 Sir Arthur Paget, Commander-in-Chief of the British army in Ireland was summoned to London.

Informed that the Army would be supported by the Navy he was told to prepare for a mass movement of men and officers from the Curragh, British army base in Co. Kildare into Ulster on March 21st 1914. Only officers with homes in Ulster could refuse to take part. When Paget conveyed these instructions to the officers in the Curragh he led them to believe that they had the choice of either going or resigning. Fifty-eight officers, including General Gough an Ulsterman whose home was not in Ulster, announced their intention to resign if they were ordered North. Alarmed, the War Office summoned Gough and the other "rebel" Commanding Officers to London. The talks, however, did not result in the expected disciplinary action but rather in the War Office giving a written undertaking not to use the Army "to crush political opposition to the policy or principles of the Home Rule Bill". The government was acutely embarrassed by the whole incident. Colonel Seely, Minister for War, was forced to resign and Liberal P.M. Asquith himself took over the War Office. The Curragh incident was not a mutiny. No military orders had been issued and therefore none had been refused. Asquith however remained convinced that if the government had ordered a march on Ulster about half the officers in the army would have refused to go.

The "Curragh mutiny" rendered impossible military action in Ulster. Intelligence of the planned military action was conveyed at once to Carson by pro-Unionist senior army officer and future military adviser to the new Northern Ireland State, Sir Henry Wilson. Carson and Craig's reaction was to return to Ulster at once, and, despite heavy British Army presence near Craigavon, to turn Craig's home at Craigavon into a military fortress. The Volunteers were put on war footing. Their vigilance was not relaxed after the immediate crisis had passed.

The Larne Gun-Running

The high level of discipline and organisation among the Volunteers throughout the whole province ensured the smooth distribution of some 24,600 German guns and around 3 million rounds of ammunition which were landed successfully on the night of April 24/25 1914 at Larne, Donaghadee and Bangor along the east coast of Ulster from a coal-boat the S.S. Clydevalley. Under the pretext of a trial mobilisation of the UVF all roads leading to the coast were sealed off by the Volunteers. Telegraph wires were cut and police and coastguards confined to barracks while the province-wide distribution of rifles and ammunition got under way. Significantly, no serious attempt was made by the police or army to prevent the mass arming of the UVF although the unloading of the Bangor consignment took place in broad daylight. Neither was any attempt made to arrest Carson or any of those responsible although the Irish Attorney-General was instructed by government to investigate the possibility of charging Carson under the Treason-Felony Act.

Just as the formation of the Ulster Volunteers had led to the setting up of the Irish Volunteers, so the Larne gun-running of April 1914 led to the Howth gun-running of July 1914 and the arming of the Irish Volunteers. By July 1914 therefore Ireland was armed to the teeth and there seemed little prospect of a peaceful political solution to the Home Rule question.

The third and final readings of the Third Home Rule Bill took place against the background of the "Curragh mutiny" and the Larne Gun-running.

A Liberal government amendment on 9th March 1914 to allow each of the

Ulster counties the option of voting itself out of Home Rule for six years after which it would automatically come under the Irish Home Rule parliament unless Westminster decided otherwise, was contemptuously dismissed by Carson as being a "sentence of death with a stay of execution for six years." Asquith was disappointed because Redmond and the Nationalists had reluctantly agreed to the "temporary exclusion" proposal. The inability of the government either to coerce successfully Unionist Ulster in the wake of Carson's total rejection or to prevent large-scale gun-running into Ulster hardened Unionist resolve not to compromise and intensified the Liberal government's desire to secure a settlement. Notwithstanding, the Third Home Rule Bill was passed by the House of Commons for the third and final time on 25th May 1914 without an amendment any more acceptable to the Ulster Unionists.

Carson, Redmond and Asquith were to find common purpose in fighting the common enemy on the continent of Europe. In return for a pledge from Carson that "a large body of Ulster Volunteers will be willing and ready to give their services for Home Defence and many will be willing to serve anywhere they are required" and a similar pledge from Redmond regarding the Irish Volunteers, Asquith, who had agreed not to enforce controversial legislation for the duration of the Great War, put forward the Third Home Rule Bill for royal assent while at the same time announcing the suspension of enforcement of Home Rule for the duration of the war and until parliament had an opportunity of making provision for Ulster by special amending legislation. Carson was not in parliament to witness Home Rule become law on September 18th 1914. The day before he had married quietly an English girl whom he had met just before the death of his first wife the previous year.

Carson and World War I

Carson was far from happy with the passing of the Third Home Rule Bill and made it clear in Belfast in early September that the suspension of Unionist opposition was only "in the interests of the country and the Empire". Anxious to show Ulster's loyalty Carson pledged an Ulster Division of 35,000 Volunteers for the war effort. Within two weeks 21,000 had enlisted. It was not until October 1915, however, that the Ulster Division, the 36th of the British army, crossed to France. Their baptism of fire came in the Battle of the Somme in July 1916. In the first two days of this first big offensive by the British army during World War I, 40,000 casualties, 5,500 of whom were from the 36th (Ulster) Division, were sustained.

Carson's chance to contribute to the war effort came in 1915 when the disastrous Dardanelles and Gallipoli campaign forced Liberal P.M. Asquith in May 1915 to form a broad coalition government which included not only Bonar Law and the Conservatives but also the first Labour government minister Henderson, minister for Education. Both Carson and Redmond were offered government posts. Redmond refused to sit in government with Carson "the leader of the Ulster revolters, who, the other day, was threatening hostilities to the forces of the Crown and the decision of Parliament." One of the most important political developments of the war years was the decline of Redmond's Irish Parliamentary Party and the consolidation of the Ulster Unionists, as Carson became Attorney General in the first Coalition government and later a member of Lloyd George's war cabinet.

Even while still a member of government Carson was the government's sharpest critic. He described the first broad-based coalition government as "twenty-three blind mice." He had nothing but contempt for Irish-born Lord Kitchener who as Secretary of State for War had overall responsibility for the British war effort. Carson claimed that Kitchener confided in him during summer 1915, "I don't know Europe, I don't know England and I don't know the British Army." When Carson discovered that Kitchener did not even read war telegrams and was not prepared to do anything effective either to win the war in the Dardanelles or to expedite the evacuation of Gallipoli, Carson resigned on October 12th 1915 although the public announcement of his resignation was not made until the next week. Carson was an even more formidable critic in opposition. From January 1916 Carson led the Conservative and Unionist backbench opposition to the government. The effectiveness of what became known as the Conservative "Ginger" Group eventually brought down the Asquith coalition government in December 1916.

Carson and 1916

The events of 1916, in particular the Easter Rising, revealed the depth of Irish dissatisfaction with the temporary settlements of the Home Rule issue in 1914. Ironically, Carson came under personal attack from staunch loyalists at the time of the Easter Rising. He was popularly seen as having given a lead in the matter of rebellion by the formation of the Ulster Volunteers in January 1913 and was inundated with hate mail in the immediate aftermath of the rebellion.

The Easter Rising 1916 forced the Liberals to re-open the whole Home Rule question. In 1916 Carson, however, had distinct advantages over his political adversary Redmond, leader of the Irish Nationalist Home Rule Party. Carson was leader of the opposition. From 1915 he had drawn close to Lloyd George, the most influential Liberal member of Asquith's coalition government and next prime minister. Both men advocated a more effective prosecution of the war through the formation of a small war cabinet to deal with every aspect of the war. When Lloyd George was asked to re-open negotiations with Redmond and Carson, Lloyd George wrote to Carson on 3rd June 1916, "let us settle Ireland promptly." Learning from the mistakes of the Buckingham Palace fiasco of July 1914, Lloyd George resolved to confer separately with Carson and the Unionists and with Redmond and the Nationalists. Lloyd George, however, was prepared only to make verbal assurances to Redmond, who reluctantly agreed eventually, to the temporary exclusion of the six Ulster counties, Fermanagh and Tyrone both of which had nationalist majorities and the four "Unionist" counties Derry, Down, Antrim and Armagh, in return for immediate Home Rule for the other 26 counties. Carson, on the other hand, received written confirmation that "the six counties are to be excluded... and are not to be included unless at some future time the Imperial Parliament pass an Act for that purpose." This was a significant new departure as, until then, the only concession available to Ulster Unionists was the "county option" offer which might only give the Unionists the four counties of east Ulster, the only ones in which there was a Unionist majority. The 1916 proposals gave Ulster Unionists effectively what they had been demanding - the exclusion of the six counties. Balfour, fellow Conservative Unionist remarked, "we have offered to us voluntarily all that civil war could give." Redmond, however, rejected utterly the whole settlement when it became clear that the intended exclusion was to be permanent. The real significance of the failed 1916 Home Rule initiative was to secure agreement, however short-lived, between Unionists and

Nationalists on the exclusion of six counties from a Home Rule Ireland. The basis of any future settlement would be along these geographical lines.

The Irish Convention

When the next and final attempt was made to reach a negotiated settlement between Unionists and Nationalists in Ireland through the Irish Convention which met between July 1917 and April 1918, Carson was a member of a new coalition government under Lloyd George, in which the Conservatives were senior partners. When Asquith finally resigned in December 1916 and Lloyd George became Prime Minister, Carson was offered the post of Lord Chancellor, the highest legal position. He declined, hoping to be appointed to Lloyd George's inner war cabinet. Opposition from within Conservative ranks jealous of Carson's influence over Lloyd George, deprived him of a post in the inner war cabinet. Instead he became First Lord of the Admiralty with rights to attend meetings of the War Cabinet only when matters relating to the Navy were being discussed. Carson was the first to admit that he knew nothing about the Navy. In his first address to naval officers he confessed, "My only great qualification for being at the head of the Navy is that I am very much at sea."

Carson's tenure of government office was far from happy. On April 30th 1917 P.M. Lloyd George, impatient with Carson's failure to implement an effective convoy system to protect merchant shipping, took the unprecedented step of taking over the Admiralty himself while Carson nominally remained in charge. Carson was finally asked to leave the Admiralty in July 1917 and to join the war cabinet.

Thus it was that when the Irish Convention of 95 delegates representing every opinion in Ireland except Sinn Fein opened on July 25th 1917 in Trinity College Dublin, Carson was no longer leader of the Ulster Unionists. Upon becoming a member of government Carson had relinquished leadership of the Unionists. Twenty Ulster Unionists attended the Convention. They were alarmed at the government's initial offer of immediate Home Rule to 26 counties with exclusion of the remaining six for a five-year period. Worse was to come. The Southern Irish Unionists were so appalled at the prospect of partition, which Ulster Unionists seemed to welcome, that they declared themselves willing to consider home rule and to co-operate with moderate nationalists in bringing about a settlement satisfactory to all. An Irish Unionist proposal in December 1917 for a measure of self-government which offered safeguards for minorities found immediate favour with Redmond and the Nationalists. When Lloyd George indicated that he would use his influence in government and parliament to ensure acceptance of the Irish Unionist proposal Carson believed that Lloyd George was about to break an earlier promise not to coerce Ulster. On January 22nd 1918 Carson resigned yet again from government and resumed leadership of the Ulster Unionists. The Convention broke up in April 1918 with the Ulster Unionists voting against all proposals and producing their own minority report of the Convention. Carson commented, "The Irish Convention gave me more trouble than almost anything I ever had to do with in relation to Home Rule". The Irish Convention marked the parting of the ways between Ulster and Southern Unionists. In the December 1918 general election Carson, who had represented the Dublin constituency of Trinity College since 1892, stood for the Belfast constituency of Duncairn. For the first time the leader of the Ulster Unionists could be said to represent Ulster Unionists in parliament.

Disillusionment and Death:

Although Carson gained a convincing victory in the North Belfast working-class constituency of Duncairn in 1918 he announced immediately afterwards, "I imagine it is likely to be my last election." The events of the last two years in particular had disillusioned Carson. While addressing a crowed of 80,000 Orangemen at the 12th July celebrations outside Belfast that year, he spoke of "the filth of politics". When offered again the post of Lord Chancellor by Lloyd George who headed a new Coalition government dominated by the Conservatives, Carson declined saying, "I long for a whiff of the Law Courts". Carson who was, according to himself, "a lawyer first and a politician afterwards" returned to his first interest. He opposed the final British initiative on Home Rule, the Government of Ireland Act 1920. Stating "I cannot vote for Home Rule and I will not vote for Home Rule" he rejected the offer of Home Rule for Ulster as well as for the rest of Ireland. Carson however had lost his battle for the Union of Britain and Ireland. For Ulster Unionists, however, the Government of Ireland Act gave them the exclusion of the six counties without a fight. On that basis Carson urged Ulster Unionists to accept. Carson, however was determined to play no part in the political life of the new Northern Ireland State. In February 1921 he resigned from the leadership of the Ulster Unionist Council. Although offered leadership of the first Unionist government of Northern Ireland, he declined. He did not attend the opening of the Northern Ireland Parliament on June 22nd 1921. Less than a month before, Carson who had declined a judgeship in 1905, had become a Lord of Appeal and a member of the House of Lords on 24th May 1921 as Baron Carson of Duncairn.

It was from the House of Lords that Carson led the attack against the Anglo-Irish Treaty which ended the War of Independence 1919-21. Carson regarded the Treaty as a betrayal of "those who, relying on British honour and British justice..." have been "deserted and cast aside." Ignoring the convention that appeal judges of the House of Lords did not engage in party politics, Carson condemned the Conservative contribution to the Treaty declaring bitterly, "I was only a puppet, and so was Ulster and so was Ireland, in the political game that was to get the Conservative Party into power".

Although ill for most of his life and always worried about his health Carson lived long enough to see his worst fears about the Treaty realised as the de Valera government of the 1930s dismantled the Treaty term by term. Carson retired as a Law Lord in 1929 but returned to the House of Lords in 1933 to protest at the Free State's abolition of the right of appeal from Irish courts to the Judicial Committee of the Privy Council in London, "the only remaining safeguard". Among his last words to the House were, "Every single promise we have made to the Loyalists in Ireland has been broken..." Significantly Carson's last "battles" were on behalf of the Irish Unionists, who he felt, were getting a raw deal from both the Free State and the British government who refused to give adequate compensation for damage incurred during the War of Independence.

Carson died on the 22nd October 1935 and was given a state funeral in Belfast. Among the tributes paid to him on his death was one from Winston Churchill, a political adversary during the Home Rule crisis, who said, "he lived to see the ascendancy of many ideas to which he was inveterately opposed,... but he lived, also to see his beloved Ulster, to whose cause he had devoted himself, firmly anchored to the United Kingdom... No name will be cherished with greater affection in Ulster than his, and few will command wider respect among all classes of Irishmen, North or South, Protestant or Catholic, orange or green."

Appraisal:
Carson has been described by Irish historian J.C. Beckett as "a patriot without being a nationalist." In 1896 Carson, insisting upon his right to oppose Conservative government policy which he felt injurious to Ireland, declared, "henceforward I am resolved to take whatever course is best for Ireland." In 1900 Carson told Balfour, "it is only for Ireland that I'm in politics". Carson firmly believed that the best course for Ireland was within the Union. When he felt that Irish interests were not being best served by union with Britain, (escalating violence forced Carson to this opinion during what he regarded as a period of Liberal misrule 1906-10) Carson told an English audience in December 1907, "I speak vehemently as an Irishman to English people, and say that if you are not prepared to govern Ireland then go out of Ireland and leave us to govern ourselves." These were indeed strange words from the champion of Unionism.

Carson's single-minded pursuance of an ideal in which he passionately believed and for which he was prepared to sacrifice "everything in fact so far as personal ambition is concerned" by his own admission, had much in common with nationalist revolutionary contemporaries whom he so vehemently opposed. Like Griffith he had no personal political ambition. He resigned from government twice and refused high office twice. Although dangerously effective in opposition, Carson was disappointingly ineffective in government and was described by contemporary Lord Beaverbrook as, "a natural revolutionary always happiest when against government".

Craig, described by Carson as his "First Lieutenant", summed up Carson's career thus, "His birth-place was Ireland, his sphere of activities largely in England, his greatest triumph saving Ulster for the Empire." Yet Ulster's victory spelt defeat for Carson's lifelong objective, the preservation of the Union of all of Ireland within the United Kingdom. Although recommending acceptance of the Government of Ireland Act 1920 granting Unionist Ulster home rule, Carson was singularly unenthusiastic about the new Northern Ireland State although his larger-than-life statue stands before the Northern Ireland Parliament building at Stormont. Carson did not want a Northern Ireland state permanently separated from the rest of Ireland. In a strange and revolutionary speech for the chosen leader of Ulster Unionism Carson said, on the eve of the passing of the Third Home Rule Bill in the Commons in May 1914, "If Home Rule is to pass, much as I detest it ... my hope and indeed I would say my earnest prayer would be that the Government of Ireland for the South and West would prove such a success in the future... that it might be even for the interests of Ulster itself to move towards that Government and come in under it and form one unit in relation to Ireland." Carson's aspirations for Ireland after Home Rule differed little from those of many Nationalists. Yet he remained implacably opposed to Nationalists. In consequence Carson's Irishness has become forgotten and he remains one of the most misunderstood leaders of the Irish Revolution.

Landmarks in Carson's Life (1854-1935)

1854   *9th February* Birth of Carson in Dublin

1877   Carson joined the Irish Bar.

1887-91 Crown Prosecutor

1892   Member of Parliament for Trinity College, Dublin.

1894   Senior member of the English Bar.

1900   Solicitor-General of England.

1910   Leader of the Irish Unionist Party, Vice-President of the Ulster Unionist Council.

1912   *September 28th* - Ulster's Solemn League and Covenant signed on "Ulster Day".

1913   *January* - Formation of UVF "Carson's Army".

1914   *March* - "Curragh Mutiny".

1914   *April* - Larne Gun-running.

1915   *May* - Carson Attorney-General in first Coalition government.

1915   *October* - Carson resigned and led the Opposition against the government's incompetent prosecution of the war.

1916   *July* - Took part in fresh discussions on Home Rule.

1916   *December* - Joined second Coalition government as First Lord of the Admiralty.

1918   *January* - Carson resigned from government again.

1918   *December* - Carson returned to Parliament as Unionist member for Duncairn in North Belfast.

1921   *February* - Resigned from leadership of the Ulster Unionist Council.

1921   *May 24th* - Entered the House of Lords as Lord of Appeal taking the title Baron Carson of Duncairn.

1935   *October 22nd* - Death of Carson.

2. Craig

Early Influences

James Craig, organiser of Ulster Unionism between 1911 and 1921 and first Prime Minister of Northern Ireland, was born near Belfast on 8th January 1871. Of wealthy Protestant parents of Scottish descent, Craig embodied all the arguments, racial, religious and economic, for preserving the Union of Protestant industrial Ulster within the United Kingdom. His father's success in business, rising within twenty years from an impoverished clerk to millionaire-owner of an international whiskey firm, was attributed to the close economic links between Ulster, mainland Britain and the lucrative markets of the far-flung British Empire. Craig and his family would certainly have endorsed the view expressed by the Belfast Chamber of Commerce to Gladstone in 1893 as the Second Home Rule Bill was under discussion, "All our progress has been made under the union. We were a small, insignificant town at the end of the last century, deeply disaffected and hostile to the British empire. Since the union and under equal laws, we have been wedded to the empire and made progress second to none . . . Why should we be driven by force to abandon the conditions which have led to that success?"

Craig's parents were Presbyterian and were determined to give Craig a strict Presbyterian upbringing. After attending a primary school run by a Presbyterian minister, in 1882 Craig was sent to public school in Scotland to complete a strict Protestant education. Craig's Protestant upbringing filled him with the general Ulster Protestant distrust of the Catholic Church which prompted him to write later, "at every stage in life from the cradle to the grave the Roman Catholic Church intervenes, exhorting and commanding her adherents to have no intercourse with Protestants . . ." Craig was to join the Orange Order, a secret society of Protestant extremists pledged to the maintenance of the Protestant ascendancy, and to become Grand Master of the Orange Lodge in Co. Down. In 1934 Craig told the Northern Ireland Parliament, "I am an Orangeman first and a politician and Member of this Parliament afterwards." To Craig, as to all Orangemen and Protestant Unionists, Home Rule from a Catholic-dominated Dublin Parliament would mean Rome Rule which would be detrimental to the cultural, religious and economic welfare of Ulster.

James Craig (1871 - 1940), the first Prime Minister, of Northern Ireland (1921- 40)

The Origins of Ulster Unionism

Craig was an impressionable fifteen-year old schoolboy when Ulster Unionist opposition made itself felt against the First Home Rule Bill in 1886. Political opposition to Home Rule within Ulster was far from being in 1886 the invincible force it was to become under Carson and Craig's guidance a quarter of a century later. The Third Reform Act of 1884 enfranchising householders gave many Catholics the vote for the first time. In 1885 the Redistribution Act broke up small Unionist pocket boroughs and redrew constituency boundaries so as to give newly enfranchised Catholic voters an advantage in enlarged county constituencies. The result was that in the 1885 general election, Nationalists who had only 3 Ulster seats in the old parliament won 17 of Ulster's 33 seats. Shocked Unionists formed the Ulster Loyalist Anti-Repeal Union in January 1886 and welcomed leading British Conservative, Lord Randolph Churchill like a king. His visit in February 1886 to Ulster was seen as a show of British Conservative solidarity with Ulster Unionism and his slogan "Ulster will fight and Ulster will be right" became the watchword of militant Unionism.

Although the Unionist majority in the nine-county province of Ulster remained small, Ulster's domination of Irish Unionism became more and more pronounced from 1886. Of the eighteen Irish Unionist MPs returned by Irish constituencies sixteen were Ulster Unionist MPs. The leading Irish Unionist MP after 1886 Colonel Saunderson, a Cavan landowner came from within the province of Ulster. Southern Unionists, unable to gain election in Irish constituencies, sought election on the British mainland. Northern Unionists preferred also to travel through Larne and Stranraer to Westminster rather than via Dublin/Holyhead as did their Southern counterparts.

Militancy, another characteristic of Ulster Unionism, also manifested itself in 1886. As the Home Rule debate reached a climax in the House of Commons in June 1886 Catholic shipyard workers were being driven from their jobs. Serious rioting and sectarian strife in Belfast and throughout Ulster only ended with the Conservative and Unionist victory in the July 1886 election and resulted in 32 people being killed and 442 arrested. Although rumours of an Ulster army were unfounded exaggerations, Ulster Unionists were determined to be better prepared when the next threat to the Union came. Unionist opposition to the Second Home Rule Bill in 1893 took three distinct forms. An Ulster Convention League was formed to organise mass demonstrations against the bill such as the Ulster Convention of June 1893 when 11,000 men marched through Belfast in silent protest against the proposed Home Rule. Such demonstrations were dress rehearsals for the monster meetings of 1911 and 1912. More significant for the future of Ulster Unionism was the creation of Unionist Clubs and their organising body the Unionist Clubs Council. By May 1893 some 200 Unionist clubs were mobilising grass roots opinion throughout Ulster. The Unionist clubs lapsed after the 1893 Home Rule scare had passed with the House of Lords rejecting the Second Home Rule Bill in September 1893. Their revival during the Conservative "devolution scare" of 1904-05 led to the formation of the Ulster Unionist Council 1905, and provided the grass roots organisation of Ulster Unionism from 1911. The militant arm of Ulster Unionism was provided by the Ulster Defence Union formed in March 1893 and backed up threats of armed resistance with actual smuggling of rifles into the province. An enthusiastic supporter of the Ulster Defence Union, which can be seen as the fore-runner of the Ulster Volunteer Force of twenty years later, was Crawford, organiser of the successful Larne gun-running of April

1914.

Before 1900, Craig's interests were financial. After an undistinguished school career, Craig served a two-year apprenticeship with a firm of stockbrokers in London. He returned to Belfast in the early 1890s where, as the son of a wealthy father, he set up his own stock-broking firm, Craig and Co., Belfast. Faith in the future of Ulster prompted Craig, the successful broker, to become a founder-member of the Belfast Stock Exchange.

Captain Craig and the Boer War (1899-1901)

The twenty-eight year old Craig, however, longed for excitement and adventure. The Boer War (1899-1901) promised both. On 17th January 1900 he enlisted with the 3rd Battalion of the Royal Irish Rifles and was quickly promoted to the rank of captain. When taken prisoner by the Boers, Captain Craig showed solidarity with the rank and file soldiers by marching with them the 200 miles to prison camp. An injury, sustained when an exploding gun had shattered his eardrum, secured Craig's early release. Upon his recovery, Craig helped to organise railway transport for the troops in South Africa. As a transport officer, Craig showed a flair for organisation which was to make him so indispensable to the Ulster Unionist movement from 1911.

Invalided out of the war in June 1901, Craig returned home filled with a new awareness of the British Empire and of Ulster's place within that Empire. The death of his father in April 1900 left Craig a wealthy man and the proud possessor of the family home, Craigavon, a huge mansion on the outskirts of Belfast. The successful entry of his brother Charles into politics as Unionist MP for South Antrim in a by-election in February 1903 prompted Craig to try a political career. His first attempt as Unionist candidate for North Fermanagh failed. In November 1903, however, he was formally selected as the Unionist candidate in his native East Down. He was duly elected as Unionist MP for East Down in the general election of January 1906 and thereafter represented the voters of County Down as Unionist MP until his death in 1940.

Early Political Career at Westminster

Craig's entry into Westminster coincided with the worst defeat ever sustained by the Conservative and Unionist Party in Britain. The Unionist representation from Ulster, however, remained undiminished. Their role from 1906 was to oppose in particular the Liberal government's Irish policy, and, while respecting parliamentary procedure, to obstruct and generally delay Liberal policy. Craig became particularly adroit at drafting amendments to Liberal Bills and thus delaying the passage of vital legislation such as the Birrell Land Act of 1909, the last of the land purchase acts. In 1907 a frustrated Birrell, Chief Secretary of Ireland, likened Ulster Unionists to "carrion crows" whose sole purpose in asking questions was to malign and misrepresent. The obstructionist activities of the Ulster Unionists from 1906, focused parliamentary attention on Ulster Unionism in much the same way as Parnell and the Home Rule party had forced attention on Home Rule thirty years before, during the 1870s.

Craig's willingness to place his time, energy and considerable resources at the disposal of the Ulster Unionist Council, formed in 1905 in order to direct and co-ordinate Ulster Unionist policy, ensured his speedy rise to a position of influence and leadership within the Unionist Council. The Unionist Council of 200 representatives was formed at the height of the "devolution scare" of 1904-05 when Ulster Unionists feared that their Conservative allies were about to betray them by considering a scheme of devolved local government for all of Ireland. The next year, the leadership of the Irish Unionists at Westminster passed from Ulsterman Colonel Saunderson to Englishman Walter Long who, with Carson, was one of the two Unionist MPs returned from Southern Irish constituencies. Although fear of Home Rule drew Southern Irish and Ulster Unionists closer and led to the setting up of a joint Committee of Unionist Associations in 1907, the Ulster Unionist Council did not disguise its Ulster character. Its stated objective as quoted in the "Irish Times" of 3rd December 1904 was, "to be the medium of expressing Ulster Unionist opinion . . . and generally to advance and defend the interests of Ulster Unionism in the Unionist Party."

Carson, Craig and the Ulster Unionist Campaign 1911-21

Ironically, the Ulster Unionists were to choose another Irish Unionist, Carson, as their leader during the dark days from 1910 when two general elections placed the Liberals once again at the mercy of the Irish Nationalists, and Home Rule again became a burning issue. As Chairman of the Irish Unionist Party from 1910 Carson was Vice-President of the Ulster Unionist Council. His unreserved acceptance by this conservative and wholly provincial body was due in no small measure to Craig who was prepared to relinquish his own position of power and authority within the Ulster Unionist movement to Carson whom he trusted implicitly from the outset. Craig became the necessary link between Carson and the Ulster Unionists. Carson was happy to lead the Ulster campaign against the Third Home Rule Bill but both Carson and the Ulster Unionist Council were anxious to leave the organisation of the Ulster Unionist campaign to Craig. Carson was to say later, "It was James Craig who did most of the work and I got most of the credit." Thus it was Craig who organised the mass demonstration in the grounds of his own home, Craigavon, in September 1911 in order to introduce Carson to his Ulster followers.

Appropriately the first tentative steps towards a separate administration in Ulster were taken at that Craigavon meeting with Carson's declaration, "the morning Home Rule passes, ourselves to become responsible for the government of the Protestant province of Ulster." Two days later, Carson and the Ulster Unionist Council appointed Craig, who within ten years was to be Northern Ireland's first Prime Minister, to lead a commission of five to draft a constitution for a Provisional Government.

Craig was host to Carson on his many trips to Ulster after 1911. Craigavon came to be regarded as Carson's Ulster home. Craigavon, Craig's home outside Belfast, became the nerve centre of Ulster Unionism from where Craig charted the course of Ulster Unionist opposition both within and outside Ulster. In April 1912 Craig master-minded an even bigger Ulster Unionist welcome in the Balmoral Show Ground for the new British Conservative leader, Bonar Law. Craig and Ulster Unionists welcomed the change in Conservative Party leadership in 1911 from Balfour who, although he admitted that in Ireland there were "two nations, two sets of aspirations, two ideals, two sets of historic memories" regarded the Unionists as "noisy Irish Protestants" to Bonar Law, whose close family links with Ulster made him sympathetic to the Ulster Unionist cause. When Bonar Law pledged

Conservative and Unionist support for Ulster in a declaration made in Dublin, "Ulster will do well to resist . . . and we will support her in her resistance to the end" his commitment to militant unionism in Ulster was not in question.

Craig's greatest achievement during 1912 was the planning of the highly successful Solemn League and Covenant campaign of September 1912 culminating in the signing by almost half a million people of Ulster's Solemn League and Covenant on "Ulster Day" September 28th 1912. It was Craig who decided on the wording of the Covenant and who masterminded Carson's ten-day speaking tour of the province prior to the mass signing on "Ulster Day."

While Craig became expert at organising mass demonstrations of loyalty and Unionist solidarity and was in turn invited as chief spokesman for Ulster Unionism to British Unionist rallies such as that held at Bleinheim Palace in July 1912, he was also capable of whipping up Unionist opposition to those who posed a threat to Ulster Unionism. A proposed visit in 1912 of Winston Churchill, son of the first Conservative champion of Ulster Unionism, Randolph Churchill, was such a threat. Regarded as the Liberal government's most forceful advocate of armed intervention in Ulster in order to coerce Ulster into accepting the government's policy with regard to Home Rule, Churchill was no friend of Unionist Ulster. Concerted Unionist opposition orchestrated by Craig, forced the Ulster Liberal Association to change the venue of a proposed Home Rule rally from the Ulster Hall, scene of Randolph Churchill's historic speech in February 1886. After a stormy passage through Belfast, Churchill eventually addressed a meeting in the Celtic Park football ground in the nationalist part of the city and made a speedy get-away by special train to Larne immediately afterwards.

The need to create organised and disciplined resistance to Home Rule led to the formation of the UVF in 1913. Craig was among the first to appreciate the potential of the Orange Order to provide the manpower for an Ulster citizen army. At Craig's instigation the Ulster Unionist Council decided in January 1913 to unite Volunteers, who had been organising and drilling with and without permission of the local Justices of the Peace, into one single military body, the Ulster Volunteer Force. Craig became political staff officer of the UVF and was closely involved with every decision taken by the UVF. In September 1913, Craig matched Carson's £10,000 subscription to an indemnity fund designed to compensate UVF men and their families for injury, loss or death in service.

Craig was an enthusiastic supporter of Crawford's scheme to run guns into Ulster from Germany and secured approval from a cautious Unionist Council for the bold and daring plan to land the guns at Larne, Donaghadee and Bangor on the night of 24-25th April 1914. It was to Craigavon, since the "Curragh mutiny" scare of the previous month, an armed fortress and headquarters of Ulster Unionist resistance, that Crawford came to announce his exciting news upon his return.

Among memorabilia of the period designed to adorn the mantle-piece of many an Ulster home or to be sent to Unionist sympathisers across the world was a popular Unionist postcard depicting a uniformed Craig holding down with one foot the nationalist leader, Redmond and holding aloft in one hand a hapless Asquith, the Liberal PM. The caption underneath summed up Unionist confidence in Craig and

Carson thus,
> "He who volunteered for England in her deadly Boer war,
> Is for Ulster volunteering a treason plot to mar.
> By his voice in Britain's Parliament he has fought the deadly foe,
> By his sword in loyal Ulster he'll lay treason mongers low,
> Then hurrah for Craig and Ulster with a hip, hip, hip hurray!
> With men like him and Carson we're quite ready for the fray."

Craig and World War I

The outbreak of the Great War in August 1914 presented Craig and the Ulster Volunteer Force with an opportunity to demonstrate their loyalty to the British Empire. It was Craig who secured War Office approval for the formation of a special Ulster division (the 36th of the British Army) formed almost exclusively from Ulster Volunteers. This was considered a propaganda coup for Craig. The Nationalist leader Redmond's request for an Irish Brigade, drawn from the 170,000 National Volunteers who broke away from the Irish Volunteers on the issue of supporting the British war effort, was steadfastly refused. Craig, however, was not destined to experience the horror of trench-warfare or to witness the slaughter of the 36th (Ulster) division during the Battle of the Somme 1916. Although Assistant Adjutant and Quartermaster-General of the Ulster Division, Craig, aged 43 years at the start of the war, twice failed an army medical. Deciding that he could best serve Ulster in politics, he resigned from the Army in April 1916. Following in Carson's footsteps, Craig joined Lloyd George's coalition government in December 1916. Although he held only minor office, Craig's inclusion in a Conservative-dominated coalition government was a singular sign of favour to Ulster Unionists. More honour was to follow. In the new year's honours list (1917) Craig received a baronetcy and became Sir James Craig.

Craig saw his duty during the war-years as winning the best possible terms for at least six counties of Ulster. The events of 1914 had shown that while Ulster Unionists had failed to prevent Home Rule from being passed they had also ensured that its enforcement would be postponed not just for the duration of the war but until special amending legislation had been enacted for Ulster. It is significant that, after September 1914, Unionists generally accepted a Dublin parliament and government as a disagreeable fact of political life and made no serious attempt to undo Home Rule for the rest of Ireland. Their main concern was to save as much of Ulster as possible from Dublin rule.

The task of reconciling Unionist demands and Nationalist aspirations prompted Liberal PM Asquith to exclaim in exasperation on 31st August 1914, the eve of World War I that he wished, "we could submerge the whole lot of them, and their island, for say ten years, under the waves of the Atlantic." Partition, however undesirable it might be to Nationalists and to Irish Unionists like Carson, was considered by Craig and Ulster Unionists from the summer of 1914 as a compromise solution. The area to be excluded became the chief bone of contention. The Liberal government's offer of the summer 1914 i.e. the county option guaranteeing Unionists only the four counties with Unionist majorities Antrim, Down, Derry and Armagh was unacceptable. The unit thus created would be too small to survive politically or economically apart from the rest of Ireland. The alternative favoured by Carson and the Conservative-dominated House of Lords in 1914, the exclusion of all nine counties of the province was equally unacceptable. In 1914 of the province's 33 MPs, only 16 were Unionist. The unpalatable truth for Unionists was that a nine-county Ulster might one day vote for union with the rest of Ireland.

The Home Rule discussions in the aftermath of the Easter Rising 1916 brought the reality of a six-county Ulster closer as, although only for a short time, Unionists, Nationalists and the British government all accepted the principle of exclusion at least of six counties, and not four, as previously offered. To Ulster Unionists, the significance of the Home Rule talks of summer 1916 was the government's written commitment that the six counties were to be permanently excluded from a Home Rule Ireland. It was the realisation that partition was to be permanent and enduring which forced Redmond and the Nationalists to break off all negotiations in 1916.

When, only the next year, the government appeared to be going back on its promise of six-county exclusion by urging Ulster Unionist members of the Convention to accept Irish Unionist and Nationalist proposals for an all-Ireland parliament, Ulster Unionists reacted sharply. Carson and Craig both resigned from Lloyd George's Coalition government early in 1918. Acknowledging the enormous political debt he owed to Carson, Craig wrote to Lloyd George thus, "It is quite impossible for me to separate myself from him in the action he has now taken and as my reliance on his judgement is so unqualified . . . I feel I have no choice but to ask you to accept my resignation."

Craig and the Creation of Northern Ireland

Unlike Carson, Craig did not feel obliged to refuse future offer of government office. In January 1919, he accepted Junior office once again in a Conservative-dominated coalition government. The electoral changes preceding the 1918 general election, the enfranchisement of women aged thirty years or over and all men 21 years and over and the redrawing of electoral boundaries to represent rapidly growing industrial areas had left Ulster Unionists with a clear Unionist majority. It gave them 22 of Ulster's then 37 seats. The 1918 General election swept away both the Irish Parliamentary Party, replaced by Sinn Féin who refused to sit in Westminster, and the Irish Unionists. The 22 Ulster Unionists alone, thanks to Sinn Féin abstention, had an effective Irish voice at Westminster after 1918.

Ulster Unionist demands for the exclusion of the "Unionist" six counties were strengthened by the coalition government's pre-election pledge on partition and the exclusion of the six north-eastern counties from a new Home Rule Bill to be drafted by the new government. Ulster Unionist interests were also protected by the choice of Long, leader of the Irish Unionist Party from 1906-10, to lead a Committee to draft a fourth and final Home Rule bill. Long's opposition to county option and his insistence upon Ulster having "a considerable area", a minimum of six counties, pleased Ulster Unionists. The appointment of Craig as Long's Financial Secretary in April 1920 was further reassurance to Ulster Unionists. Craig was seen as Ulster's watchdog over the new Government of Ireland Bill introduced in February 1920 and finally passed into law in December 1920. Long's illness during 1920 meant that Craig frequently carried out his duties at the Admiralty (Long was also First Lord of the Admiralty). Craig was, therefore, in close contact with Long and was able to exercise considerable influence over the terms of the Government of Ireland Act which provided for the partition of Ireland into two separate states each with its own separate Home Rule parliament subordinate to the Imperial Parliament at Westminster to which both were obliged to send representatives. Craig, upon being informed in November 1919 of the government's intention to introduce a new bill maintained close contact with the Ulster Unionist Council. The changes recommended by Craig, therefore, were also those demanded by the Ulster Unionist Council. Craig's first concern and biggest triumph was to ensure that the Northern Ireland state to be created would consist of just the six north-eastern counties demanded by Ulster Unionists since 1914. Long's drafting committee had favoured the creation of a nine-county state. Craig, however, knowing that Unionists would never have more than a slender 3/4 seat majority in a nine-county provincial state, defeated the nine-counties proposal and secured government approval for a six-county state within the first month of parliamentary discussions on the bill. In the words of fellow-Unionist, Dixon, Craig had "scored nothing less than a triumph."

Further "triumphs" were to follow. Craig had been happy with the initial plan to set up single-assembly parliaments in Dublin and Belfast. A House of Lords amendment designed to give Southern Unionist peers representation in an upper house, a Senate, was opposed by Craig who had no desire to accommodate hostile minority opinion in a representative senate. Craig's submissions on 5th November 1920 ensured that the Northern Ireland Senate would reflect the Unionist majority in the Northern Ireland House of Commons. With the exception of two permanent members, the Lord Mayor of Belfast and the Lord Mayor of Derry city, the 24 Northern Senators were to be elected by the House of Commons. Craig did not consider the proposed Council of Ireland, to be composed of 20 members drawn from each parliament, as a serious threat to Ulster separatism especially as the nationalist majority in Southern Ireland remained unimpressed and rejected the bill in its entirety. Craig believed that the British government's acceptance of a "safe" six-county Northern Ireland state meant that the pious aspiration "to the eventual establishment of a parliament for the whole of Ireland" would remain an empty platitude.

Craig was unable, however, to change the government's determination to use proportional representation in elections to the new parliaments. As early as 1912 the Liberals saw PR as a means of protecting minorities and had used PR in local government elections in Ireland in 1920. Craig interpreted the stipulation that elections must be held under PR for the first three years after enactment of the Government of Ireland Act as meaning that thereafter PR could be replaced by simple majority. PR was abolished as early as 1922 in local elections and in 1929 in general elections.

Craig's close involvement with every aspect of the Government of Ireland Bill during its passage through parliament ensured its acceptance by Ulster Unionists who became its only supporters in Ireland. Craig's brother, Charles, summed up Ulster Unionist opinion in March 1920 thus, "We would much prefer to remain part and parcel of the United Kingdom . . . but we have many enemies in this country," and "We see our safety, therefore, in having a parliament of our own . . . and therefore I say that we prefer to have a parliament, although we do not want one of our own." Thus it was that on December 23rd 1920 the Government of Ireland Bill became law.

It came into operation on 3rd May 1921 with elections to both parliaments to be held 3 weeks later. The Southern nationalist majority rejected the Government of Ireland Act. The Anglo-Irish Treaty of December 1921 was needed in order to settle the Irish question in the rest of Ireland. Ironically, Ulster Unionist acceptance of the Government of Ireland Act meant that the area which had so steadfastly opposed Home Rule since 1886 was the only area to accept the kind of limited Home Rule envisaged by the successive Home Rule bills in 1886, 1893 and 1912.

The Government of Ireland Act gave Northern Ireland control over its own affairs. Even before the Government of Ireland Bill was on the statute book, Northern Ireland had, at Craig's instigation, its own Assistant Under-Secretary responsible for Northern affairs in Belfast. Craig was also instrumental in securing government approval for an armed unionist police force, the Ulster Special Constabulary, recruitment to which began one month before the Government of Ireland Bill became law. The reformation of the Ulster Volunteers in July 1920, in response to the threat posed by the War of Independence, was disquieting to the government who did not want another unofficial army in a war-torn land.

The Ulster Special Constabulary, drawn largely from the ranks of the UVF, was legally policing the Northern Ireland state when elections were held in May 1921 to determine the political future of the state.

Craig, Northern Ireland's First Prime Minister (1921-40)

Unionist confidence in an overall Unionist majority in the Northern Ireland elections was such that on 25th January 1921, almost four months to the day before the May elections, Carson was offered and declined premiership of a Unionist government in favour of Craig who assumed leadership of the Ulster Unionist movement on 4th February 1921. Craig said at this time, "All my political career has been bound up with Ulster." Thereafter the rest of his life was bound up with Northern Ireland.

The general election of 24th May 1921, the first ever to be held within the British Isles under the PR system, was a public test of everything that Craig and Ulster Unionism stood for. Craig represented the campaign thus, "If Ulster listens to me and if Ulster believes in me, as I believe she does, I will carry them through." The overwhelming Unionist victory, with every Unionist candidate who stood, elected, was a personal triumph for Craig and vindication of his convictions. Forty of the fifty-two members of the Northern Ireland Parliament were Unionist. The remaining twelve seats went to 6 Sinn Féin and 6 Nationalist candidates elected in the nationalist areas of West Belfast, Fermanagh, Tyrone, Armagh and Derry. All twelve candidates declined to take their seats. When the Northern Ireland Parliament met in early June to elect the Senate, the monopoly of Unionist power in the House of Commons ensured a totally Unionist Senate. There was thus no parliamentary opposition to the Unionist government announced at the first assembly of the Northern Ireland House of Commons on June 7th 1921.

Craig's election victory in May 1921 was all the greater because de Valera the Sinn Féin leader and President of the Irish Dáil had chosen to oppose him in Co. Down. Sinn Féin fielded 20 candidates in the election which was seen as a contest between the opposing ideologies of Unionism/Republicanism - partition versus the unity of Ireland. De Valera's decisive defeat (he polled just over 16,000 votes against

30,000 for Craig) was seen a defeat for Republicanism and unity in Northern Ireland.

The new parliament was formally opened amid great pomp and ceremony by King George V on June 22nd 1921. Intended to be a Westminster Parliament in miniature, its powers were so limited by the Government Act of Ireland that the Northern Ireland Parliament was often described as little better than a glorified county council. It was not empowered to alter the Northern Ireland constitution as laid down by the British-enacted Government of Ireland Act. All matters relating to the Crown, peace and war, the armed forces, treason, treaties with other states, trade with any place outside of Northern Ireland, naturalisation, domicile, cables and wireless, air, navigation, lighthouses, coinage and the issue of bank notes and negotiable instruments, weights and measures, trade marks, copyright and patents were all to be dealt with by the imperial parliament at Westminster where Northern Ireland interests would still be represented by thirteen members. In addition, in order to encourage the two parliaments envisaged by the Government of Ireland Act of 1920 to unite, Westminster reserved postal service, savings banks, designs for stamps, registration of deeds, land purchase, the supreme court of Northern Ireland and practically all taxes, hoping to transfer these considerable powers to an all-Ireland parliament. Most important of all, section 75 of the Government of Ireland Act made the Northern Ireland Parliament subordinate in every respect to the Westminster Parliament. "Notwithstanding the establishment of the parliament of Northern Ireland . . . the supreme authority of the parliament of the United Kingdom shall remain unaffected and undiminished over all persons, matters and things." Section 75 justified British government intervention from 1969 which eventually led to the suspension of the Northern Ireland parliament and government in March 1972 and the reimposition of direct rule from Westminster just over fifty years after the setting up of the state.

The Early Years

The seeds of the failure of the Northern Ireland state were sown during the premiership of Craig, its first premier. Craig's first address as government leader held out the promise of a non-partisan government pledged to "look to the people as a whole" and "probe to the bottom of those problems that have retarded progress in the past." Most significantly, in his speech of 23rd June 1921 he declared, "every person inside our particular boundary may rest assured that there will be nothing meted out to them but the strictest justice . . . We will be absolutely honest and fair in administering the law." Circumstances and events both inside and outside the state militated against such pious aspirations.

The Northern Ireland State was born in the midst of the violence of the War of Independence. Raging in the South since 1919, the war spread during 1920 to Belfast and the North. Sectarian rioting in Belfast and the expulsion of Catholic workers from the Belfast shipyards in the summer of 1920 were seen as Unionist reprisals for the IRA murder of high-ranking police officers with Ulster connections. In a wave of attacks on not just Catholic and Protestant areas of Belfast, but also in Bangor, Banbridge, Lisburn and Ballymena between July and September 1920, 62 people were killed, 200 were wounded and thousands, mainly Catholics, were driven from their homes and jobs. The Ulster Special Constabulary, formed at Craig's instigation to keep order, was seen as the Ulster Volunteer Force made legal. Ulster Volunteers were openly encouraged in a memorandum from their commanding officer Colonel Spender in October 1920 "to do all they can to make the Special Constabulary Forces a success." All categories "A" full-time and paid, "B" part-time and paid, "C" an unpaid reserve, became "legitimate" targets of IRA attack after their formation in November 1920. In addition, the Dáil imposed a boycott on all goods and services from the Protestant North-east from August 1920.

Ironically the truce, following upon King George V's plea for peace at the opening of the Northern Ireland parliament in June 1921, did not ease Craig's difficulties. The truce heightened Northern Ireland's security problems. The military terms of the cease-fire of 11th July 1921 meant that thirteen battalions of the British Army in Northern Ireland stood aside while sectarian violence escalated during August and September 1921 culminating in a week of rioting in November and resulting in 27 deaths and 92 injuries. The orgy of murder and violence precipitated the transfer of police powers from Westminster to the Northern Ireland government on November 22nd 1921 giving the Craig government responsibility for law and order and control of the police forces in Northern Ireland.

Whilst "a satisfactory solution of the age-long Irish problem" which the King requested in Belfast in 1921 was in Craig's interests (the transfer of powers to the NI Parliament had been postponed because of the South's non-acceptance of the Government of Ireland Act), Unionists dreaded the prospect of an Anglo-Irish settlement and feared betrayal by a war-weary British government anxious for peace at any price.

De Valera's conviction that the coercion of the majority in Northern Ireland would be as grave a mistake as had been British coercion of the rest of Ireland down the centuries and his assurance to the British in August 1921 to that effect, prompted Craig in September 1921 to make a friendly overture to the South, "We here are prepared to work in friendly rivalry with our fellow countrymen in the south and the west . . . we are prepared to work for the betterment of the people of Ireland, not to quarrel, not to continue political strife. . . ". Nonetheless, Craig, who had attempted one abortive meeting with de Valera in May 1921 before the general election, refused to meet de Valera or the Irish delegation during the Treaty talks July-December 1921. Summoned to London both in July and again in November at a critical stage of the Treaty negotiations, Craig reminded Lloyd George, the British PM, that it was "as a final settlement and supreme sacrifice in the interests of peace the Government of Ireland Act was accepted by Northern Ireland although not asked for by her representatives. "Stung by the comment of the then Conservative and Unionist leader in the House of Commons, Austen Chamberlain, that "the six counties was a compromise . . . illogical and indefensible and you could not raise an army in England to fight for that" Craig and the Northern Unionists adopted a stubborn intransigent stance. "What we have we hold" and "not an inch" became popular Unionist slogans as Northern Ireland went again on the defensive.

In his dealings with Lloyd George, Craig had a distinct advantage over Griffith and the Irish delegation. Whilst Lloyd George's resignation threats filled Griffith with dread they were welcomed by Craig who cherished the hope that Lloyd George's coalition government would fall and be replaced by an all Conservative government. Far from being intimidated Craig returned from the November talks with a definite time-table for the transfer of powers from London to Belfast. One of the greatest achievements for the Craig government in 1921 was the transfer of substantial powers which made possible the setting up of a Northern Ireland civil service and a NI courts system. Despite forebodings about the Treaty, the Northern Ireland government was setting up the machinery of a separate state and taking control of its own affairs.

Craig did not conceal his dismay at the terms of the Anglo-Irish Treaty of 6th December 1921. In a strongly-worded letter of protest to Lloyd George on 14th December 1921, during the Westminster debates on the Treaty, he described Northern Ireland's right to opt out of the united Ireland formally acknowledged by the terms of the Treaty as "a complete reversal" of declared imperial policy that "Ulster should remain out until she chose of her own free will to enter an all-Ireland Parliament." Equally rejecting the Boundary Commission's right to take "territory from an established Government without its sanction", Craig reserved the right of dissenting from the appointment of the Boundary Commission provided for in Article 12 of the Treaty. With remarkable foresight in 1921 Craig prophesised that "in years to come the British nation will realise the advantages in having in Northern Ireland a population which is determined to remain loyal to British traditions and citizenship."

Whilst the Westminster debates on the Treaty in mid-December 1921 did not rival the Dáil debates in intensity they were colourful. One Unionist MP from Northern Ireland, paraphrased Lloyd George's post-war election promise to make England "a country fit for heroes to live in" saying that he "was now making Ireland a country fit for murderers to operate in." Notwithstanding, the Treaty was approved by both the Commons and the Lords with even such former champions of Ulster Unionism as Bonar Law voting acceptance.

Craig - Collins Meetings 1922

Dáil acceptance of the Treaty on 7th January 1922 brought the threat of the Boundary Commission closer. Collins, the leader of the Provisional Government in the South, hoped that the Boundary Commission could start its study in July although he also made it known that he was prepared to drop demands for a Boundary Commission if Craig and he could reach mutual agreement. With this in mind and against a background of spiralling violence in Northern Ireland, Craig met Collins in London on 21st January 1922. During a three-hour meeting, Collins is reputed to have confided in Craig that he had so many troubles in Southern Ireland that he was anxious to establish "cordial relations" with Northern Ireland. Both showed a willingness to alter the Treaty by abandoning the Boundary Commission. Collins agreed to call off the boycott of Northern Ireland goods which was as damaging to the Southern economy as it was to the Northern. In return, Craig promised to use his influence to have the Catholics expelled from the Belfast shipyards reinstated. A second meeting in Dublin on February 2nd revealed how far apart both sides were on the border issue.

Failure to reach agreement on the border sparked off a border war as nationalists in border areas of Fermanagh, Tyrone, Armagh and Derry who had hoped to be returned peacefully to the Free State showed that they, assisted by IRA border units, were prepared to fight for inclusion. The seizure of unionist hostages by IRA flying columns in ill-defended rural areas of Fermanagh and the much-publicised "battle" of Clones of 11th February 1922 when a party of eighteen Ulster Special Constables en route from Newtownards to Enniskillen were attacked at Clones railway station by the IRA, revealed a lack of border security. Craig's appeals for additional armed forces fell on deaf and unsympathetic British ears. Winston Churchill who as Colonial Secretary was responsible for Irish affairs reminded Craig that British army strength in Northern Ireland had been increased from thirteen to nineteen battalions and rebuked Craig for permitting violation of Free State territory and asked for assurance that such violation would not recur. The British government feared that unchecked sectarian violence in Northern Ireland would provoke a Southern invasion of the North and undo all their work to solve the Irish question. In June, Lloyd George told Churchill that in the two years since 1920, 400 Catholics had been killed in NI without a single person being brought to justice.

The need to find a peace formula prompted Churchill to bring Craig and Collins together again in London on 30th March 1922. There, Churchill countersigned on behalf of the British government an eleven-point agreement under the impressive title "Heads of Agreement Between the Provisional Government and Government of Northern Ireland." Paper agreements to have half-Catholic, half-Protestant police patrols in mixed districts and to set up a Catholic Advisory Committee to advise on selection of Catholic recruits for the Special police came to naught as the Northern Ireland Parliament passed a draconian Civil Authority (Special Powers) Act renewed annually until 1928 and made permanent in 1933, which gave the Minister of Home Affairs the power "to take all such steps and issue all such orders as may be necessary for preserving the peace." Further he could delegate these wide-ranging powers to any member of the new RUC which in June 1922 replaced the RIC as the armed police force in Northern Ireland. Under Field-Marshal Sir Henry Wilson, Unionist MP for North Down at Westminster since February 1922 and until his assassination in London on the eve of the Civil War in the South in June 1922, military advisor in Northern Ireland, and also under his successor Major General Solly-Flood, Northern Ireland turned into a police state. By mid-1922 there were 50,000 policemen "armed and equipped to overawe nationalists and Catholics" according to the local nationalist newspaper the "Fermanagh Herald" of 27th November 1920. Lloyd George, on 30th May 1922, compared Craig's special police to Mussolini's Blackshirts in Italy. Yet Lloyd George resisted all Collins's pleas to let British troops take control in the north and preferred to subsidise the Special Constabulary rather than to keep large numbers of the British Army tied up in Ireland.

Craig used the short-lived Collins-de Valera pact of May 1922 as a pretext for dropping all pretence of friendship with the South. Fearing that the pact was a prelude to a united attack on the North and knowing that Collins since March had been supporting pro and anti-treaty IRA units by supplying them with arms for use in the North, Craig went on the offensive in the Northern House of Commons in May 1922 and gave the Unionists a new slogan when he declared defiantly, "What we have now we hold."

The outbreak of the Civil War in the South in June 1922 diverted IRA attention from the North. The rigorous application of internment without trial and curfew in areas of unrest, permissible under the Special Powers Act, imposed an uneasy calm on the troubled Northern state but not before 230 people had died in political disturbance in Belfast alone. The year 1922 had demonstrated that the Craig Government could rule only by the use and the threat of force.

The Boundary Commission

Craig knew that sooner or later the border issue would have to be faced. Changes in government during 1922 in both Britain and Southern Ireland made him more hopeful of a favourable outcome. The new all-Conservative government of Bonar Law from October 1922 made Craig more confident in his dealings with the new government of Cosgrave who became head of the first Free State Government. The Civil War in the South was ample illustration of the difficulty the Free State government was experiencing in ruling its existing territory and strengthened the argument for maintaining the status quo. The relative calm in Northern Ireland compared with the South also strengthened the North's argument for retention of existing boundaries. Craig knew that the longer a decision was delayed the stronger would be the North's case. Consequently, although he first met Cosgrave in November 1922 and discussed the setting up of a Boundary Commission with Cosgrave in London in April 1924, Craig delayed the appointment of a Northern Ireland Commissioner, forcing Britain's first labour PM Ramsay McDonald in August 1924 to amend the Treaty and make the Northern appointment himself. Notwithstanding, Craig managed to have the Boundary Commission postponed until November 1924 by which time the Conservatives under Baldwin had returned to office in Britain. Craig's reluctance to allow the Boundary Commission was all the more ironical as it had been Craig who had first suggested a Boundary Commission in 1919. In December 1919 he was heard to favour "a vote in those districts on either side immediately adjoining that boundary."

No plebiscite was to be permitted when the Boundary Commission consisting of Co. Antrim born Catholic, Eoin McNeill representing the Free State government, JR Fisher, British-appointed Ulster Unionist and Justice Feetham of South Africa finally met in November 1924. Amid threats from Craig to resign and to lead Unionists in their fight "to defend any territory . . . unfairly transferred", the British-appointed "neutral" chairman, Justice Feetham, chose to interpret Article 12 of the Treaty in Northern Ireland's favour by emphasising "economic and geographic conditions" rather than the wishes of the people. A general election in April 1925 in NI fought on the Unionist boundary slogan "Not an inch" seemed to confirm Unionist determination to resist change. Timely Unionist gains in disputed counties Fermanagh and Tyrone, due to Nationalists and Sinn Féin splitting the nationalist vote, strengthened Unionist claims to a six-county NI state. When it became clear that a majority report could be presented to the governments and, once presented, the Commission's findings would have the force of law, McNeill realised that his and the Free State's viewpoint mattered little. McNeill's resignation not only from the Commission on November 20th 1925, but from the Free State government a few days later following an accurate "leak" to a Conservative newspaper the "Morning Post", that only minor boundary changes were envisaged in the Commission report which was about to be published, prompted the Cosgrave government to take immediate action to suppress the report and seek direct talks with both the Craig and Baldwin governments.

Craig knew that in the tripartite talks which followed he held all the advantages. For the Free State the alternative to a no-change border was the unfavourable Boundary Commission findings which proposed giving part of Donegal to Northern

Ireland in return for gains elsewhere to the South. Either way the six-county state of Northern Ireland was to remain intact. Before the tripartite agreement affirming no change on the border was signed by Cosgrave, Craig and Baldwin, the British PM, in London on 3rd December 1925, Cosgrave was resigned to no territorial change. The tripartite talks concentrated on agreeing an acceptable financial "compensation" for the Free State government. Craig, whose own government had difficulty in meeting its financial commitments to Britain under the terms of the Government of Ireland Act 1920, revelled in describing the Free State as a poverty-stricken country unable to pay its share of the UK public debt as laid down in Article 5 of the Treaty. Both Articles 5 and Articles 12 relating to the modification of the border were revoked. The Irish Free State was released from its obligation to contribute an as yet unspecified amount to the British public debt. Of far greater significance, however, was the agreement to abandon the Council of Ireland, the intended bridge between the two parliaments. The abandonment of the Council of Ireland in 1925 meant that all three interested parties, NI, the Free State and Britain concurred with Craig's view as expressed to Collins in January 1922, "For the present, an all-Ireland Parliament was out of the question, possibly in years to come — 10, 20 or 50 years." Craig's final comment on the subject of an all-Ireland Dublin Parliament is interesting, "He would erect no barriers round a Dublin Parliament but in no case would he pass through them himself."

For Craig, the outcome of the border issue was an unqualified success. The agreement not to alter the border was a vindication of his "Not an Inch" policy. Grateful and jubilant Unionists held religious services of thanksgiving throughout the province. A grateful NI Parliament, whose powers were greatly enhanced by the transfer to it of powers reserved to the Council of Ireland by the Government of Ireland Act (1920), presented Craig in mid-December with a silver Celtic cup. Appropriately, "Not an Inch" was engraved on its base. Further honour was accorded to Craig when his name appeared in the new year honours list. In 1926, Sir James Craig became Lord Craigavon. Craig's greatest achievement in 1925 was to secure Free State recognition of a six-county NI state. Cahir Healy, Nationalist MP for Fermanagh, despondently expressed the betrayal of the Northern Nationalists thus, "The new leaders agree to partition forever." Among the important political consequences of the boundary controversy was the entry of the ten Northern Nationalist MPs into the NI Parliament. Nationalist leader, Devlin, MP for West Belfast, took his seat after the April election, an indication that, even before the border issue had been decided, Northern Nationalists were reluctantly coming to the conclusion that their future lay within Northern Ireland. The Boundary agreement also led to political change in the Free State. De Valera decided to leave Sinn Féin which refused to recognise the Dáil and to form a political party, Fianna Fáil, which in 1927 entered the Dáil and led the parliamentary opposition to the Cosgrave government.

Craig, in his address to the NI Parliament on the boundary agreement, spoke of, "a new era . . . in Irish history" and expressed the hope that "cordial relations" between the two states would lead to co-operation on trade and looked forward to meetings between the two governments "to smooth over those small but irritating difficulties that are bound to arise . . . between two neighbouring States". The reality was that forty years were to pass before the historic meeting between the two heads of government, O'Neill and Lemass in January 1965 rocked the Unionist community to its foundation and set in motion the train of events which led to the downfall of the NI regime in 1972.

In another respect the 1925 boundary agreement ushered in a new era. The British government, convinced that peace must follow such a satisfactory agreement, withdrew all subsidy from the Ulster Special Constabulary. Craig had no choice but to order the disbandment of categories "A" and "C" on December 10th 1925. The voluntary part-time "B Specials" remained but were stepped down. The first phase of the NI "Troubles" were over. All looked forward to a period of peace and hopefully prosperity.

Northern Ireland Under Craig:
Alienation of Catholics

Although the Government of Ireland Act (1920) contained built-in safeguards for religious minorities (Section 15 expressly prohibited the NI Parliament from discriminating on religious grounds,) the Catholic community never overcame its initial hostility and suspicion of the NI regime. The 1926 census, the first undertaken in the new state, revealed that Catholics represented the largest single denomination (Catholic 33·5%, Presbyterians 31·3%, Church of Ireland 27%, Methodists and others 8·2%) in the state. Yet the Craig government made no effort to woo the Catholic/Nationalist minority. From the outset Nationalists were regarded as enemies of the state. In 1921 "rebel" Nationalist county councils were dissolved. Unionists resolved to have proportional representation, introduced into local and parliamentary elections, as a safeguard for minorities by the 1919 Local Government (Ireland) Act and the Government of Ireland Act 1920, respectively abolished. Craig had expressed his opposition to PR as early as 1909 when he submitted arguments against PR to an Electoral Reform Commission at Westminster. Within a year of taking office the Local Government Act of 1922 had abolished PR in local elections. County and rural district constituencies were redrawn so as to ensure permanent Unionist domination of local government. The charge of "gerrymandering", the redrawing of constituency boundaries in such a way as to create artificial Unionist majorities in areas where Nationalists were in a majority e.g. Fermanagh, Tyrone and Derry city and the system of plural voting in local elections whereby owners of business and property had more than one vote while non-ratepayers had no vote at all, eventually led to the Civil Rights Demonstrations of the late 1960s and the termination of the NI regime when it proved unable to contain the civil disorder from 1968.

Whilst only one local government election in 1920 was held under PR two general elections (in 1921 and 1925) were held before PR was swept away totally by the Method of Voting and Redistribution of Seats Act 1929. The 1925 election returned four Independent Unionists and three Labour MPs. Fear of the proliferation of small parties (encouraged by PR and multi-member constituencies), which might vote with the Nationalists against the government, prompted the Unionists to seek both to abolish PR and to introduce single-member constituencies before the next general election in 1929. Craig, in his campaign for abolition of PR, maintained that the electorate did not understand the PR system of voting and feared that "by an actual mistake they might wake up to find Northern Ireland in the perilous position of being submerged in a Dublin parliament."

The replacement of PR by simple majority representation in single member constituencies and the redrawing of constituencies in order to give Unionists a permanent parliamentary majority came just as Nationalists had decided to work within the Northern parliamentary system. The electoral changes of 1929 further polarised Northern politics and Northern society. Labour representation fell to one MP in 1929. Northern politics developed along rigid two-party lines with only one issue before the electorate Unionism versus Nationalism. Political apathy was another consequence of the electoral changes. The hopelessness of attempting to dislodge firmly-entrenched Unionists resulted in elections being uncontested. In 1933 thirty-three of NIs fifty-two MPs, including three-quarters of the Unionist candidates, were returned unopposed. The opposition were doomed to perpetual opposition while the government ruled, confident that there was no political alternative to it.

Education

Although a small number of Catholics belonged to the Unionist Party, Catholics were generally perceived as Nationalists and therefore opposed to the setting up of the state. Nowhere was this more evident than in the attitude of Catholic teachers who refused to recognise the NI regime and resisted the transfer of responsibility for education from Dublin to Belfast in February 1922. Some 800 teachers in primary and secondary schools, encouraged by the payment of subidies by Collins and his successor Cosgrave until November 1922, initally refused salaries from the Northern government.

Lord Londonderry, Northern Minister of Education, hoped to solve the educational impasse by creating a state system of free compulsory non-denominational education. Non-denominational education was as unacceptable to Protestants as it was to Catholics. The Catholic Church, however, from the outset refused to take part in any discussions on state education. Protestants, on the other hand, dominated the Lynn Committee formed in 1921 in order to frame proposals for the Education Act 1923 which, with amendments largely inspired by Craig in 1925 and 1930, became the basis of state education in Northern Ireland. The amendments made state schools "safe for Protestant children" - Craig's own comment in the NI Parliament in April 1930. The appointment of Protestant teachers was assured by the nomination of Protestant clergy to local education selection committees. Simple Bible instruction, acceptable to Protestants but not to Catholics, was made compulsory. The form of state education which emerged during the first ten years of the NI state ensured the continuation of segregated education, with Catholics labouring under the double grievance of having to support their own disadvantaged under-funded Catholic schools while, at the same time, supporting through their rates and taxes, the state schools which have remained almost exclusively Protestant in character.

The Economy

The acid test for the Craig administration in the eyes of the Irish Unionist supporters was the extent to which it maintained parity of living standards with the rest of the United Kingdom. One of the cruel ironies of the time was that the powerful economic reasons for the industrialised North-East remaining within the United Kingdom no longer held. In the early 1920s the old-established ship-building and linen industries went into permanent decline. Employment in the Belfast shipyards fell from around 20,000 in 1924 to just over 2000 in 1933, the first time in over a century that Belfast had no new ship in the pipe-line. Underlying the sectarian violence of the 1920s and mid 1930s was the spectre of mass unemployment. At the same time as Catholic workers were being physically ejected from their jobs, Protestant workers were being dismissed and laid off in thousands. For a brief period in 1932, with unemployment reaching new levels throughout the United Kingdom as the Great Depression paralysed industrial output everywhere, Catholic and Protestant workers threatened to join together in their common economic misery. A Unionist government recommendation to Protestant employers to employ only Protestants ensured that economic difficulties found expression once again in sectarian strife.

Belfast, again, erupted in religious war in the summer of 1935 resulting in 11 dead and nearly 600 injured.

The economic problems of Northern Ireland were made worse by the financial and economic restrictions placed on the NI government by the Government of Ireland Act 1920. Fourteen of the seventy-six articles of the Government of Ireland Act 1920 dealt with financial provisions and effectively removed control from the Belfast government over the imposition and collection of four-fifths of government revenue. Essentially control of revenue lay with Westminster while responsibility for government expenditure was assumed by the NI government. In addition, Northern Ireland, as part of the United Kingdom, was obliged to contribute to the imperial exchequer. A fixed annual contribution in 1921 of almost £8m proved too high. During the 1930s the imperial contribution fell to as little as £10,000. Craig's prediction of 1925 that "the contribution, instead of being paid by Northern Ireland to Great Britain, may be paid by Great Britain to Northern Ireland in order to preserve the same standard of living amongst the population as prevails on the other side" was fulfilled.

Craig's "not an inch" attitude endeared him to Ulster Unionists.

Parity in living standards and social services with British citizens on the UK mainland was not conceded by Britain until 1938. The Simon declaration by the British Chancellor of the Exchequer Simon in May 1938 within days of the return of the Treaty ports to Eire, guaranteed equality in social services and standards with the rest of the UK. Unemployment throughout the inter-war period, however, ran at a higher level in Northern Ireland than in most other areas of the UK except during the worst years of the Great Depression. In 1925, almost a quarter of the work force was out of work. During the 1930s, the annual average never fell below 20%. With the exception of a short-lived boom during the war-years 1939-45, Northern Ireland has become a financial liability to the rest of the United Kingdom. R. J. Lawrence in his book "The Government of Northern Ireland" summed up the achievements of the Craigavon years thus, "On the ramshackle foundations of the Act of 1920 he and his colleagues had built not a half-way house but a lean-to whose stability depended on ties that bound it to Britain.

Final Years

From his first days as Prime Minister, Craig spent an ever-increasing amount of time away from the new state. During the first year 1921-22, Craig crossed to Britain thirteen times in order to win better conditions for Northern Ireland. On the pretext of being an ambassador for Northern Ireland, Craig undertook long business trips abroad and became increasingly out of touch with events at home. For Craig, the highlight of the 1930s was the opening of Stormont Parliament by the Prince of Wales in November 1932. It was made the occasion of a great unionist demonstration which served to distract loyalists from the economic ills of the day.

By 1940, the year of his death, Craig was a tired old man leading a tired old government. Four of his six government ministers had held office since 1921. Yet Craig resisted all pressure to resign. In 1938, in response to de Valera's 1937 constitution claiming jurisdiction over the whole island and to the Anglo-Irish Agreements of 1938 which he saw as further British concessions to a hostile government, he called a general election on the border issue. Victory at the polls in 1938 gave him his fifth successive election victory. He proudly boasted to the British newspaper, the Daily Express, that he was "the one politician who can win an election without even leaving his fireside." Two years later, he was dead. His death in November 1940 occurred at a critical time during the war. The summer of 1940 saw union with Britain under threat as PM Churchill appeared willing to trade unity for an end to Irish neutrality. For Northern Ireland, the Anglo-Irish discussions between April-July 1940 represented the greatest threat to NI's constitutional position since the Treaty talks of 1921. Appropriately, Craig's last significant speech in the NI Parliament less than one month before his death on November 24th 1940 was in denunciation of a motion that Northern Ireland should unite with the South. To the end, Craig was the champion of Ulster Unionism. A cabinet colleague and future Northern Ireland Prime Minister, Sir Basil Brooke, paid tribute to the memory of Craig thus, "Ulster can never repay the debt it owes to him and might never appreciate all he meant to her."

Appraisal

The names of Carson and Craig are synonymous with Ulster Unionism and the birth of the Northern Ireland state. Whilst Carson was the adopted son of Ulster, Craig was the true son. An Ulsterman first, then a Briton but never an Irishman, Craig devoted his political life to the maintenance of Unionist Ulster within the United Kingdom because he was convinced that union with Britain was in Unionist Ulster's best possible interests. His relationship with successive British government can be best summed up in his comment to Kevin O'Higgins, Minister for Home Affairs in the first Free State government at the tripartite talks in 1925 leading to the Boundary Agreement, "Anything I can do to help you get what you can off those fellows, I will."

As Northern Ireland's first premier, Craig, during his long premiership, had the opportunity to influence the development of the new state. Craig, however, never quite made the transition from leader of a sectional interest to government leader representing all the people within the new state. Failure to win the trust of a large minority within the community ultimately led to the collapse of the Northern Ireland state. The seeds of Northern Ireland's failure were sown by the sectarian policies of the Craigavon years which ensured the permanent alienation of 1/3 of the population. Craig's proudest boast about Northern Ireland was that it had "a Protestant Parliament and a Protestant State."

As leader of Ulster Unionists, Craig had few critics. As Prime Minister, Craig's shortsightedness, his unwillingness to consult government colleagues prior to, and worse still, after decisions were taken, above all, his determination to stay in office long after failing health made effective government impossible, drew from one government critic the sharp rebuke that it was not in Ulster's interests for him to maintain his "tired and jaded men" until "the hand of God removes him." It was, however, that stubborn streak of character that endeared him to Ulster Unionists. Although perhaps not the most competent of Prime Ministers, to NI Unionists, Craig was a popular Prime Minister. His personal, almost presidential, tours of the state and his willingness to speak and listen to ordinary people enhanced his popularity. A senior civil servant, although critical of Craig's leadership, in 1938 summed up his appeal thus: "he had a hold over the people of the province as Carson's successor which no one else had."

Landmarks in Craig's Life (1871-1940)

1871 *January 8th* — Born into a wealthy family in Co. Down.

1906 Entered Westminster Parliament as Unionist MP for East Down.

1911-14 Carson's "First Lieutenant" during the Ulster Unionist campaign against Home Rule.

1916 *December* — Became junior member of Lloyd George's Coalition government.

1918 *January* — Resigned with Carson from government in protest at Irish Convention findings.

1919 *January* — As junior member of a new Coalition government Craig exercised an important influence over the drafting of the Government of Ireland Bill.

1921 *February 4th* — Assumed leadership of Ulster Unionist movement.
May 24th — First elections to a Northern Ireland Parliament.
June 22nd — Formal opening of the Northern Ireland Parliament.

1921-40 Premiership of Craig.

1925 Boundary Agreement signed by Craig, Cosgrave and Baldwin.

1929 Abolition of PR in elections gave Unionists a monopoly of power.

1940 *November 24th* — Death of Northern Ireland's first Prime Minister.

3. Griffith

Early Life and Influences

Arthur Griffith, founder of Sinn Féin and founding father of the Irish Free State, was born on 31st March 1871 in Dublin. His father was a printer. Young Griffith's formal education ended at fifteen years when he left school in order to become an apprentice printer. He continued his education through reading and membership of numerous literary societies which were mushrooming in Dublin in the last quarter of the nineteenth century as part of the Anglo-Irish cultural revival. Through membership of the Leinster Literary Society he met a fellow school-mate, William Rooney whose political judgment he came to admire and whom he considered as "the destined regenerator of his people." Rooney's premature death in 1901 forced Griffith to assume leadership of the political movement, Cumann na nGaedheal, formed in September 1900 in order to give political expression to the Gaelic and nationalist revival of the last years of the nineteenth century.

Ill health and the threat of unemployment forced Griffith in his mid-twenties to seek work for a brief period in South Africa. There, Griffith took the Boer side against Britain in the critical period before the Boer War (1899-1902). His first truly political and anti-British statements were made in the Boer Republic of the Transvaal when he stated categorically "the Boer and no one but the Boer owned the Transvaal . . . God Almighty had not made the earth for the sole use of the Anglo-Saxon race." Griffith's sympathy for the Boers was shared by many Irishmen who like Griffith saw the Boer struggle against British domination as being similar to the Irish struggle to liberate Ireland from British rule.

The year 1898 was the centenary anniversary of the 1798 republican-inspired rebellions to liberate Ireland. Griffith, in Johannesburg, formed an Irish Society in order to link the Boer and Irish struggles. Just one month after celebrating the centenary anniversary of the '98 rebellions in style, Griffith left South Africa leaving fellow founder-member John McBride to form an Irish brigade of members of the Irish Society which fought with distinction during the Boer War using effective guerila tactics to be copied by the Irish during the War of Independence twenty years later. Back in Dublin, Griffith's contribution to the Boer War was to set up "the Transvaal Committee" among whose members were Maud Gonne, who was to marry the Irish hero of the Boer War, Captain John McBride, and James Connolly future socialist leader in the 1916 Rebellion. The main concern of "the Transvaal Committee" was to whip up public sympathy for the Boers and antipathy against the British and more practically to discourage recruitment in Ireland to the British Army. The visit by the aged Queen Victoria to Dublin in April 1900 at

Arthur Griffith (1871 - 1922)

a critical stage of the Boer War, was roundly condemned by Griffith as a recruiting gimmick. He regarded her as having been sent over, "in her dotage . . . to seek recruits for her battered army." The military difficulties experienced by Britain during the Boer War demonstrated to many Irish nationalists that the great might of the British armies might not be as invincible as they were led to believe.

Griffith's contribution to the 1898 centenary celebrations in Ireland was to launch a newspaper called the "United Irishman." Yeats was among the nationalist writers of the literary revival who contributed to Griffith's "United Irishman."

In September 1900 Griffith formed his own first political movement Cumann na nGaedheal. Seen as an umbrella organisation representing all shades of nationalist opinion it required only of its members that they should declare themselves advocates of an Irish republic while at the same time recognising "its present inability to lead Ireland to victory against the armed might of her enemy army." John O'Leary, the veteran Fenian became Cumann na nGaedheal's first president. The IRB of which Griffith was a member at this time, actively supported Griffith's ventures. At a convention of Cumann na nGaedheal in October 1902, Griffith, in calling upon members of the Irish Parliamentary Party to refuse "to attend the British parliament or recognise its right to legislate for Ireland" was advocating political abstention from Westminster, the cornerstone of Griffith's political philosophy.

Griffith was not the first to advocate parliamentary abstention. Both O'Connell and Davis whom Griffith greatly admired, had considered it during the Repeal of the Union campaign in the 1840's while Parnell had also considered withdrawal from Westminster during the dark days of the Land War in 1881. Griffith, however, looked to the success of the Hungarian experience in Central Europe for a contemporary analogy. In a series of newspaper articles in the "United Irishman" in 1904 Griffith outlined his "Hungarian policy." The articles were later produced in book form under the title "The Resurrection of Hungary, A Parallel for Ireland." The parallel was not totally accurate. The multi-racial Austrian Empire in Central Europe had little in common with the British Empire. An Anglo-Irish Ausgleich could not hope to bring the benefits to Britain that the creation of the dual monarchy Austria-Hungary, by the Ausgleich compromise of 1867, had brought to Austria. Yet the Hungarian policy held enormous attraction for Griffith. It represented a political alternative to both parliamentarianism and to violent revolution. Francis Deak had won independence for Hungary, not in Vienna the Austrian capital, but by withdrawing from the Imperial Parliament in Vienna and setting up a Hungarian parliament in Budapest, the Hungarian capital. The common link, the monarch, was to Griffith as essential to the Anglo-Irish relationship as it was to Austria-Hungary. In the "United Irishman" of August 1903 Griffith, whose grandfather was of Ulster Protestant farming stock, made his own position clear "We hold that the subsistence of the connection between this country and Great Britain in any form is not for our country's good, but we recognise the existence of a large mass of our countrymen who believe . . . that provided the countries retain each their independence and exist co-equal in power, the rule of a common sovereign is "admissable". Griffith looked to a period of intense patriotic activity by Anglo-Irish Protestants during the eighteenth century for an Irish parallel. Grattan's Parliament of 1782 which had forced upon the British Parliament the Renunciation Act of 1783 renouncing the right of the British Parliament to legislate for Ireland, was taken as the Irish model. Describing himself as a "King,

Lords and Commons man" Griffith echoed O'Connell who in moving Repeal of the Act of Union in the House of Commons in 1834, stated that he saw Ireland as "another and distinct country, subject to the same King but having a Legislature totally independent of the Legislature of Great Britain." Griffith was an avowed anti-partitionist. Dual monarchy was a platform upon which to unite the country.

Griffith was also influenced by the warmth of the welcome afforded to the new king, Edward VII during a state visit in 1903. The Nationalist newspaper the "Cork Examiner" remarked upon "the honest unaffected welcome extended by the people of all classes". Griffith realised that the monarchy was still popular. Nevertheless, he formed a National Council of literary and public figures such as Yeats and Edward Martyn who, with Lady Gregory had started the Abbey Theatre, to protest officially against the royal visit. Their campaign succeeded in stopping Dublin Corporation from making a loyal address to the royal visitors. After the royal visit the National Council remained in being. The first National Council Convention met in November 1905 using for the first time the slogan "Sinn Féin" which Griffith said, "are exactly the two words which express my meaning."

Formation of Sinn Féin

Like Cumann na nGaedheal, Sinn Féin was an umbrella organisation embracing all shades of nationalist political opinion excluding the Irish Parliamentary Party. In April 1907 the Sinn Féin League was formed by the fusion of Cumann na nGaedheal and the recently formed Dungannon clubs. The Dungannon Clubs formed in 1905 by IRB enthusiasts Bulmer Hobson and Denis McCullough, sought respectability by association with the legal political movement Cumann na nGaedheal. The National Council joined in September 1908 and the new movement became known simply as Sinn Féin.

Sinn Féin meaning "Ourselves", not "ourselves alone", adopted the policies already outlined by Griffith. The Dungannon Clubs were separatist and had difficulty in accepting Griffith's concept of dual monarchy. Clinging tenaciously to the concept of a dual monarchy, Griffith endeavoured to mollify separatists by saying "I am a separatist. The Irish people are not separatists. I do not think that they can be united behind a separatist policy. But I do think it is possible to unite them on this policy." As a further gesture to the Dungannon Clubs the first objective was the creation of a Council of Three Hundred made up of 103 elected local government delegates drawn from County Councils, Corporations and District Councils who, together, with the King, would form the governing body in Ireland.

Griffith had clear ideas as to the type of government he expected from an all-Irish democratically-elected assembly. National self-reliance was the keynote of Sinn Féin's economic policy. Griffith looked again to Europe for an economic success story for a self-governing Ireland to follow. Protectionism was the secret of Imperial Germany's economic success at the turn of the century. The German protectionist, Friedrich List's book, "National System of Protection" became the basis for Griffith's policy of economic nationalism. Economic independence was for Griffith as important as political independence. Self-sufficiency in industry as well as agriculture was important to Griffith who stated, "a merely agricultural nation can never develop to any extent a home or a foreign commerce." Among fifteen practical ways to demonstrate economic independence, Griffith advocated the boycott of goods paying duty to the British Exchequer, and the replacement of British manufactured goods by protected Irish goods.

Sinn Féin put its policies to the test in a by-election in 1908 ironically caused by the resignation of the elected Irish MP, C. J. Dolan who withdrew from Westminster in order to stand on the abstentionist policy of Sinn Féin. Sinn Féin's defeat (S.F. candidate Dolan 1,157, I.P.P. candidate 3,105 votes) in its first political contest did not detract from the significance of the first abstentionist votes cast. Griffith commented thus, "From the day the representatives of Ireland first crossed the sea to sit in an Alien Parliament — that fatal January 1st 1801 — until Friday last, no vote has been cast in an election in Ireland in denial of the authority of that Parliament to rule Ireland."

Election defeat in 1908 demonstrated a lack of popular support for what one contemporary nationalist journalist D.P. Moran scornfully called the "Green Hungarian Band". An attempt to launch the newspaper "Sinn Féin" which had replaced the "United Irishman" as Griffith's newspaper in 1906, as a daily in 1909, ended in financial disaster in January 1910. Sinn Féin's eclipse coincided with the raised expectations of the Irish Parliamentary Party of gaining Home Rule from a British Liberal Party who, following two general elections in 1910, relied upon the support of the Irish Parliamentary Party in order to curb the power of the Conservative-dominated House of Lords. The price of Irish parliamentary support from 1910 was the same as that exacted by Parnell in 1886 — a Liberal commitment to Home Rule. Liberal Prime Minister Asquith's pledge to "set up in Ireland a system of full self-government in purely Irish affairs" drove moderates, attracted to Sinn Féin by Griffith's dual monarchy concept, into the ranks of the constitutional parliamentary party who in 1912 seemed to have achieved their objective at last when the Third Home Rule bill was finally passed in the British House of Commons. At the same time Sinn Féin was losing its extremist supporters. As early as 1906 Bulmer Hobson whose Dungannon Clubs were to merge with Sinn Féin in 1907, stated in their weekly paper "The Republic", "We stand for an Irish republic . . . no compromise with England, . . . will satisfy the national aspirations of the Irish people." Extremists like Sean McDermott, who, as a Dungannon Club recruit, organised the Sinn Féin by-election campaign in 1908 could not be satisfied with Griffith's cautious non-revolutionary programme and had become revolutionary leaders in the revitalised IRB movement which from 1907 was again actively planning for armed insurrection. Although he relied heavily on the IRB for funds, Griffith had left the IRB organisation by 1910. Only the failure of both the Parliamentary initiative on Home Rule and the failure of revolution in Easter Week 1916 could enable Sinn Féin to rise again as an acceptable alternative to both parliamentarianism and armed insurrection.

Transformation of Sinn Féin (1916-18)

Griffith, although he is popularly depicted as a pacifist, joined the Irish Volunteers and helped in the distribution of guns at the Howth gun-running in July 1914. Despite strict censorship of all nationalist newspapers Griffith managed to keep an anti-war paper "Scissors and Paste" — an amalgam of selected cuttings from British newspapers and translations from German newspapers — until its suppression in 1915. Griffith was present at the IRB-convened meeting in the Gaelic League

Headquarters in Parnell Street on September 9th 1914 and endorsed the IRB sentiment expressed there that England's dilemma should be Ireland's opportunity.

Griffith, like McNeill, was unconvinced about the value of a rebellion that was doomed to failure. Unlike McNeill, Griffith, however, offered his services to the rebels on Easter Monday but was told that "they wanted his pen and his brain to survive the fight for their memory — and not to join in."

The "Sinn Féin" Rising 1916

Griffith knew that non-participation would not save him from arrest and imprisonment after the inevitable collapse of the rebellion. For long Sinn Féin had been regarded in the public mind, both in Ireland and in Britain, as the public anti-British, extra-parliamentary, and therefore to many, revolutionary political movement in Ireland. MacNeill's Irish Volunteers after the Woodenbridge split in September 1914 were popularly called "Sinn Féin Volunteers." Whatever doubts the public may have had about Griffith's role in the Easter Rising were dispelled when official government communiqués referred to the "Sinn Féin Rebellion" and when Griffith was arrested on 31st May 1916 the day on which the first three of the fifteen post-Rising executions took place. Griffith, interned until Christmas 1916 in Reading gaol, was one of 1,841 sympathisers interned in British jails.

The transformation of Sinn Féin which, on its own admission in October 1915, was "on the rocks" into a national political alternative to the Irish Parliamentary Party was the biggest political development between 1916 and 1918. Wrongful association with the Easter Rising was largely responsible. Faulty British intelligence may have led to mistakes on the British side but there is evidence to show that the British government hoped to use the rebellion to crush Sinn Féin which they regarded as a potentially dangerous revolutionary movement. Members of the British government in Dublin Castle spent Easter Sunday debating about when to order the mass arrest of "Sinn Féiners." When public sympathy swung behind the executed martyrs of Easter Week 1916 the suffering Sinn Féin internees equally benefited. Volunteer, IRB and Sinn Féin prisoners were treated as one group by both the British prison authorities where they shared the same cells and prison conditions and by the largely IRB-organised Prisoners' Dependents Associations who did not differentiate between prisoners in the distribution of aid. Sinn Féin, therefore, gained the political credit from the Rising. Republicans who had little in common with Griffith's moderate opinions, knew that after 1916 they could only find political expression in Sinn Féin the political alternative to the then despised Irish Parliamentary Party.

The decline and demise of the Irish Parliamentary Party coincided with the rise of Sinn Féin in the two years after the Rising. The Irish Parliamentary Party became identified with party leader Redmond's condemnation in the immediate wake of the rebellion which he said had attempted to make Ireland the "catspaw of Germany" and which was both "treason to the cause of the allies" . . . and to the cause of Home Rule. Irish nationalists regarded Redmond's willingness in July 1916 to consider partition as even a temporary solution to the Irish question, as even greater treason. Although Redmond withdrew the Irish Parliamentary Party from the Home Rule talks when it became clear on July 11th that the proposed exclusion of six counties from a Home Rule Ireland would be "permanent and enduring", public opinion was shocked that he could consider even temporary partition. Dillon, the next and last leader of the

Irish Parliamentary Party, assessed the situation thus, "Enthusiasm and trust in Redmond is dead, so far as the mass of the people is concerned."

By-election results in 1917 and 1918 demonstrated the truth of this statement. In February 1917 Count Plunkett, father of the executed signatory of the 1916 Proclamation of Independence, Joseph Plunkett, became the first abstentionist M.P. when he was elected to represent North Roscommon and refused to take his seat at Westminster. He was followed by Volunteer prisoner, McGuinness, who won the Longford by-election in May, the July East-Clare by-election victory of de Valera, "the accepted leader of the men of Easter Week," and the August success of S.F. candidate, Cosgrave, in Kilkenny. These 1916 men, while not subscribing fully to Sinn Féin policies, were happy to accept Sinn Féin nomination and adopted the Sinn Féin policy of political abstention from Westminster. Further common ground was found in the desire by all to place Ireland's case for independence before the international Peace Conference at war's end and in Sinn Féin's refusal to participate in the British-proposed Irish Convention, set up in July 1917 to attempt to find a solution acceptable to both Unionists and Nationalists.

De Valera was to use Griffith's willingness to have the sovereignty of Ireland determined by international opinion as a first step towards the rewriting of the Sinn Féin constitution and his own domination of Sinn Féin. A formula acceptable to all shades of political opinion represented in the umbrella organisation of Sinn Féin ran thus, "Sinn Féin aims at securing international recognition of Ireland as an independent Irish Republic. Having achieved that status the Irish people may by referendum freely choose their own form of Government." Griffith, who had no personal ambitions for leadership, actually proposed de Valera for Presidency of Sinn Féin, and on October 25th 1917 handed over a vibrant organisation, which had grown in the period April-October 1917 from 11,000 to 250,000 members, to those who rejected totally his concept of a dual monarchy.

The militancy of the "new" Sinn Féin was evident in the demonstrations following the death of Sinn Féin supporter, Ashe. His death in September 1917 while on hunger-strike "made 100,000 Sinn Féiners out of 100,000 constitutional nationalists" according to the London newspaper "Daily Express." As early as February 1918 Dublin Castle was considering the mass arrest of Sinn Féin leaders and the suppression of the movement. Fear of armed resistance and preoccupation with the need to extend conscription to Ireland forced them to propose action. The "Conscription Crisis" caused by the introduction of the Military Service Bill in the House of Commons on April 10th, 1918, designed to enable the British Army to call up at least 150,000 Irishmen, was an unqualified success for Sinn Féin. Griffith, always an outspoken opponent of conscription, had said in Reading gaol in 1916, "Ireland must fight conscription with tongues, pens, sticks, stones . . . swords, guns." Griffith's triumph was complete when the Irish Parliamentary Party belatedly adopted the abstentionist tactics of their political opponents by withdrawing en bloc from the House of Commons on 16th April 1918, in protest at the passing of the Military Service Act. Griffith was present at the all-party anti-conscription meeting in the Mansion House in Dublin two days later when a Sinn Féin resolution drawn up by de Valera was adopted, not just by the Mansion House conference but also by the Catholic hierarchy, who set aside the following Sunday as a day of special anti-conscription protest outside Catholic churches throughout the country. When the trade union movement agreed to hold a 24-hour anti-conscription general strike on April 23rd 1918 it was as if Sinn Féin had been able to marshal the whole country, with the exception of the Unionist North-East, against conscription.

The government, thoroughly alarmed at the prospect of a country united behind Sinn Féin, decided to implement its earlier plan to crush the movement. The alleged "German Plot" of May 1918 was the excuse used by Field Marshal Lord French, the new Viceroy, to order the arrest of seventy-three Sinn Féin leaders on the night of 17th May 1918, among them both de Valera and Griffith. Thus it was that Griffith was elected abstentionist M.P. for East Cavan on June 19th on the election slogan "Put him in to get him out." Neither could the imprisoned Griffith share personally in Sinn Féin's spectacular success in the December general election 1918 when the return of 73 Sinn Féin M.P.s made possible Griffith's primary political objective, the setting up of an Irish assembly of elected abstentionist M.P.s to legislate for Ireland.

Griffith and Dáil Eireann

Griffith, still imprisoned in Gloucester jail, was unable to attend the historic opening of the First Dáil Eireann on January 21st 1919. Only 27 Teachtaí Dála (TDs) were present at the first meeting of an elected Irish political assembly since 1800. The imprisoned de Valera and Griffith were deputised with Plunkett to attend the Paris Peace Conference which had opened on the previous day, January 20th 1919, in order to present the Irish claim for international recognition of Ireland's right to independence. It was however Seán T. O'Ceallaigh, first President of the Irish Republic in 1949, and not Griffith, who pleaded in vain for admission to the Paris Peace Conference.

Griffith was released in March 1919 when fears that an influenza outbreak in post-war Britain would make martyrs of the Irish prisoners. Two of them had already died. On April 1st 1919 Griffith was one of 52 TDs who attended the second meeting of the First Dáil. Griffith became Minister for Home Affairs and deputy to de Valera, head of the first Dáil government.

As Minister of Home Affairs and from June 1919 until December 1920 as acting head of government during de Valera's absence in America, Griffith was able to put into practice the theories of alternative government propounded by him fifteen years before.

Griffith's objective to create alternative institutions of government which would eventually supplant unpopular British institutions began to take shape against a background of terrorism and violence as the War of Independence intensified.

By May, the Dáil was having to meet secretly and in September 1919 was declared illegal. Notwithstanding, the Dáil met six times in 1919 and three times under intense harassment during 1920. Government departments also managed to function under almost impossible conditions. Sinn Féin and arbitration courts were one of the success stories of the First Dáil and were actively encouraged and developed by Griffith as Minister for Home Affairs. Seen as a popular alternative to the British courts of justice, the "Dáil Courts" were standardised and established nationally by Dáil decree in June 1920. Parish Courts and District Courts were supplemented by circuit court sittings three times a year and a Supreme Court sitting in Dublin. By July 1921 over 900 Parish Courts and over 70 District Courts were in operation. A republican police force was called into being in order to enforce Dáil

Court decrees. Sinn Féin courts won the grudging approval and respect of even Southern Unionists. Lloyd George's secretary Tom Jones in his Whitehall Diary of events in Ireland quoted a Limerick landlord thus, "Sinn Féin rules the country — and rules it admirably". Regarding Sinn Féin courts, he said, "they administer justice in a most thorough fashion." The success of Griffith's "alternative" government is summed up by Calton Younger in "Ireland's Civil War", thus, "for all the flaws in the system of clandestine government, the Dáil, with its control of local government, its courts and its police was governing more effectively than was the Irish Government centred upon Dublin Castle." To Griffith, that was the key to independence and the real achievement of the period.

Griffith would have liked to have made some progress towards economic independence. A social and economic programme the "Democratic Programme", aimed at securing Labour and Trade Union support for the Dáil and perhaps at gaining international socialist recognition for the Dáil regime, was announced at the first meeting of the First Dáil in January 1919. The ideas expressed in the "Democratic Programme", "We declare that the nation's sovereignty extends . . . to all its material possessions . . . all the wealth and all the wealth-producing processes within the nation" accorded in many respects with Griffith's earlier teachings on economic nationalism.

The ever-intensifying War of Independence prevented Griffith from implementing much of his fifteen-point plan for political and economic independence drawn up in 1905. This included protection for industry and commerce, the establishment of an Irish merchant shipping service, national control over transport and fisheries and the reform of education as well as the setting up of an Irish court system and national civil service and withdrawal of all voluntary co-operation with British institutions in Ireland.

Griffith, anxious to demonstrate the efficiency and stability of Dáil government, knew that the War of Independence militated against the smooth-running of government. Griffith was anxious to establish Dáil control over the Volunteers who threatened to become a law unto themselves during the early years of the War of Independence. In August 1919, largely upon Griffith's insistence, Volunteers were asked to swear allegiance to Dáil Eireann and became the Irish Republican Army. It was not, however, until after de Valera returned from the U.S. in December 1920 that the Dáil began to assume responsibility for the actions of the IRA and played a much greater part in directing the war. It is to his credit that, although not in total agreement with the conduct of the war, Griffith, acting President of the Dáil until his arrest in November 1920, placed no restrictions on those who were conducting the war. Indeed only one member of the Dáil, Roger Sweetman, resigned in January 1921 in protest at the War of Independence.

It is one of the many ironies of the time that Griffith, and not the "physical" force advocates, suffered arrest and imprisonment in Mountjoy on November 26th, 1920 in the wake of the "Bloody Sunday" atrocities. One reason put forward for his arrest was to make Griffith more accessible and perhaps more amenable to British peace overtures. Peace talks, initiated by British Prime Minister, Lloyd George, and conducted by a special emissary, Archbishop Clune of Perth, Australia, with the imprisoned Griffith against the background of the burning of Cork city in December 1920, failed. The initiative passed to de Valera who had returned in December upon hearing of Griffith's arrest. Griffith languished in jail until the peace negotiations following the opening of the Northern Ireland Parliament in June 1921, made possible his release on June 30th 1921. His release came in time to enable him to attend the signing of the truce on July 8th which took effect at noon July 11th 1921, thus bringing to an end the War of Independence.

Griffith and the Treaty Negotiations

Griffith was among those who accompanied de Valera on the first round of treaty talks in London in July 1921. For the first time, Dominion Status, was offered by Britain and external association proposed by de Valera. Both were rejected but Griffith considered the British proposals "pretty good." Dominion Status, affording the same independence to Ireland as was enjoyed by the other self-governing members of the British Empire, e.g. Canada, Australia, New Zealand and South Africa, was to Griffith an enormous improvement upon Home Rule proposals which, from 1914, had threatened to partition the country. It accorded most closely with Griffith's own concept of dual monarchy.

Griffith's chief objection to participation in the Treaty delegation talks of October 1921 was his failing health. Imprisonment on three different occasions since 1916 and the stresses and frustrations of public life were taking their toll. Although only fifty years, Griffith was just ten months from death when he led the Irish Treaty delegation to talks in London on October 11th 1921. Griffith was also unhappy about the anomalous position of the Irish Treaty delegates. The British insisted on the Treaty delegates being plenipotentiaries empowered "to negotiate and conclude" a Treaty. Specific government instructions, however, drawn up by de Valera on October 7th and reiterated on December 3rd when negotiations reached a critical stage, stipulated that no draft treaty could be signed without submitting it to Dublin first.

Griffith, appointed Minister for Foreign Affairs in the Second Dáil government formed in August 1921, was described by Birkenhead, one of the British delegates, as "more clever than de Valera . . . is the real power in Sinn Féin." From the start the able experienced British delegation saw Griffith and Collins as the leaders of the Irish delegation and singled them out for private consultation. Griffith had his first meeting with Lloyd George alone in the home of British delegate Winston Churchill on October 30th 1921. This was the first of many private meetings at which Griffith compromised himself and, as chairman of the Irish delegation, the other delegates, by giving personal undertakings which honour later demanded he uphold but which, he knew, could never be acceptable to the Dáil government in Dublin.

The Treaty negotiations revolved around two main issues Unity and Status. To Griffith, they were indissolubly linked. Dominion Status was an acceptable concession to Northern Unionism in the same way as dual monarchy proposed in the "United Irishman" in July 1904 to "a large mass of our countrymen who believe . . . that the rule of a common sovereign is admissable," (the "United Irishman" of July 2nd, 1904). The Ireland of 1921 was very different to the Ireland of 1904. The Government of Ireland Act (1920) had set up two independent Home Rule Parliaments and had divided Ireland into two separate states. After June 22nd, 1921 when the Northern Ireland Parliament was opened, negotiations with Ulster had to be made with the elected Unionist government of Craig. Griffith, on October 26th 1921, told the British delegation "no Irishman could ever discuss an association with the

British Crown until the 'essential unity' of Ireland was agreed to by the parties." Griffith pinned his hopes on the hitherto neglected sections of the Government of Ireland Act providing for a Council of Ireland consisting of twenty representatives from each parliament which might, in time through mutual consent of each parliament, lead to an all-Ireland parliament. Craig, in a series of discussions with Lloyd George in early November, made clear that no concessions to Irish unity would be made by a people who had accepted the Government of Ireland Act only "as a final settlement and supreme sacrifice in the interests of peace." Unable to move Craig, Lloyd George was to use every ploy possible to get Griffith to agree to accept Dominion Status without getting any firm commitment from Ulster on 'essential unity.' Lloyd George used the threat of resignation and replacement by a Conservative Unionist government led by Bonar Law, who was of Ulster stock and had espoused the Ulster Unionist cause since 1911, as a weapon to intimidate Griffith into accepting a Boundary Commission to draw up a boundary between the two states to "conform as closely as possible to the wishes of the population." Griffith was led to believe that all of Fermanagh and Tyrone and parts of Down, Derry and Armagh would all join Southern Ireland and that the rest for economic reasons would quickly follow. On November 13th, Griffith, without the knowledge of the other delegates, effectively accepted the British proposals on Ulster. As the strategy of the Irish delegation in the event of non-agreement, was to force a break on Ulster and not on the question of Ireland's relationship to Britain, Griffith's written undertaking to Lloyd George effectively left the Irish delegation without a bargaining counter. When, during the final negotiations on December 5th, Lloyd George dramatically produced his "agreement" with Griffith, to the initial disbelief of the other delegates who knew nothing about it, Griffith knew that he was honour-bound to sign as he had already agreed to dominion status provided there was agreement on Ulster. Lloyd George's insistence on a unanimous decision by the delegation as a body on the Articles of Agreement proposed, made an individual decision, by Griffith alone, impossible. Griffith led the signing of the Anglo-Irish Treaty at 2.20 am on December 6th 1921.

Treaty Debates

Throughout the long Treaty debates, Griffith emphasised the practical tangible benefits of the Treaty. The release of 4,000 Irish internees on December 7th 1921 was just one of the immediate benefits which Griffith hoped would win over cabinet, Dáil and people to the Treaty.

Although Griffith was disappointed at de Valera's rejection of the Treaty, he was encouraged by the 4/3 decision for the Treaty in the Dáil cabinet. During the long historic Dáil debate on the Treaty Griffith proposed on December 19th 1921 the motion for acceptance. His pro-Treaty, Dáil speech reiterated the practical benefits . . . "peace with England, alliance with England, confederation with England, an Ireland developing her own life . . ." He explained the real achievement of the Treaty thus: "It is the first Treaty . . . since 1172 signed on equal footing. It is the first Treaty that admits the equality of Ireland . . . We have brought back the flag; we have brought back the evacuation of Ireland after 700 years by British troops . . . we have brought back to Ireland her full rights and powers of fiscal control." To anti-Treaty republican critics who accused him of betraying the Republic he pointed out that in, the weeks of on-going negotiation before the Treaty delegation talks of October 1921, no mention was made of the Irish Republic. Dismissing de Valera's alternative Document No. 2 as "merely a quibble of words" he vowed "so far as my power or voice extends not one young Irishman's life shall be lost on that quibble." He ended by calling on "Irish people everywhere to ratify this Treaty, to end this bitter conflict of centuries."

Dáil acceptance of the Treaty on January 7th 1922 and the resignation of de Valera as President of the Dáil and, since August 1921, President of the Republic, two days later, left the first position in the state to Griffith, who, on his own admission, had no political ambitions. Understanding fully the anomaly of his position as President of an assembly and a republic which he was pledged to destroy, Griffith, ever a democrat, pledged to "keep the Republic in being until such time as the establishment of the Free State is put to the people to decide for or against." Until the Free State came into existence on the first anniversary of the signing of the Anglo-Irish Treaty on the 6th December 1922 the Republic remained in being although both Griffith and his successor Cosgrave saw their task as preparing for a smooth transfer of power to the new Irish Free State.

Griffth and the Drift to Civil War

In a sense both Griffith's Dáil government and Collins's Provisional Government were "provisional." Both would be swept away by the new Free State Constitution. Yet Griffith was impatient to bring about a permanent government and played a major role in the drafting of a Free State Constitution acceptable to both the Irish people and the British government. To achieve this, Griffith, although in rapidly declining health, crossed again to London to argue the merits of the new constitution. When the first Irish draft proved unacceptable to the British, Griffith, finally giving vent to pent-up frustrations, suggested that Lloyd George and de Valera "should share the government of Ireland between them as one was as impossible as the other." Election victory in June 1922 was a personal triumph and vindication for Griffith. His pro-Treaty Sinn Féin Party won 58 seats against 35 Anti-Treaty seats. Both the Treaty and the constitution of the Irish Free State, which had been published only on the morning of the election, had been accepted by the people. Griffith always regarded that the decision of the people, "our masters" would be the final judgment on the Treaty. [Griffith had sought an early election and had opposed both the postponement and the Collins-de Valera pre-election pact.]

Griffith had always advocated democratic rule by elected representatives. This for Griffith was the great merit of the proposed Council of Three Hundred and of Dáil Eireann. Consequently, he deplored and condemned the attempt by the militant minority to impose their anti-Treaty views upon the majority. Although his health was steadily deteriorating Griffith proved to be a more resolute and decisive leader than Collins in the six months after the acceptance of the Treaty. Griffith showed increasing impatience and dissatisfaction at Collins's failure to assert his authority over the IRA. He expressed particular alarm at the race between pro and anti-Treaty members of the IRA for possession of evacuated British army barracks. It was at Griffith's instigation that the Army Convention of March 26th 1922 was banned. He feared a military coup d'état and urged Collins to move against the Four Courts garrison in June 1922, thus precipitating civil war. Not prepared to compromise on principles, he opposed Collins's attempt to reach an understanding with the anti-

Treaty members of the IRA in the agreed Army Document of May 1st 1922. Similarly, he disapproved strongly of Collins's clandestine support for border units of the IRA who were mounting terrorist attacks in the six county state. Griffith hoped through co-operation with the Northern Ireland government to expedite the reunification of Ireland. Griffth co-signed with Collins the second Collins-Craig agreement of 30th March 1922.

Before the June election 1922 Griffith, worn out with the cares and burdens of state, told his wife that he would retire in August. His death on August 12th 1922 was the final retirement of a man who literally gave his life for Ireland. His death in the critical first months of the Civil War was received with mixed feelings. A contemporary who described Griffith as "a lifelong friend" said that he had "made such a chaos of Ireland as must cloud his eternity." Other tributes were more fulsome. Although Griffith was President of a Dáil and Republic not recognised by Britain, the King sent condolences to Griffith's widow and Lloyd George and the other members of the British Treaty delegation sent a special message of sympathy to Collins and the Provisional Government. The feelings of those who appreciated Griffith's contribution to Irish political life were summed up by General Seán McEoin of the National Army, "Griffith sacrificed his life — a life of great ability — for the Irish people."

Appraisal

Griffith, journalist, writer and intellectual, was the political theorist of the Irish Revolution. Not a "physical force" extremist, mainly because the history of Ireland demonstrated that violence does not pay, Griffith spurned equally the constitutional alternative of parliamentary agitation. Reaching back into history for an Irish precedent and drawing also from contemporary European experience, Griffith presented a reasoned argument and comprehensive political and economic programme for self-government won by extra-parliamentary activity. The political weapon of Sinn Féin, abstention from the British parliament at Westminster, is still practised by Sinn Féin over eighty years after its formation.

Griffith, often called the forgotten man of the Irish revolution, was among the most misunderstood of the Irish revolutionaries. To many such as "physical force" activist Cathal Brugha who died fighting during the first week of the Civil War, he was not a revolutionary at all. Yet he was fiercely nationalistic and opposed anything and anybody English. He could never overcome antipathy towards Childers whom he called a "damned Englishman." He acted as a catalyst enabling major change to come about. Pre-1916, his Sinn Féin movement and its predecessor Cumann na nGaedheal enabled separatists and those disillusioned by parliamentary politics to come together. In 1917, although not fully espousing the republican cause of the revolutionary activists, he enabled de Valera to take control of a "republicanised" Sinn Féin. Similarly, during the War of Independence, although not approving of terrorism, he gave Collins a free hand in conducting the war. Yet Griffith was an exponent of non-violent passive resistance and was an inspiration to Gandhi who led his country, India, to independence from Britain in 1947.

During the Treaty debate Griffith said, "I have not now and never had an ambition about either political affairs or history." Notwithstanding, Griffith became President of an Irish state free for the first time in 700 years from British rule, with its own flag and army and enjoying the same degree of independence as any of the dominion states. Griffith, the political realist among the Irish Revolutionaries, appreciated the practical benefits of the Treaty.

Griffith showed greater political realism in relation to the Ulster problem than any of the other revolutionary leaders. It was to accommodate the Ulster Unionists that the concept of dual monarchy was formulated. Always opposed to partition and prepared to sacrifice full independence in the interests of "essential unity" it was Griffith's greatest political disappointment that the Treaty sacrificed total independence without securing unity. Griffith's premature death at the age of fifty-one years left much of his life's work undone. It is a measure of the insurmountable nature of the difficulties he courageously confronted that, seventy years after his death, the task of reconciling different traditions and aspirations in Ireland and thereby bringing about reunification, remains to be done.

Landmarks in Griffith's Life (1871-1922)

1871	*March 31st* — Born.
1897-98	Formed an Irish Society sympathetic to the Boers in South Africa.
1899	Launched the "United Irishman" to commemorate 1798 rebellions.
1900	Cumann na nGaedheal political umbrella organisation formed.
1903	National Council formed initially to protest at King's visit.
1904	"The Resurrection of Hungary — A Parallel for Ireland" published.
1908	*September* — Formation of Sinn Féin.
1908	Defeat of Sinn Féin candidate, Dolan, in North Leitrim By-election.
1916	Easter Rising mistakenly called a "Sinn Féin Rebellion".
1916-18	Transformation of Sinn Féin.
1918	*December* — Sinn Féin victory in post-war general election.
1919	*January 21st* — Abstentionist Sinn Féin MPs formed Dáil Eireann.
1919	*April* — Griffith, Minister for Home Affairs and Vice-President of the Dáil.
1919-20	*June 1919 - November 1920* Griffith controlled the Dáil government in de Valera's absence in the US.

1921 *July* — Accompanied de Valera on first round of Treaty talks in London.

1921 *October* — Led the Irish delegation which on December 6th signed the Anglo-Irish Treaty.

1921 *December 19th* — Griffith proposed acceptance of the Treaty in the Dáil.

1922 *January 9th* — Griffith replaced de Valera as President of the Dáil and the Irish Republic.

1922 *June* — Griffith sought British approval for an Irish draft constitution of the Irish Free State.

1922 *June 16th* - Election victory for Griffith's Pro-Treaty party.

1922 *August 12th* — Death.

4. Collins

Early Life

Michael Collins, the most colourful leader during the War of Independence and signatory of the Anglo-Irish Treaty of 6th December 1921 which made possible the Irish Free State for which Collins gave his life on August 22nd 1922, was born near Clonakilty, Co. Cork in 1890. The youngest of eight children, Collins took the emigrant-ship to London in 1906 in order to work in the British Civil Service. One year later both his parents were dead. His father was seventy-five years old when he was born.

The Ireland in which Collins grew up was the Ireland of the G.A.A. and the Gaelic League. Collins, moving in Irish circles during his ten-year stay in London, found the same Gaelic and nationalist movements in London. He joined the G.A.A.'s Geraldine Club in London and learned Irish at a London branch of the Gaelic League. As in Ireland, the secret society, the I.R.B. had infiltrated the Gaelic movements in London. In 1909 Collins joined the I.R.B. This step has been called "the most eventful... in his whole life". Collins became President of the Supreme Council of the I.R.B. in 1919. Leon O'Broin a biographer has observed, "Everything of consequence he did subsequently in the political or military spheres turned on the taking of that oath."

Collins became a founder-member of the London company of Irish Volunteers when formed in August 1914. The London Volunteers were branded pro-German as they steadfastly resisted all pressure to get them to join the British war effort. Indeed it was the threat of conscription of unmarried men between the ages of eighteen and forty-one years from January 1916 which prompted Collins to return to Ireland where conscription did not apply. Collins therefore found himself in Dublin during Easter Week 1916.

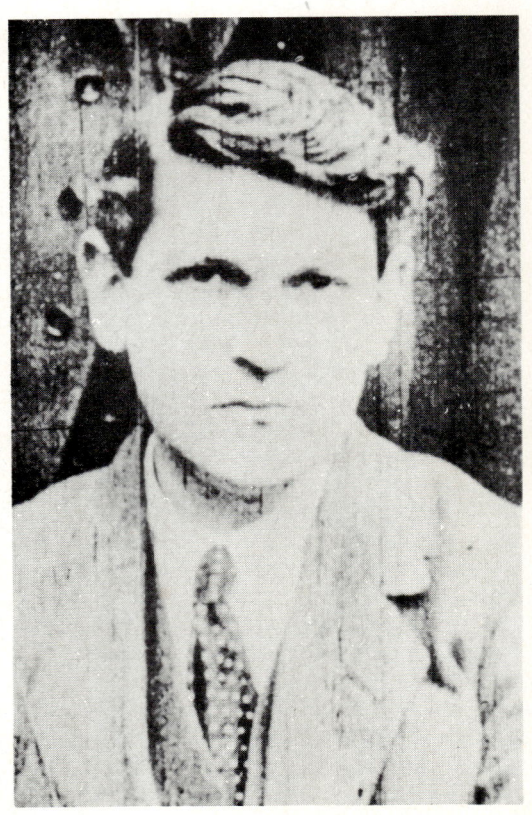

Michael Collins (1890-1922)

Collins and the Easter Rising 1916

As I.R.B. treasurer for London and the South of England Collins quickly came to the notice of Mac Dermott, generally acknowledged to be chief organiser within the I.R.B. military council of the Easter Rising. Anxious to remain in Dublin for what he was assured would be a "manoeuvre out of the ordinary", Collins took a job with Craig Gardner firm of accountants. Collins was assigned to Plunkett, Director of Military Operations as his aide-de-camp and took his place beside Pearse, Connolly and the leaders in the G.P.O. during Easter Week. Collins, was described by Desmond Fitzgerald, father of future Taoiseach, Garret Fitzgerald and quarter-master, responsible for feeding the rebels in the G.P.O., as "the most active and efficient officer in the place". Collins's own verdict on the Rising was "I think the Rising was bungled terribly". Although he expressed admiration for Connolly, Plunkett, and MacDermott and was saddened by their executions, he was sharply critical of "panic decisions and a great lack of very essential organisation and co-operation." During his internment after the Rising in Frongoch in Wales, Collins had plenty of time to contemplate the reasons for failure in 1916 and to determine that such mistakes would not be made again.

Collins's role in the 1916 Rising however was minor. He was among the first batch of internees to be released in the new British P.M. Lloyd George's "Christmas amnesty" of December 1916. Like so many other places of detention, Frongoch prison became a "university of revolution". Collins emerged, determined to revitalise the I.R.B. and reorganise the Volunteers, the two forces necessary to launch a war of independence.

Rise to prominence and power:

Collins's first appointment after his release was as Secretary of the National Aid Association and Volunteers' Dependents Funds. The I.R.B. was anxious to extend its influence in the Volunteers and wanted to demonstrate its concern for the welfare of Prisoners and their dependents. The post gave Collins an opportunity to demonstrate his efficiency as an organiser and to make personal contact with Volunteers and their families, many of whom were later to feel that they owed a personal debt of gratitude to Collins. The "army of contacts" which was to play such a vital role in the War of Independence was already forming.

Collins was a member of the new Supreme Council of the I.R.B. which was formed after the release of the remaining prisoners in June 1917. It was I.R.B. President Ashe's death on hunger-strike in September 1917, however, which gave Collins the opportunity to become Secretary of the Supreme Council and one of the three-man Standing Executive which made all I.R.B. decisions.

In October 1917 the I.R.B. supported de Valera's Presidency of Sinn Fein. De Valera was however no longer a member of the I.R.B. Despite careful scrutiny of all delegates attending the Sinn Fein Ard Fheis on October 25th, Collins only managed to scrape last place on the executive, which was not I.R.B.-dominated. The I.R.B. were more successful in their domination of the Volunteers at the Volunteer Convention next day. Collins became Director of Organisation and the I.R.B. took three of the top five posts in the Volunteers. De Valera however was President and the Chief of Staff, Brugha was also a non-I.R.B. man. The power-struggle which was to be a factor in the Civil War was already manifesting itself. The seeds of the "Army

Mutiny" of 1924 were already sown.

The "conscription crisis" of the early months of 1918 drove thousands of young men into the ranks of the Volunteers. The Irish Volunteers in 1918 were as determined as they had been in 1914 not to fight for any cause other than that of Ireland. The "conscription crisis", plus Collins's reorganisation of the Volunteers which included the publication of a Volunteer news-sheet, An t-Óglach, directed and distributed by Collins, turned the Volunteers into a national army.

The mass of arrests of Sinn Féin members and Volunteers in May 1918 as a result of the so-called "German plot" removed practically all the leadership of the revolutionary movement with the exception of Collins and Brugha. Ironically Collins who had been arrested for a seditious speech in April 1918 was actually released on bail at the time of the mass-arrests.

This, plus the fact that he took refuge at the height of the police searches in mid-May in the house of the President of the I.R.B. after it had been raided and the I.R.B. President McGarry arrested, probably secured his escape. Collins's successful evasion of arrest in May 1918 enabled him to take control of the revolutionary movement. With the leading I.R.B. men in jail until 1919 all I.R.B. decisions were taken by Collins who became President of the I.R.B. in 1919. The rapidly-growing Volunteer army was shaped and formed by Collins who combined the posts of Director of Organisation and Adjutant-General of the Volunteers from March 1918.

As most of the Sinn Féin executive were in prison at the time of their biggest political test to date, the post-war general election in December 1918, it fell to Collins and his cohorts to engineer the Sinn Féin electoral victory (S.F. won 73 seats against its election rival the Irish Parliamentary Party's 6 seats). Collins was elected unopposed for his native Cork county. By ruthlessly eliminating moderates from the Sinn Féin selection lists Collins ensured that the First Dáil would not stand in the way of the War of Independence which started coincidentally on the same day as the First Dáil assembled on January 21st, 1919.

Collins and the War of Independence

The imprisonment of Sinn Féin and Volunteer leaders until March 1919 left the conduct of the War of Independence to Collins, Director of Military Organisation. Characteristically, Collins, although at liberty, did not attend the first meeting of the First Dáil in January 1919. He was in England organising the escape of de Valera from Lincoln jail in February 1919. Collins's skill and success in "springing" political prisoners and his equally spectacular success in evading arrest, made him the "pimpernel" of the Irish revolution and enhanced his reputation both among his own men and among the enemy forces. By 1920 Collins had become the most-wanted man in Ireland with a price of £10,000 on his head.

Despite the personal danger, upon his appointment as Minister of Finance at the second meeting of the Dáil in April, 1919, Collins was determined to set up an efficient government department. He studied banking and economics and set up Finance Department offices in Harcourt Street, head-quarters of Sinn Fein and in Mary Street. Collins had the onerous task of raising much-needed finance in order to make the Dáil government a reality. A Dáil Eireann National Loan floated in 1919 exceeded its £250,000 target within one year. The collection of close on £358,000 by Collins's Department of Finance, working against the most-overwhelming odds, was one of the success stories of the First Dáil.

Collins's main interest however was in the military conduct of the War of Independence. Although the Soloheadbeg incident of January 21st 1919 which sparked off the War of Independence was undertaken by local Volunteers acting on their own initiative, Collins rejoiced in the isolated attacks on R.I.C. men and R.I.C. barracks. These had the double advantage of arming the Volunteers with seized police guns and seriously depleting the ranks of the R.I.C. This first stage of the War of Independence reached a climax in the celebratory burning down of over 300 abandoned R.I.C. barracks at Easter 1920.

Collins as Director of Intelligence since mid-1919 had played no small part in the assassination of selected members of the R.I.C. Collins's notorious "Murder Squad" formed in July 1919 was singularly successful in identifying and assassinating keymen in the detective section of the Dublin Metropolitan Police, known as the G Division. The assassination of Detective-Sergeant Smith on July 30th 1919 was the first of many political assassinations by Collins's "Squad" which by 1920 had rendered the "division" an impotent force in the fight against political crime in Ireland.

The most wanted man in Ireland

MICHAEL COLLINS M.P. (Dublin City and Cork W.R.), age 28, height 5ft.11, complexion fresh.

Police Photo of Collins as it appeared in the Police Gazette in December 1920.

The success of Collins's "Squad", known irreverently as the "twelve apostles", was due in no small measure to the success of Collins's intelligence service. At every other period in Irish history revolution had failed because of prior government intelligence of the intentions of the revolutionaries. For the first time in republican revolutionary history, Irish intelligence was superior to the long-established British intelligence service. Collins's intelligence network was so all-pervasive that it was not possible for any person or indeed any message verbal or written to enter the country without Collins hearing of it. His network of agents in the ports and on all ships coming to Ireland enabled wanted men such as de Valera, considered an escaped convict in 1919, to leave Ireland and ensured a steady supply of imported arms and ammunition for the war effort. Collins used the contacts he had made during his first days at work as a junior Civil Servant in the British Post Office to monitor "official" mail and to tap selected telephones. An early breakthrough was the decoding of classified R.I.C. messages. Collins had "friends" and agents working for him in the most unlikely places including Scotland Yard, the headquarters of the detective division of the British Police, and most sensational of all, within the "G Division" of the DMP which Collins was committed to exterminate. Four recruits within the "G Division", Kavanagh, Mac Namara, Broy (appointed Garda Commissioner by the de Valera government in 1933) and Neligan, fed Collins a constant supply of information about British government and police activities. On one occasion Broy, a confidential typist at G Division headquarters, admitted Collins to police headquarters and gave him free access to official files. Collins was as well "briefed" on British political and military policy in Ireland as any member of the

Dublin Castle staff. By contrast, British Intelligence had no clear picture of what Collins looked like. Collins walked the streets unarmed, frequented the haunts of senior British personnel and joked about the "elusive" Collins to unsuspecting police and military patrols who were desperately trying to track him down. Another irony was that the nerve-centre of Collins's international intelligence service was close to Dublin Castle, the headquarters of British rule in Ireland and remained undetected throughout the War of Independence.

One consequence of the selective assassination techniques used by Collins' "Murder Squad" was to reinforce the popularly held belief, especially in British government circles, that the "troubles" in Ireland were caused by a small number of dangerous men. Lloyd George was adamant, "You don't declare war against rebels". When however, General Macready, commander of the British army in Ireland, reported early in 1920 that the RIC was on the point of collapse, the war moved into its second and most deadly phase with the arrival of "Black and Tans" in March 1920. Many of them still wore the Khaki uniform of a World War I British soldier. Most had joined in order to escape post-war unemployment and all were determined that, having survived four years of trench war-fare, they were not going to die at the hands of unknown assassins in Ireland. As policemen they were useless according to General Macready, "The value of a policeman lies in his knowledge of a locality and its inhabitants of which these RIC recruits were necessarily ignorant". Winston Churchill, the Secretary of State for War, urged that a special force of 8,000 ex-soldiers be sent at once to Ireland. It has been estimated that 12,000 men enrolled in the RIC between January 1920 and its formal disbandment in August 1922. In addition an Auxiliary Division of the RIC was formed in August 1920 of British officers who were paid £1 per day, double the wages of a Black and Tan who were such an indisciplined body that their commanding officer Brigadier-General Crozier said that he had resigned his command in February 1921 rather than lead them.

A serious escalation of the war coincided with the arrival of the "Black and Tans". The police murder on March 20th 1920 of the popular Cork Lord Mayor, MacCurtain who was also Commandant of the Cork Brigade of the IRA (the Volunteers from April 1919 were regarded as the national Irish Republican Army) and the murder by the "Squad" a few days later of an elderly magistrate, Alan Bell who had been summoned from Belfast to confiscate money lodged to Collins's National Loan in Dublin banks, led to reprisal warfare and the indiscriminate sacking of towns such as Tuam, Mallow, Balbriggan, Cork city and Ennistymon. Such Black and Tan atrocities caused Macready to consider them as much an obstacle to peace as were the Irish Terrorists while Field-Marshal Wilson, future military adviser to the new Northern Ireland state, declared prophetically that the government had embarked on a suicidal policy that would lead to the British being put out of Ireland.

The war reached new and frightening proportions in the autumn of 1920. The Restoration of Order in Ireland Act of August 1920 fell far short of placing the whole country under martial law as General Macready wanted but allowed internment without trial and set up military courts. Martial law could be imposed in a troubled area at the discretion of the military commander. The Act gave "carte blanche" to the Black and Tans who quickly acquired a reputation for thuggery and brutality which was to shock public opinion not only in Ireland but in Britain. The arrest in August of Terence MacSwiney, Lord Mayor MacCurtain's successor in Cork, followed by a seventy-four day hunger-strike ending in his death in Brixton prison on October 25th, 1920, set the scene for a month of escalating terror. November, the worst month of the entire war, opened with the execution of an eighteen-year old medical student Kevin Barry on November 1st, 1920.

Bloody Sunday 1920:
The murderous activities of Collins's "Murder Squad" reached a bloody climax on the morning of November 21st 1920. For some time Collins had known that the primary objective of Major-General Tudor, the newly appointed Police Chief, was the elimination of "the murder gang". For that purpose, specially selected British Secret service agents known as the "Cairo Gang" had been brought to Dublin and were living as ordinary citizens throughout the city. Collins's intelligence agents among hotel porters and house servants soon identified individual members of the "Cairo Gang". Plans were carefully laid for the shooting simultaneously at different locations of British agents early on Sunday morning November 21th 1920. Eleven men were killed in the multiple shooting but events had not gone exactly as planned. Not all the members of the "Cairo Gang" were eliminated, whilst some of those killed were ordinary officers of the regular army. Also two of Collins's men McKee and Clancy, who had planned the assassinations, had been arrested just hours before the operation got under way. Their execution later that night, allegedly while attempting to escape from Dublin Castle, incensed the people of Dublin who were still reeling from the shock of all the events of Bloody Sunday.

Collins's first reaction to the reports of frenzied attacks by maddened Black and Tans and Auxiliaries on innocent passers-by was to try to have the hurling game in Croke Park between Dublin and Tipperary cancelled. The crowds were already gathering for the afternoon game and the G.A.A. was powerless to prevent it. Collins's worst fears were justified. Believing that the assassins had come to Dublin with the match crowds, the Black and Tans launched a full-scale attack on the unarmed spectators and players. Within minutes twelve people had died including one player and sixty others were wounded. Known as the "Bloody Sunday" massacre the Black and Tan atrocity of the afternoon more than cancelled out the wave of revulsion felt at the cold-blooded IRA killings of the morning. The campaign to have the Black and Tans removed and to find a peace formula gathered momentum both in Ireland and Britain.

The month of November closed with the spectacular ambush at Kilmichael Co. Cork by Tom Barry Commandant of the Cork No. 3 Brigade of the IRA on a convoy of Auxiliaries on November 28th 1920. All but one of the Auxiliaries were killed by Tom Barry's flying column of about 40 Volunteers. The war was entering into its third and final phase as increasingly larger units of IRA men (flying columns) engaged the British forces in guerilla war. The response of the Black and Tans to the Kilmichael ambush and to another smaller ambush outside Cork city on December 11th 1920 was to place Co. Cork under martial law and to burn down part of Cork city on the night of 11th December. After that night of looting and pillage the Auxiliaries wore burnt corks in their caps as a new "badge" of authority.

Although such outrages were condemned in both Britain and Ireland the unofficial policy of reprisal was given official sanction in January 1921 when Macready, Commander of the British army in Ireland, ordered that "punishments including ...the destruction of houses or property might be carried out against any person or persons ... considered implicated in ... outrages against the Crown forces." The first of these "official reprisals" was the burning of 7 houses at Middleton in Co. Cork on January 1st 1921. Not surprisingly the Collins family home in West Cork was also burned to the ground in a separate incident.

The decision by the IRA to mount large-scale operations was endorsed by de Valera, recently returned from the U.S., but was viewed with some apprehension by Collins, who understood the serious military implication of a major defeat. Consequently Collins was unenthusiastic about the attack on the Customs House in Dublin planned for May 1921. Involving all the Dublin units of the IRA it was regarded as the biggest operation of the whole war. From a military viewpoint it was disastrous. With over eighty men killed, wounded and captured, the Dublin IRA, was finished as a fighting force. Not even Tom Barry's victory at Crossbarry, West Cork in March 1921 when Barry's flying column had inflicted heavy Black and Tan casualties during a 2 hour battle could cancel out the devastating effect of the Customs House fiasco.

Mass search operations by combined British army and police units, such as the Crossbarry "battle" was designed to prevent, had seriously affected morale and had reduced actual numbers in the IRA. By mid-July 1921 there were 4,500 IRA men interned in special internment camps such as Ballykinlar, Co. Down. Collins himself had many narrow escapes. On New Year's Eve files relating to Dublin Castle and the "G Division" of the DMP were seized in a raid on one of his haunts. From then on British Intelligence was on top of the situation. The arrest of Broy, one of Collins's "inside" men in the "G Division" led to the break-up of his spy network within the RIC detective division. In the week after the Customs House attack in May, British police activity intensified. Three different places used by Collins as offices were raided prompting him to observe that the enemy was "very close on the heels of some of us".

Lack of ammunition in particular was a crucial factor in the final stages of the war. The large-scale operations of the last phase of the war made enormous demands on both men and ammunition. Collins told the IRB of which he was President that by June 1921 there were "only 1,617 men in active service units with perhaps one weapon per man but scarcely one cartridge per shotgun". In his direct manner he commented after the truce to the British Chief Secretary in Ireland Sir Hamar Greenwood, "we were astounded. We thought you must have gone mad". Collins, the military realist, accurately assessed the situation thus, "we were unable to beat him out of the country by force of arms. But neither had he beaten us". The choice for the Lloyd George government after two years of costly "troubles" (since 1919 the cost of maintaining British rule in Ireland was £20m per annum) was a full-scale military war. It was felt that the war-weary British public in the depressed post-war British economy, would not tolerate another war until at least a peaceful alternative (the offer of a truce with both sides retaining arms) was tried and failed.

Collins, unlike some of his comrades, among them Erskine Childers who dreamed of repeating a Howth-style gun-running in order to arm the IRA with continental arms and continue the struggle, was under no illusions that once the truce was signed on July 11th 1921 there could be no going back. "Once a truce is agreed and we come out into the open, it is extermination for us if the truce should fail ...

We shall be ... like rabbits coming out from their holes". For Collins therefore, the Treaty negotiations in which he was to play such a key role simply had to succeed.

Collins and the Treaty

De Valera told the Dáil that he regarded Collins as "absolutely" vital to the delegation" to be sent to London for the Treaty negotiations starting on October 11th, 1921. Whilst Collins had expressed a desire to accompany de Valera on the first round of talks in July immediately after the truce, he was a most reluctant Treaty delegate. He felt that his inclusion on the Irish delegation would of itself be an obstacle to a settlement. To the British, Collins was the uncompromising extremist creator of the "Murder Squad" which had wreaked havoc on British interests in Ireland. Collins was intensely unhappy with his role as a negotiator. To the uncompromising military commander, negotiation smacked of compromise. He of all people should not be seen to compromise. Collins the realist knew that compromise was inevitable but felt that the Irish delegation would have to give away less if he, Collins, were known to be at home possibly organising a fresh war of independence.

Collins made it clear that he accepted only "in the spirit of a soldier who acts against his judgement at the order of a superior officer". From the outset, Griffith who was less than twelve months away from death at this time, had asked Collins to act as unofficial leader of the delegation in London. After the introductory meetings the British detached Griffith and Collins from the rest of the delegation and worked out the terms of the proposed treaty with them. Not only had Griffith and Collins agonising decisions to take regarding primarily Ireland's relationship with Britain and the position of Ulster, they also had the task of persuading the other delegates Barton, Gavan Duffy and Duggan who, because they were excluded from much of the negotiation process, came to regard the leaders with distrust and suspicion. Even before the delegation was split, Collins voiced his misgivings, "Who then do I trust? Beyond Griffith no one?"

With regard to the most crucial issue at stake during the Treaty negotiations, the relationship between Britain and Ireland, Collins was an early convert to Dominion status. There is strong evidence to suggest that as early as July 1921 the IRB had decided not to fight against Dominion status. Childers, secretary to the Irish delegation was regarded as the Dominions expert of the delegation, but Collins had spent much time studying the evolution of dominion states. On November 28th Collins presented a prophetic and sensational paper "On the Wider International Aspects of an Anglo-Irish Settlement" in which he stated dramatically, "A new era is dawning, not for Ireland only but for the whole world... The problem of associating autonomous communities can only be solved by recognising the complete independence of the several countries associated." In 1921, the "Balfour Declaration" of 1926 that the Dominions were "autonomous Communities within the British Empire" and the Statute of Westminster 1931 granting parliamentary sovereignty to the dominion parliaments were still a long way off. Yet Collins's thinking clearly foreshadowed such developments and led to his conviction that the Treaty could be a "stepping-stone" to independence.

Collins's realism dominated the final stages of the Treaty negotiations. The bitter and inconclusive discussions in the Dáil on December 3rd on the Treaty proposals brought back by the Irish delegation for Dáil and cabinet consideration, left Collins, the decisive man of action, confused and angry. He was angry not just because personal animosities of old rivals (Brugha, the Minister for Defence had always resented Collins's control of the IRA) coloured the discussions. Brugha condemned the decision to split the delegation, remarking that the British knew what they were doing in deliberately picking the weakest men on the Irish side. Griffith and Collins took this as a personal insult. Collins was also angry because the only alternative to the Treaty proposals that the cabinet had to offer was external association which was no more acceptable to the British then than it had been when first mooted by de Valera in July 1921. Collins, unaccustomed to failure, could not bear to think of almost two months of wasted talks.

Collins refused to accompany the delegation to the resumed talks with the British delegation on December 4th. When the expected break-down in the negotiations did not take place Collins was persuaded by Griffith to make one last effort to reach agreement where all others had failed. Collins's meeting with Lloyd George on the morning of December 5th determined the form and content of many of the Articles of Agreement for a Treaty.

The discussion ranged around Ulster, trade, defence and the oath. On the oath Collins won what was regarded as a personal triumph when his formula for an oath, drawn up by the IRB, expressing allegiance primarily to the Constitution of the Irish Free State, and thereafter faithfulness to His Majesty, won acceptance. On defence and trade, Lloyd George, happy that dominion status and an oath of allegiance were acceptable, was prepared to make concessions. On defence Britain had been adamant on its exclusive right to defend the coasts of Ireland. To that end Britain insisted on the retention of port facilities at Cobh, Berehaven and Lough Swilly. In time of war the Irish Free State was required to provide "such harbour and other facilities as the British Government may require". In addition Ireland was not allowed to build a navy. Collins, the military commander, succeeded in having the above conditions made provisional "until an arrangement has been made between the British and Irish Governments whereby the Irish Free State undertakes her own coastal defence..." Ireland was allowed to have "such vessels as are necessary for the protection of the Revenue or the Fisheries". A review of the defence arrangements was to be held in five years, not ten years as the British had originally hoped. Collins was above all anxious to establish total independence for the Irish army. This was conceded. The word "local" was deleted from the reference to "defence forces" in deference to the man who over the past two years had been forging a national army out of isolated Volunteer units.

On trade there were also concessions with the agreement that both sides should be free to impose tariffs on each other's goods. Collins's "concession" enabled de Valera, rapidly becoming Collins's arch-enemy, to wage the economic war of the 1930s. On Ulster, Collins the realist knew that, since the opening of the Northern Ireland Parliament on June 22nd, 1921, the Irish case for unity had been weakened. Although he continued to insist on the original Irish demand for Unionist Prime Minister Craig's assent to the principle of an all-Ireland parliament, Collins favoured the idea of a Boundary commission first suggested by him on October 14th. He was easy to persuade that a Boundary Commission would give the Irish Free State two whole counties (Fermanagh and Tyrone) and parts of three others (Derry, Armagh and Down).

Lloyd George's dramatic intervention at a critical stage in the afternoon talks with Collins, Griffith, and Barton showed his understanding of the mind of Collins in particular. Collins, the military leader, appreciated fully the significance of the ultimatum- sign or else war within three days. The flourishing of the two letters, one of which had to be sent to Craig that night by special train and destroyer; one holding the hope of a peaceful solution and the other the threat of all-out war which Collins knew the Irish could not win, introduced the necessary note of urgency to ensure that no attempt would be made to contact Dublin before signing. Lloyd George, knew that Collins would decide quicker under pressure. At 2.20 am. on December 6th 1921 the Treaty was signed. The two months of endless discussion and suspense had finally borne fruit.

Collins was under no illusions as to what the reaction to the Treaty might be. Within hours of signing he was writing to a friend, "Will anyone be satisfied at the bargain?... early this morning I signed my death warrant." The cabinet debate on the Treaty on December 8th 1921 revealed the divisions which were already evident in the pre-Treaty discussions of December 3rd. Collins expected Brugha and Stack (in whose badly-run department of Home Affairs the ever-efficient Collins interfered without apology or leave) to vote against. De Valera's rejection of the Treaty was not however, based on personal animosity. Nevertheless tension between Collins and de Valera had been growing. Collins the decisive man of action had always shown impatience with de Valera's slow deliberations, remarking on one occasion that the Paris Peace Conference would be over before de Valera had agreed a draft submission for Irish admission. He was disappointed that de Valera should choose to absent himself in the U.S. for much of the war. He resented his criticism of the war effort upon his return and resisted fiercely his suggestion that he, Collins, should go to America in 1921, stating angrily that he would not get rid of him as easily as that.

Collins's contribution to the Dáil debate 14 December - 7 January "In my opinion it gives us freedom, not the ultimate freedom that all nations desire... but the freedom to achieve it" was prophetic. Tragically Collins was not to live to see that "ultimate freedom." Ironically it fell to Collins's political opponent, de Valera, to develop to their fullest potential, the freedoms won in the despised and rejected Treaty. Cabinet and Dáil approval of the Treaty caused de Valera and anti-Treaty TDs to resign, casting Griffith and Collins in the role of political leaders. Griffith replaced de Valera as President of the Dáil while Collins became Chairman of the Provisional Government, the government recognised by Britain and required under the terms of the Treaty in order to effect a transfer of power and to draw up a constitution for the Irish Free State.

Drift to Civil War

On January 14th 1922 Collins was chosen as Chairman of the Provisional Government by an assembly of sixty pro-Treaty members and the four Unionist members for Trinity of the Parliament of Southern Ireland elected in May 1921 under the terms of the Government of Ireland Act of December 1920. This Act provided for two Home Rule parliaments, one in Northern Ireland and the other in Southern Ireland. Collins was also Minister of Finance in Griffith's Dáil government. For the first time, Collins, who had led during the War of Independence from a position subordinate to both the Minister of Defence Brugha and to the Commander-in-Chief of the IRA Mulcahy, was in a true position of command.

Two days later on January 16th 1922 Collins had a personal triumph when he presided over the formal surrender of Dublin Castle, the centre and hated symbol of British administration in Ireland for centuries. Collins saw the practical benefits of the Treaty in the speedy evacuation of British troops and the replacement of the despised RIC and feared Black and Tans with an unarmed Garda Síochána. Beggar's Bush Barracks was the first British army barracks to be evacuated and became the Irish Army headquarters. The haste with which the British abandoned their posts in Ireland created problems for Collins and the Provisional Government and indirectly led to Civil War.

A serious consequence of Collins's participation in the Treaty negotiations in London from October to December 1921 was to remove Collins from his position of authority within the IRA. An unfortunate consequence of the truce was to enable armed rebels, no longer under the iron discipline of Collins, to become a law unto themselves. Whilst a majority of the Headquarters staff of the IRA accepted the Treaty, a sizeable minority of officers and brigade commanders opposed it. During the Dáil debate on the Treaty a signed declaration against the Treaty from brigade commanders had sparked off an attack on the bona fides of Collins. The IRB of which Collins was President had declared itself for the Treaty on December 10th 1921. Yet both the IRA and the IRB were pledged to "support and defend the Irish Republic". The anomaly of Collins's pro-Treaty stance was evident to many IRA officers. To men like Rory O'Connor and Liam Lynch an Irish Republican Army could not be expected to support a Free State dominion of the British Empire.

The surrender by departing British forces of their barracks to local IRA units created real security problems for Collins and the Provisional Government. A raid by anti-Treaty members of the IRA on the vacated RIC barracks in Clonmel on February 26th before Free State troops could take possession was the first open act of rebellion by the anti-Treaty IRA. The seizure of RIC arms, in the opinion of General Tudor, British chief of the RIC since 1920, "had put the rebels in relatively a better position than the forces of the Provisional Government". The race for possession of evacuated British bases between anti-Treaty Irregulars and the National Army which Collins was hoping to forge out of the pro-Treaty forces led to a bizarre situation in Limerick when pro-Treaty, anti-Treaty and British forces were all in possession of military bases in Limerick during a critical brief period in March 1922. Hostilities were avoided however by the withdrawal of both pro- and anti-Treaty forces and the occupation of Limerick by "neutral" forces under Liam Lynch who was still prepared to accept direction from Mulcahy, the new Minister for Defence.

Such incidents, however, prompted Mulcahy to ban the Army Convention requested by army officers on January 11th 1922. The prohibition, however, resulted in pro-Treaty officers observing the ban and staying away from an illegal anti-Treaty dominated IRA convention on March 26th 1922. As predicted, the army Convention reaffirmed its allegiance to the Irish Republic. More significantly however, the IRA members present reverted to the position of the Volunteers in 1917. Supreme control passed to a sixteen-member Executive appointed by the Convention. The authority of the Dáil and the Minister of Defence were repudiated. Mac Eoin the pro-Treaty Army Chief-of-Staff who was not present at the rebel Army Convention, described the sixteen-man Executive as "an Executive to supplant both the Dáil and the

Provisional Government and it was to all intents and purposes a government they formed". On April 14th the seizure by O'Connor and members of the Executive of the Four Courts and other public buildings in Dublin brought Civil War one step closer. The attack by Free State forces on the Four courts on the morning of June 28th and the forcible ejection of the rebel military junta brought hostilities to a head.

Churchill, colonial Secretary and British government spokesman for Ireland thought that the events of April 1922 would lead to a showdown between the rebels and the long-suffering Provisional government. Collins, however, was determined to explore every avenue before using force against former comrades-in-arms. An "Army Document" of May 1st 1922 signed by Collins and both pro-and anti-Treaty officers, was repudiated by O'Connor in the Four Courts but the evacuation on May 8th 1922 of buildings seized by the rebels other than the Four Courts held out the promise of a reunited army and the aversion of civil war.

One of the demands made by the "Army Document" was for an "agreed election", the first election to be held to the new Free State parliament and the first opportunity for the people of Ireland to vote on the Treaty. Feverish political activity resulted in the Collins-de Valera pact of May 20th 1922. This seven-point "pact" threatened to remove the Treaty as an election issue. Collins and de Valera, both members of Sinn Féin, agreed to draw up a national panel of pro- and anti-Treaty S.F. candidates reflecting their existing strength in the Dáil. The Minister of Defence would represent the Army. Of nine other ministers, five would be pro-Treaty four against. The pact, however, applied only to Sinn Féin candidates. The "pact" was deplored by Griffith who remarked angrily "you have given them everything" but was defended by Collins as a last attempt "to avoid strife."

Neither the pact nor the proposed Free State Constitution which Griffith and Collins submitted to the British Government for approval in early June was acceptable to the British. Of a draft-Constitution in which there was no mention of an oath of allegiance, Churchill said "The distance between their Constitution and the Treaty is almost as great as when the Prime Minister began his negotiations with Mr. de Valera". Agreement however to British amendments which brought the Free State Constitution back to the terms of the Treaty, showed that Collins and Griffith were not prepared to return to pre-Treaty conditions. Two days before the June 16th election Collins told electors in his native Cork "to vote for the candidates you think best of". Collins's repudiation of the "election pact" rendered a political solution impossible. The publication of the amended Constitution on polling day shattered all trust the anti-Treaty candidates had in the Provisional Government. The election results, pro-Treaty 58 Anti-Treaty 35, revealed a decisive majority for the Treaty. Demand, especially from Britain, to remove the rebel Four Courts garrison intensified.

The assassination of Sir Henry Wilson, the recently appointed military adviser to the Unionist government in Northern Ireland, in London on June 22nd 1922 was for Britain, the last straw. British cabinet instructions of the day which included the re-occupation of Dublin and the retaking by force of the Four Courts were only rescinded when the Free State forces, using artillery supplied by the British, attacked the Four Courts on June 28th 1922. Ironically the assassination of Wilson was carried out by two of Collins's men based in London during the War of Independence. They went to their deaths without divulging who had ordered Wilson's murder. It is not inconceivable that Wilson's death was the last tragic act of the Bloody Sunday killings of November 21st 1920. It is more likely however that the order to kill Wilson was a recent one given in response to escalating violence against the Catholic population of Northern Ireland. By June 1922 80 Catholics had died and 188 had been wounded since the signing of the Treaty. Collins who had earlier entertained hopes of co-operating with Craig, the Northern Ireland Prime Minister, had agreed in January 1922 to end a Southern boycott on Northern Ireland goods in return for a promise of protection for Catholics living in Protestant areas. The Collins-Craig agreement of January 21st did not, however, secure the return to work of 9000 Catholics driven from their jobs in the Protestant-dominated Belfast shipyards and factories. A further agreement of March 30th did little to protect the Catholic minority from police violence. Collins decided that secret support for the largely anti-Treaty units of the IRA working within Northern Ireland and along the border might achieve the double purpose of protecting the beleaguered Catholic minority and reuniting the IRA in a new war of independence in Northern Ireland. Consequently Collins was prepared to supply arms secretly to the active IRA units operating in the border areas.

In June 1922 Collins had warned the British government that he was "not prepared to hold up the hands of the Ulster government while Catholics were being murdered". The British government, however, immediately blamed the rebel Four Courts garrison for the assassination of Wilson and demanded their immediate removal.

The kidnapping on June 26th of the Deputy Chief-of-Staff of the pro-Treaty National Army, General "Ginger" O'Connell, was the pretext used to justify the dawn attack on the Four Courts on June 28th 1922. Neither the surrender of the two hundred strong Four Courts garrison after two days of sustained bombardment nor the lifting of the O'Connell Street siege five days later, discouraged the rebels who decided to abandon the capital and consolidate their position in the country-side. The attempt to seize and hold strategic buildings in Dublin had failed in 1922 just as it had failed in 1916.

Collins who knew how successful guerilla war tactics had been in rural Ireland during the War of Independence was determined not to let the Irregulars, who at the start of hostilities outnumbered the national army by four to one, become entrenched in the Irish provinces. On July 12th 1922 a War Council was formed with Collins as Commander-in-Chief. Although Collins had assumed responsibility for the military conduct of the War of Independence this was the first time that sole command was in his hands. He threw himself into the military task with his usual speed and efficiency but with little of the enthusiasm which had fired his actions during the War of Independence. He hoped to terminate hostilities by a quick decisive victory while at the same time trying to use his influence with former comrades to heal divisions.

From the outset Collins was determined to bring the war to the rebels. Never a desk commander, Collins resolved to move freely around "his" country and personally to oversee military operations. The fall of Limerick and of Waterford on 20/21st July 1922 shattered Republicans' hopes of setting up a "Munster Republic". Effective use of British troopships overcame the transport problems of the National Army. Simultaneous landings at Passage West and Youghal ensured the collapse of Cork city by August 12th, 1922, the day on which Griffith, co-founder with Collins of the Irish Free State, died of heartbreak, disillusionment and exhaustion. Collins cut short a southern tour in order to attend his funeral but returned to Cork on August 20th despite fears for his safety. "No one's going to shoot me in my own county," he asserted with the same careless abandon he had shown during the War of Independence when he had walked around Dublin unarmed. The trip to Cork was a success. Collins was gratified by the goodwill of the people and received a warm welcome from his own people in his native Clonakilty on August 22nd 1922. August 22nd was a busy day with meetings in Roscarbery, Skibbereen and Bandon. In the fading evening light, Collins and his party, driving in an open touring car between a Crossley tender and an armoured car, were ambushed at Béal na mBláth. Collins was killed possibly by a ricochet bullet. His assassin has never been brought to justice. Theories abound as to who killed Collins and more importantly as to why he was killed. A controversial figure throughout life, Collins has remained controversial in death.

Collins's violent death shattered all hope of reconciliation and a speedy end to hostilities. It was generally believed that one purpose of Collins's military tour of the South was to make contact with rebel leaders and to use his influence with IRB men in particular who had taken the anti-Treaty stand. Collins was mourned by Free Stater and Republican alike. "Everyone looked on him as a sort of bridge" was a contemporary opinion echoed by many. The untimely deaths of Griffith and Collins left the new state without its founders. The Civil War was destined to become a protracted bloody affair with just under 4000 sacrificing their lives, as Collins had, for what they believed to be right for Ireland.

Appraisal

Collins emerges as the romantic hero figure of the period 1916-22. The elusive "Pimpernel" of the War of Independence had caught the imagination of all and won the grudging admiration of British Prime Minister, Lloyd George who said that his services would have been worth twelve brass hats to Britain during the Great War. Yet Collins's greatest contribution to the Ireland of his day was his realism. Collins the realist knew that a truce was absolutely essential in July 1921.

Equally he appreciated the impossibility of returning to a pre-truce position and therefore the absolute necessity of reaching a settlement. The Treaty negotiations and debates turned Collins, the young soldier, into a national and international statesman.

Hailed by a contemporary as "the most outstanding leader of them all... who did more to free Ireland than any Irishman", Collins was also regarded as the "lost leader". Collins, the uncompromising leader of the War of Independence, had become the man of compromise. With reference to the comment that in signing the Treaty he may have signed his death warrant, he remarked with that black humour which characterised his attitude to life and death, "ridiculous - a bullet might just as well have done the job five years ago". The real tragedy of Collins's death was that it took place during a Civil War between former comrades-in-arms. His death underlined the real tragedy of the independence struggle in Ireland which left Irishmen bitterly divided and fighting each other. Collins's vain attempt to prevent this cost him his life and robbed the young state of a promising founding father.

Landmarks in Collins's Life (1890 - 1922)

1890   *October 16th*   Born near Clonakilty in Co. Cork.
1906-16   The London years.
1909   Joined the IRB.
1914   Founder member of the London Volunteers.
1916   Minor revolutionary role in Easter rebellion.
1917   *October* - Member of Sinn Féin executive and Director of Organisation within the Volunteers.
1918   *May* - Collins successfully evades arrest during the alleged "German Plot" conspiracy.
1919   *January - July 1921*
War of Independence.
Director of Military Organisation.
Director of Intelligence.
Minister of Finance in First Dáil.

Michael Collins (1890 - 1922)

1921   *October - December*   Key member of Irish Treaty Delegation.
1921   *December 6th* - Anglo-Irish Treaty signed.
1921   *December 8th* - Dáil cabinet approved the Treaty.
1922   *December 14th - January 7th*   Dáil approval of the Treaty, 64 for, 57 against.
1922   *January 14th* - Collins Chairman of Provisional Government.
1922   *January 16th* - Hand-over of Dublin Castle, the seat of British rule in Ireland, to Collins.
1922   *April 14th* - Seizure of Four Courts by rebel IRA executive.
1922   *June 28th* - Attack on Four Courts garrison.
1922   *June 28 1922 - May 24 1923* - Civil War.
1922   *July* - General Collins, Commander-in-Chief of the National Army.
1922   *August 22nd* - Assassination of Collins in Béal na mBláth ambush.

5. Cosgrave

Early Influences

W. T. Cosgrave, Griffith and Collins's successor and leader of the Irish Free State during the crucial formative years 1923-32 was born in Dublin on 6th June 1880. His father was a licensed vintner and member of Dublin Corporation. Young Cosgrave showed early signs of following in his father's footsteps. Upon leaving school he went to work in his father's licensed premises. In 1909 he was elected Sinn Féin Councillor on Dublin Corporation. Thus began an almost unbroken thirteen years in local government. Administrative experience gained during his years as councillor and alderman made him the obvious choice for the post of Minister of Local Government in the First Dáil Government in April 1919.

The most exciting political development of the early years of the Twentieth Century, the formation of Sinn Féin, left a deep and lasting impression on the young, politically-aware Cosgrave. Griffith was to exercise a life-long influence on Cosgrave who was present at the first Sinn Féin convention in the Rotunda in Dublin in 1905. He launched his own political career by forming a branch of Sinn Féin in the Usher's Quay ward of the City. As well as being a Sinn Féin Councillor on Dublin Corporation from 1909 he worked tirelessly on behalf of the Sinn Féin party machine. In 1915 he became chairman of its Estates and Finance Committee. Before his election in 1917 as Sinn Féin abstentionist M.P. for Kilkenny, Cosgrave was a member of the Mansion House Committe, the central directing body of Sinn Féin.

W. T. Cosgrave (1880-1965)

Although Cosgrave was over thirty years old and a respectable city councillor he did not hesitate to commit himself to the armed struggle for independence. An early member of the Volunteers after their formation in 1913, Cosgrave was a lieutenant in the Fourth Dublin Battalion which seized the South Dublin Union on Easter Monday 1916. Cosgrave fought alongside Cathal Brugha whose spirited defence of the building when it came under heavy fire on Easter Thursday inspired the 60-strong garrison to hold on until the cease-fire order came on Easter Saturday. Six years later Cosgrave and Brugha were to find themselves on different sides in another deadly struggle, the Civil War. Brugha's refusal to surrender then cost him his life at the end of the first week of fighting in Dublin city centre on July 5th 1922.

Cosgrave, whose half-brother was killed during the Easter Rising, was regarded by the British as a key figure. Among the first to be courtmartialled on May 4th with Major John MacBride, he was sentenced to death. MacBride was executed. The death sentence on Cosgrave was commuted to life imprisonment. Like de Valera whose death sentence was also commuted, Cosgrave served his sentence in an English jail,

Portland Jail, until the general amnesty of June 1917 released both men. De Valera and Cosgrave were destined to play a vital role in the political future of their country. They were elected within weeks of each other as Sinn Féin abstentionist M.P.s. De Valera, the newly elected Sinn Féin M.P. for East Clare, actively canvassed for Cosgrave during the Kilkenny by-election in August 1917. Cosgrave's two to one victory over Magennis, the Irish Parliamentary Party's candidate, showed that the stature of the Dublin Councillor and Easter Rising survivor was high, not just in Dublin but throughout the country. Cosgrave was among the seventy-three Sinn Féin activists arrested and imprisoned in May 1918 as part of the so-called "German plot". His enhanced popularity as a result of his re-arrest ensured his election for North Kilkenny in the general election of December 1918. Along with other released Sinn Féin members, he attended the second meeting of the First Dáil on April 1st 1919 and was pleased to be made Minister for Local Government in the first Sinn Féin administration.

Dáil Minister of Local Government

The Department of Local Government set up and administered by Cosgrave from 1919 was one of the success stories of the First Dáil and illustrated admirably Griffith's principle of alternative government. Sinn Féin's success in the sphere of local government was due largely to a measure passed by the Conservatives as part of their "Kill Home Rule with Kindness" policy, the Local Government Act 1898. Although not regarded as revolutionary at the time, the decision to allow elected county urban and rural district councils meant that Sinn Féin was able to take control of local authorities in many parts of the country and to gain valuable political and administrative experience at local level. A councillor himself, Cosgrave had little difficulty in gaining the confidence of other elected Councillors. Victory in the local government elections in January and June 1920 gave Sinn Féin control of 72 of the 127 town and city corporations and of 28 of 33 County Councils. Cosgrave felt strong enough in mid-summer 1920 to recommend to Sinn Féin councils to sever all links with the British operated Local Government Board whose officials were being politely ignored. By October 1920 practically all councils outside of Unionist Ulster had transferred allegiance to Cosgrave's Department of Local Government. The burning down of the Customs House in Dublin in May 1921, the last major operation of the War of Independence, represented the final blow to the old system. The Customs House was the headquarters of the Local Government Board. Destruction of local government records symbolised the destruction of centuries of British civil administration in Ireland. Cosgrave's success in local government was all the more striking as much of his administrative work was done while he and his department were on the run. Cosgrave became a master of disguise. Despite continual harassment and raids on offices, the Department of Local Government was one of the few really effective departments established by the illegal Dáil Èireann in 1919 and 1922. Much of the credit was due to Cosgrave's able assistant, O'Higgins who impressed Cosgrave by his diligence and by his strength of character. O'Higgins remained by Cosgrave's side during the dark days of the Civil War and the difficult years thereafter until his assassination in 1927 robbed Cosgrave and the new state of its strongest and most able minister.

Cosgrave and the Treaty

The success of his Department of Local Government did not blind Cosgrave to the reality that real power in Ireland between 1919 and 1922 still lay with the British and that political independence had to be negotiated. To Cosgrave, the political realist, negotiation must mean a compromise settlement. Cosgrave's initial concern was that the best possible team of negotiators should go to London. Cosgrave alone recorded his opposition to the fact that de Valera, President of the Second Dáil, was not leading the Irish Treaty Delegation to London for the second round of Treaty talks. In a defeated Dáil motion on 14th September 1922 Cosgrave, commenting that it was a pity to have "their best player among the reserves", proposed that de Valera should lead the delegation. Misgivings about the composition of the treaty delegation did not prevent Cosgrave from giving whole-hearted support to the Treaty and its signatories from the signing. Cosgrave insisted upon a full cabinet discussion on the Treaty. His vote for the Treaty at the subsequent cabinet meeting on 8th December 1922 ensured cabinet acceptance of the Treaty, as the voting split 4 for, 3 against. Cosgrave was the only non-signatory among the 7 members of the government to vote for the Treaty. Cabinet acceptance meant that the Treaty had to be placed before the Dáil for full Dáil debate. In the Treaty debate which followed Cosgrave's support remained constant, "I have not got the constitutional lawyer's mind, the solicitor's mind or even the mind of an idealist but an ordinary businessman's mind and I see nothing objectionable in it absolutely." Privately he remarked colourfully. "Everybody wants to lap up the milk but nobody wants to recognise the cow." Subsequent events demonstrated that even though the anti-Treatyites wanted to dismantle the Treaty they did not want to surrender the privileges and benefits gained by the Irish state from its special relationship with Britain secured by the Treaty.

After the Dáil acceptance of the Treaty, Cosgrave was considered to be firmly and irrevocably within the Pro-Treaty group. A member of both Griffith's Pro-Treaty Dáil government and of Collins's Provisional Government, Cosgrave rated number three behind Griffith and Collins in Pro-Treaty ranks. When Collins became Commander-in-Chief on July 12th 1922 Cosgrave took his place as Chairman of the Provisional Government. Upon Griffith's death, one month later, Cosgrave became acting President of the Dáil. When the new Dáil, elected in June 1922 finally met on September 9th 1922, Cosgrave was confirmed in his position as President of the Dáil. Dual government effectively came to an end as Cosgrave also led the Provisional Government. Until peace was restored in mid-1923 Cosgrave held a variety of posts as key ministers, in particular O'Higgins who was an Assistant Adjutant-General and General Mulcahy, Minister of Defence in the National Army concerned themselves chiefly with the conduct of the civil war.

Cosgrave in command 1922-32

At forty-two years Cosgrave became leader of a government and of a state whose structures and institutions had yet to be formed. An ongoing civil war threatened both his government and the state for which he was responsible. To "implement the Treaty, enact the Constitution, support and assist the National Army and ask Parliament if necessary for any powers thought necessary to restore order, to expedite a return to normal conditions and to speed reconstruction and reparation" were Cosgrave's stated objectives as he assumed office. On September 18th, just nine days after he took over leadership he put the Constitution Bill for the Irish Free State before the Dáil. Cosgrave was lucky that the difficult work of drafting a constitution acceptable to both British and Irish governments had been accomplished by his predecessors Griffith and Collins in June 1922. He was also lucky that his trusted and able henchman, O'Higgins, had been present during the drafting and the negotiations held in London on amendments to the Irish draft. O'Higgins successfully steered the Free State Constitution Bill through a Dáil which was boycotted by Republican anti-Treaty members. On October 25th 1922 the Pro-Treaty Dáil which from September had regarded itself as a constituent assembly whose task was to approve a constitution for the new state, passed the Constitution. On December 5th 1922 eve of the first anniversary of the signing of the Anglo-Irish Treaty the British Parliament at Westminister passed the Constitution and the Irish Free State was born just one year after the signing of the Treaty which made it possible. On December 7th 1922 a Dáil deputy was shot dead in a Dublin street, a timely reminder that political initiatives alone would not end the military struggle in the land.

Cosgrave and the Civil War

Cosgrave had been present at the combined meeting of the Provisional Government and the National Army presided over by Griffith at which the decision to attack the Four Courts and bring hostilities into the open on 28th June 1922 was taken. Unlike Collins who sought to excuse the waywardness of former comrades-in-arms, Cosgrave condemned utterly all who took up arms against the Treaty. Strong and definite action were promised in order to restore peace, order and security, his immediate objectives when he came to power in September 1922. Just as Cosgrave was lucky that the Constitution had been agreed before he took office so was he lucky that, by September 1922, the National Army had established its superiority. After the fall of the Munster Republic in July, depleted Anti-Treaty Irregulars were reduced to fighting a sporadic guerrilla war in remote rural areas. Nonetheless Cosgrave and O'Higgins, the new Minister for Home Affairs, took the military threat posed by the Irregulars seriously. In the Dáil O'Higgins called for special powers to set up Army Courts empowered to inflict severe penalties including death on those convicted of possession "without proper authority" of firearms, ammunition or explosives, of arson, looting or the destruction of private or public property, of taking part in or aiding and abetting attacks on the National Forces or of the breach of any order made by the Army Council. On September 27th the Dáil passed the Special Powers Acts. On October 10th Special Emergency Powers were granted to the Army but they were not to become applicable until October 15th. Cosgrave who always accepted the democratic rights of opponents of the Treaty to hold what he called "an attitude of opposition on constitutional lines to the Government policy" announced a general amnesty to all "engaged in insurrection and rebellion against the State." Activists were given until October 15th to surrender their arms and renounce participation in the armed struggle. Thereafter the full rigours of the Special Powers Act would be invoked.

Cosgrave successfully enlisted the moral support of the Catholic Church in the government's conflict with the Irregulars. On the same day as the Government announced Special Emergency Powers to the Army, October 10th, a joint pastoral issued by all the bishops condemned in unambiguous language the activities of the

Irregulars, "the guerrilla warfare now being carried on by the Irregulars is without moral sanction, and, therefore, the killing of National soldiers in the course of it is murder before God, the seizing of public and private property is robbery, the breaking of roads, bridges and railways a criminal destruction, the invasion of homes and the molestation of citizens a grievous crime." Stressing that "in all this there is no question of mere politics" the Hierarchy took the ultimate step of excommunicating those who persisted in acts of terrorism and impressed upon all the duty of supporting the national government. This was the strongest statement from the Catholic Hierarchy since its pre-election pronouncement in May 1922 "that the best and wisest course for Ireland is to accept the Treaty".

Despite the strictures of the Catholic Church, in particular the admonition "There is no other government and cannot be, outside the body of the people" on October 26th 1922, the day after the Dáil passed the Free State Constitution Bill, the Irregulars announced the setting up of a republican government of which de Valera was proclaimed president. From November 30th the names of thirty Dáil deputies were placed on the Irregulars' death list. They had voted for the Special Powers Act which was being enforced with ruthless rigour. One of the first victims was Englishman Erskine Childers whose Howth Gun-running in July 1914 had made the 1916 Easter Rising possible. As Secretary to the Treaty delegation Childers vehemently opposed the Treaty. A propagandist rather than an activist for the Irregulars he was arrested on November 10th 1922 for possession of a tiny pistol given to him by Collins as a souvenir. Childers was tried and found guilty by a military court on the day that the first executions under the Special Powers Act took place. (On November 17th four practically unknown men were executed for possession of guns in Dublin). One week later Childers was executed. Dáil deputies were moved to protest at what one deputy, Gavan Duffy, described as the execution of "one of the noblest men I have ever known" simply because he was a political opponent.

The assassination, however, of Dáil Deputy Hales on December 7th and the knowledge that Dáil deputies were "legitimate" targets of attack to the Irregulars hardened attitudes. The government's response to the assassination of Hales was swift and ruthless. The execution of O'Connor, Mellows, McKelvey and Barrett, one from each of the four provinces of Ireland and all imprisoned since the fall of the Four Courts on June 30th and therefore not responsible for recent atrocities, showed that the government was prepared to apply the Special Powers retrospectively. Cosgrave had repeatedly warned that Irregular prisoners were not going to be treated as prisoners of war. The execution of the four rebel leaders on 8th December 1922 was a chilling warning to other political prisoners that they were also under death sentence. In all seventy-seven Irregulars were executed by the Cosgrave administration.

The executions had a demoralising effect on the diminishing Irregular forces. The new year saw a campaign of arson and terror against families of TDs and Senators of the Free State Parliament which had come into being on December 6 1922. The father of O'Higgins who as Minister for Home Affairs, had voted for the execution of Rory O'Connor was murdered. Sir Horace Plunkett, founder of the Irish Co-operative movement, chairman of the Irish Convention of 1917, the last attempt to secure agreement between Nationalists and Unionists on Home Rule, and recently appointed Senator in the Irish Free State, had his home destroyed by Irregulars who embarked upon a campaign of arson and destruction of the homes of Irish Unionists. The Irregulars knew however that burning the homes of the rich Anglo-Irish would not win the Civil War. By spring 1923, 13,000 men had been taken prisoner. Only 8,000 Irregulars remained at large. By contrast, government forces had grown from 7,000 in June to 60,000 by the autumn. Recruitment to the Free State forces reached the rate of 1,000 per day. Some high-ranking Irregular officers were seeking means of ending the Civil War by January 1923. It was not however until after some of the worst atrocities of the seven years of civil strife 1916-1923 such as the Ballyseedy massacre in Co. Kerry when, on March 7th Free State troops tied nine Irregular prisoners to a log and blew them up, and until after the death of die-hard Irregular Commander-in-chief Lynch on April 10th 1923 that the pleas of the Republican leader and President of the rebel republican government, de Valera, were listened to on May 24th 1923.

Counting the Cost

The dumping and hiding of arms (there was no official ceasefire) ended seven years of intermittent strife and unrest. In numbers killed and in destruction done, the Civil War surpassed both the Easter Rising 1916 and the War of Independence (1919-1921) the other two bloody chapters in the story of Ireland's twentieth century struggle for political independence. Apart from the fifteen executions after the Easter Rising four hundred and fifty were officially listed as dead. Nine were reported missing. Between the Easter Rising in 1916 and the Treaty in 1921, 600 IRA Volunteers died in action. Crown casualties between January 1920 and July 1921 were some 525 killed. Even if one takes into account the 752 civilians and IRA who were killed between January 1919 and the truce in July 1921 these were much fewer than the estimated 4,000 - 5,000 deaths of the Civil War period. Army deaths alone between January 1922 and April 1924 were 800 according to government sources.

The economic toll of seven years of war and destruction was immense. An estimated £2.5m of damage was done mainly to city centre premises in Dublin during Easter week 1916. The bill for damage done to Dublin property during the first week of fighting in the Civil War was £5m. Whilst £1^{3}/4m was paid out in compensation claims after the Easter Rising 1916 the Free State government was paying out £1.7m in compensation as late as 1926/'27. Destruction to property, both public and private, was greater during the Civil War than during the War of Independence. Heavy reliance by the National Forces on public transport meant the systematic destruction by the Irregulars of railways, roads and bridges throughout the country. This, coupled with the destruction of creameries and public works, brought the bill for material damage to over £30m. In addition, the cash cost to the government of crushing the Irregulars was reckoned by O'Higgins to be £17m. Cosgrave had given an undertaking as early as 1920 that claims to compensation for injury or loss due to the "necessary operations of the National Forces" would be met. Seven per cent of national expenditure went on compensation claims in 1923/'24. During the 1920's compensation and defence of an insecure regime ranked among the five heaviest charges on national expenditure and added to the economic difficulties of an already crippled economy.

The Irish Free State

The most important task facing the Cosgrave administration upon the restoration of peace in May 1923 was the establishment of institutions of state in accordance with the terms of the Irish Free State Constitution.

The Free State Constitution came into force on December 6th 1922 just one year after the Treaty was signed. On the same day the Senate (the upper house of parliament) came into being. Half of its sixty members were to be nominated by the head of government who was to be called the President of the Executive Council. Cosgrave was anxious to honour assurances given by his predecessor Griffith to Southern Unionists that, despite being a minority, they would have representation in the upper house. Of the first thirty Senators to be nominated, sixteen were Southern Unionists. Others were drawn from literary and arts circles such as W.B. Yeats and Oliver St. John Gogarty. The other thirty were to be elected by the Dáil, the lower house. The sixty senators were to be retired in groups of fifteen over three year periods and be replaced by senators elected at three year intervals by votes of citizens over thirty years of age. The Unionists pressed hard for real powers for the Senate. The Senate however, like its British counterpart from 1911, the House of Lords, could not reject bills passed by the lower house. It could hold up legislation for 270 days and in cases of contentious legislation demand a joint session of both houses to discuss all the issues. The Senate did not conflict with the Dáil or the Executive Council (government) during the Cosgrave Years 1922/'32. Under de Valera the Senate proved such an obstacle to legislation, in particular to the proposed constitutional changes, that the de Valera government sought its dissolution even before the new 1937 constitution was drawn up.

The Dáil was intended to be the dominant house. Its membership was initially fixed at 153 TDs elected by proportional representation by universal suffrage of adults aged 21 years or over at least once every six years. The Dáil elected not just the President of the Executive Council but also approved each of the President's nominees for posts on the Executive Council.

The powers of the President of the Executive Council were less extensive than his British counterpart, the Prime Minister, or his successor, the Taoiseach. Cosgrave, unambitious and unassuming, was happy to stress the role of the Executive Council as a body in decision-making. His ministers in the main were strong dominant personalities to whom Cosgrave was happy to allow independence of action. In 1937 he said, "Ministers in my view ought to possess security and a measure of independence." Cosgrave preferred to be regarded as "a leader among equals". "The chairman not the chief" is how political analyst, Brian Farrell has described the role of Cosgrave as president of the Executive Council during the first decade of the Irish Free State.

Article 17 of the Constitution required all members of the Oireachtas to take the oath of allegiance as expressed in Article 4 of the Anglo-Irish Treaty. When a number of pro-Treaty deputies declared on 6th December 1922 their intention not to take the oath and to retire from the Dáil, Cosgrave, who, frequently during his ten-year period as leader spoke of retiring, astounded everybody by announcing that, although he had no personal objections to the oath, he also would not take the oath and leave the Dáil. So shocked were the would-be "rebels" that they agreed to take the oath. All returned to the Dáil and a major political crisis at a critical stage of the Civil War was averted.

After an initial 8-year period, extended in 1929 by a further 8 years, amendments to the Constitution could only by done by popular referendum. Theoretically a petition by 75,000 voters could force the government to hold a referendum. Fianna Fail attempted to invoke the right to referendum and to initiate constitutional amendment in 1927 in order to force a referendum on the oath of allegiance or, failing that, to secure the suspension of the Electoral Amendment Act of 1927 which compelled elected TDs to take their seat or to forfeit it. The fear that enemies of the state might use the rights of the people in order to undermine the foundations of the state, prompted the Oireachtas (the King and two houses of parliament) to restrict the referendum right to members of the Oireachtas who had taken the oath, and to abolish the initiation of laws or constitutional amendments by the people in a measure accompanying the Electoral Amendment Law of 1927.

The Constitution of the Irish Free State allowed for a sovereign state with a special and visible relationship with the United Kingdom to emerge. The institutions of state were based upon the Westminster model. It was hoped however to adopt only what was good of the British system. The Irish Free State Constitution was seen as an evolution of the British system of government and of Dáil Eireann, its immediate predecessor. Unlike the Constitution of Dáil Eireann which was intended to be a provisional constitution for an independent republic which the Constitution makers hoped to make a reality, the Constitution of the Irish Free State was intended to be a permanent and definitive document. Within fifteen years it was replaced by a new constitution.

First Cumann na nGaedheal Government 1923-27

The first elections under the Constitution were held in August 1923. The events of 1922-23 had ensured that the greatest political divide in the Free State would be on the issue of the Treaty and the Civil War. Whilst both pro- and anti-Treaty candidates had fought the June election in 1922 under the Sinn Féin name the official launch in the Mansion House, Dublin, in April 1923 of the pro-Treaty party under Cosgrave which assumed the name of Griffith's first organisation, Cumann na nGaedheal, ensured the development of a two-Party political system. Although other political parties, notably Labour, founded in 1912 and therefore the oldest political party in independent Ireland, became influential, the biggest political parties remained the pro-Treaty, Cumann na nGaedheal/Fine Gael and the Anti-Treaty Sinn Féin/ Fianna Fail parties. Until 1927 the anti-Treaty Opposition Parties (Sinn Féin and from 1926 Fianna Fail) refused to take their seats in the Dáil and remained outside the parliamentary process. Thus it was that Cumann na nGaedheal with only 63 seats had an over-all majority over the other political parties represented in the Dáil (Labour 14, Farmers 15, Independents 17). The abstention of the 44 Sinn Féin TDs - 29% of the total - gave the Cumann na nGaedheal government an overall majority which they never won at the polls.

The first Cumann na nGaedheal administration 1923-27 was headed by Cosgrave, President of the Executive Council. O'Higgins became Vice-President and Minister of Home Affairs. The first Protestant to hold cabinet office in independent Ireland, Ernest Blythe, became Minister of Finance. Joseph McGrath who was to resign over the first major crisis after the ending of the Civil War, the Army Mutiny of 1924, became Minister for Industry and Commerce. Eoin MacNeill, founder member of the Gaelic League in 1893 and of the Irish Volunteers in 1913 and an eminent scholar and educationalist was appointed Minister for Education. Desmond Fitzgerald 1916 activist and father of future Taoiseach Garret Fitzgerald became Minister for External Affairs while Mulcahy remained Minister of Defence. Four "extern" ministers selected by the Dáil remained outside the Executive Council but were responsible for the government departments of Agriculture, Local Government, Posts and Telegraphs and Fisheries respectively.

The composition of the first Free State government reflected continuity with the past. The strong men of the new regime were those who had brought the state safely through the Civil War, Continuity, especially continuity with the British past, was also evident in the take-over of existing British systems of government. Nowhere was this more evident than in the transfer of the British Civil Service to the authority of the provisional government on April 1922. A total of 20,415 civil servants transferred. Only 131 members of the civil service of the Irish Free State came from the much-vaunted Dail Eireann administration. Ninety-eight per cent of the Irish Civil Servants in the first 10 years were former British civil servants. One of the first to join the Irish Civil Service, Joseph Brennan, became Secretary of the Department of Finance 1923/'27, the most senior position in the Irish Civil Service. As chairman of the first commission of inquiry into the civil service 1932-35 he noted, "Under changed masters the same main tasks of administration continued to be performed by the same staffs on the same general lines of organisation and procedure".

The Irish Civil Service aimed at retaining what was good in the British system and eliminating what was seen to be wasteful and inefficient. Thus a civil service commission was set up to ensure that new entrants would be by competition and that appointments would be made on merit and not by political patronage. The Ministers and Secretaries Act 1924 pruned down the unwieldy forty-seven departments and boards under the British system into a stream-lined eleven departments of which the department of finance with its control over spending by other departments was the most important. An administrative takeover therefore rather than an administrative revolution took place during the first years of the new state.

The legal system established by the Courts of Justice Act (1924) reflected the desire to preserve a reformed British system of justice. The Courts of Justice Act abolished both the British and the Sinn Féin courts. In their place it established District Courts presided over by paid District Justices with jurisdiction over minor matters. The Circuit Court came next with jurisdiction over most criminal and civil matters. Above the Circuit Court was the High Court with full jurisdiction over civil and criminal matters and sole original jurisdiction to try the constitutional validity of all laws. The highest court in the land was the Supreme Court presided over by the chief justice and two other judges of the High Court and was the final arbiter in Ireland in matters relating to the Constitution. The final court of appeal against decisions made in the Irish courts rested in London with the Judicial Committee of the Privy Council. Although the right of the individual to apply for leave to appeal to the Judicial Committee of the Privy Council was enshrined in the Free State Constitution the Cosgrave administration successfully resisted attempts to enforce appeal decisions on the Irish courts. The Imperial Conferences of 1926 and 1930 were used to render the Judicial Committee of the Privy Council, what O'Higgins called it, "a useless court and an unnecessary court".

The laws administered by the Irish courts were in the main British laws. Like the

Civil Service the personnel remained unchanged. As late as 1932 with the de Valera anti-Treaty administration in office, all seven high court judges and two of the three supreme court judges all bore the KC (King's Counsel) after their name. Almost seventy years after the foundation of the state the Irish inns of court where barristers of the legal profession are trained is still called the King's Inns.

The setting up of an unarmed police force, Garda Siochana marked the most striking departure from British practice in Ireland. In 1924 O'Higgins proudly remarked, "there is in Ireland a phenomenon which was never seen in the days of British administration, an unarmed police force functioning from Donegal to Cork with the complete goodwill and co-operation of the people." The creation of an unarmed police force operating from September 1922 when the Civil War was raging, was an act of confidence in a peaceful future, and a lasting achievement of the Cosgrave era. By the end of 1922 2,000 guards drawn mainly from the ranks of pro-Treaty IRA occupied 190 Garda stations throughout the country. Under Garda Commissioner Eoin O'Duffy, the police force grew. It offered what was difficult to find in Ireland during the 1920's, "security, the chance of promotion and a degree of esteem in the public eye" according to Conor Brady who has written a history of the Garda Siochana, "Guardians of the Peace". The presence of an unarmed police force, totally loyal to the state, lessened the gravity of the Army Mutiny 1924, the first serious crisis of the post-Civil War period.

The "Army Mutiny"

The "Army Mutiny", potentially the most serious security crisis in the history of the state, occurred within twelve months of the ending of the Civil War. Two main sources of unresolved conflict lay at the root of the problem. The government's determination to establish civil authority over the army, many of whose members had been a law unto themselves since 1916, made a clash with the army almost inevitable. The second source of tension contributing to the "army mutiny" of 1924 were the divisions within the army. Distrust had always existed between the Irish Volunteers and the secret oath-bound members of the IRB. Collins as Commander-in-Chief and President of the IRB managed to unite all factions of the army. His successor, General Mulcahy also a member of the IRB Supreme Council was less successful in cementing the differences between opposing factions of the army. The "Old IRA" - pro-Treaty members of the IRA who were not members of the IRB - began to voice their dissatisfaction. On 6th June 1923 in a confidential ultimatum to Cosgrave, officers Tobin, Ennis and Dalton who had provided the nucleus of Collins's Murder Squad during the War of Independence and who had formed the IRAO, Irish Republican Army Organisation to represent the "Old IRA" in 1922, listed their grievances. Their major grievance was the political one that the Cosgrave administration was not moving fast enough or at all towards the full independence promised by Collins. Cosgrave was reminded that both Collins and the pro-Treaty IRA regarded the Treaty only as a stepping stone towards the republic. More practical grievances were the threat, and for some the reality, of peacetime demobilisation. Defence expenditure remained one of the highest charges on the national expenditure. The army estimates for 1923/'24 were, however, cut from £14.75m to £10.15m. Further drastic cuts were planned for the next financial year. Recommendations to reduce the 50,000 strong army to 35,000 raised urgent questions about demobilisation. The IRA was particularly anxious that "old IRA" veterans of the Civil War and the War of Independence should not be compulsorily demobbed. Yet the Army Council and General Mulcahy, Minister of Defence and Army spokesman within the government, responsible for selection of officers and men for demobilisation, were strongly influenced by the IRB. The June 1923 interview with Cosgrave and Mulcahy failed to resolve any of the issues although Mulcahy promised to listen to future representations.

Demobilisation of ordinary soldiers from July 1923 and of officers from September 1923 confirmed Tobin's worst fears that IRB men, despised "trucileers", those who had joined the Irish army after the truce and the Treaty, and hated and distrusted ex-British soldiers who had joined the National Army rather than return to Britain in 1922 to almost certain demobilisation and unemployment, would be retained, while "old IRA" veterans of the War of Independence would be demobbed. Disaffection grew within the ranks of the army as Tobin campaigned secretly among officers from summer 1923, prophesying gloomily "that inside a year… the British ex-personnel serving in the army would be in control of all the administrative posts and… the IRA officers… would be demobbed." Tobin and the IRAO were fortunate in having the support of a government minister, McGrath, Minister for Industry and Commerce and since, February 1923, director of the CID, the criminal investigation department created by Collins out of military intelligence staff who had proved so effective during the War of Independence. The CID included Tobin, Dalton and Ennis, the officers at the centre of the Army Mutiny. The decision in October 1923 to disband the CID intensified opposition. McGrath dissented from the Executive Council decision. In vain McGrath argued in government discussions on "army reorganisation" in February 1924 for "a detailed list of those whom it is proposed to demobilise."

Matters came to a head when a decision was taken to demote or dismiss practically all members of the IRAO. Tobin and Dalton responded on 6th March 1924 by issuing a second ultimatum to Cosgrave. They demanded the dismissal of the IRB-oriented army council, the immediate cessation of demobilisation and army reorganisation and a meeting to discuss their interpretation of the Treaty. The government acted swiftly. Tobin and Dalton were arrested. McGrath resigned in protest from the Executive Council and sided openly with the "mutineers". Rumours of resignation and desertion threatened a national crisis.

Cosgrave was ill and O'Higgins, Vice-President and Minister for Justice, undertook to defuse the situation. O'Higgins was determined through solving the current crisis to assert the government's authority over the military forces. As early as March 1923 when the army estimates for 1923/'24 were being decided O'Higgins had stated "that a very grave mistake had been made in accepting the position in which there was a joint Minister (for Defence) and Commander-in-Chief and that the position of the army in respect to government was most unsatisfactory." O'Higgins's first step in March 1924 was to appoint the then Garda Commissioner, O'Duffy as General-Officer-Commander of the army to investigate the grievances. O'Duffy's appointment over Mulcahy was seen as a triumph for the concept of civilian control. Garda Commissioner O'Duffy was responsible to the Minister for Justice, O'Higgins. The crisis seemed to have eased when Tobin and Dalton withdrew their ultimatum on March 11th 1924 having received assurances from ex-Minister McGrath, who acted as intermediary between the "mutinous" officers and the government, that a committee of inquiry was to be set up and that there would be no further arrests or victimisation. Tension again flared one week later when, on the orders of a senior member of the army council and, with the knowledge of Mulcahy, though not of O'Duffy, armed soldiers surrounded equally armed mutinous officers in a pub in Dublin city centre. A possible civil war between rival factions of the army was averted only by the timely intervention of McGrath and by O'Higgins's decision to root out all factions within the army. Determined to prevent what he called an "alphabet war" within the army by rival factions IRA/IRB O'Higgins demanded the resignation of the IRB officers in the Army Council. Mulcahy, the IRB Commander and Minister for Defence, voluntarily resigned. Cosgrave himself took over the post of Minister of Defence. Undertakings were given to mutinous officers (only about 100 officers were involved, 41 of whom were senior officers above the rank of captain. Disaffection did not spread to the rank-and-file soldiers) that no action would be taken against them if they returned to their posts. By April 17th 1924 O'Duffy was able to report to the government that he had "the co-operation of the responsible officers... and the loyalty of the rank and file." The crisis was over.

The "Army Mutiny of 1924" cost the government two ministers and eight deputies who resigned in protest. The army lost many of its longest-serving soldiers. Tobin and his IRAO comrades who were not reinstated but were instead offered improved retirement terms, protested vainly that "in the name of 'discipline' the large majority of the old soldiers of 1916-21 have been driven out of the army". The failure of the 'Army Mutiny" demonstrated once again the government's ability to defeat revolution from within and to win what O'Higgins called the "age-long struggle for mastery in its own house. Its failure represented a triumph for consitutionalism. The Army would no longer play a role in the political life of the state. The government's control over the reorganised Army which became the official armed forces of the state by the Defence forces (Establishment) Order of October 1st 1924 was total. O'Higgins asserted with authority, "Those who take the pay and wear the uniform of the state, be they soldiers or police, must be non-political servants of the state."

An important political consequence of the "Mutiny" was the emergence of O'Higgins as the dominant member of government. The resignation of two government ministers revealed deep divisions within the Cosgrave administration. The whole episode also illustrated Cosgrave's willingness to allow others (notably O'Higgins) to take over in time of crisis. Cosgrave's reliance on O'Higgins both during the Army Mutiny and during the next crisis, the Boundary Settlement, which was already brewing, meant that O'Higgins's assassination in 1927 was a blow, not just to the Free State but also to Cosgrave, who relied so heavily upon him.

Relations with Northern Ireland

Relations between Northern Ireland and the Irish Free State during their first formative years were crucial for the future of both states. Although Cosgrave had been an advocate of the Belfast boycott during the War of Independence in retaliation for attacks upon Catholics, a "pacific and friendly disposition" to the Craig administration in N.I. was urged by the Northern Committee set up in August 1922 by Cosgrave "to consider the question of the policy to be adopted to the Belfast government". The inclusion of a Protestant, Blythe from the border county

Monaghan, on the Northern Committee was evidence of a conciliatory policy. In a forceful 8-page argument presented to the government on August 9th 1922 Blythe pointed out that full acceptance of the Treaty implied recognition of the Northern government. The shift in policy became more pronounced after the death of Collins. On October 2nd, Cosgrave, the new leader announced that his government had no objection to Northern Catholics taking a declaration of loyalty to the northern government. One month later as the Southern Government decided to stop payment of northern teachers' salaries, Cosgrave and Craig the Northern P.M. met for the first time in London. "We got on very well together", was Craig's comment after the meeting.

The hope expressed by Blythe in August 1922 that conciliatory gestures might make the Northern government reconsider voting out of the All-Ireland state brought into being on 5th December 1922 by the enactment of the Irish Free State Constitution Act was rudely dashed when within the month stipulated in the Treaty of December 1921 the N.I. administration had opted out of the Irish Free State. The Free State government had then to invoke Article 12 of the Anglo-Irish Treaty providing for a Commission to "determine in accordance with the wishes of the inhabitants, so far as may be compatible with economic and geographic conditions, the boundaries between Northern Ireland and the rest of Ireland." As early as October 1922 the Cosgrave government had set up a north-east boundary bureau. The securing of a Boundary Commission acceptable to all interested parties, the Irish Free State, Northern Ireland, and the U.K. became the main concern of Cosgrave's northern policy over the next two years.

The Boundary Commission

The Civil War and the difficulty which the Irish Free State was experiencing in 1922-23 in establishing control over its twenty-six county state, were set-backs to those who hoped to persuade a Boundary Commission to extend the jurisdiction of the Irish Free State. The prospect of victory in the Civil War meant that the Executive Council pressed for the setting up of the Boundary Commission from the end of January 1923. In July 1923 Eoin MacNeill, a Catholic from the N.I. county of Antrim, was chosen as the Free State Commissioner. The chairman Justice Feetham from South Africa was not appointed until June 1924, almost twelve months later. Craig delayed in appointing a N.I. Commissioner until he was informed that if he refused to nominate a Commissioner, the British government would nominate the N.I. Commissioner. On October 10th 1924 the British Labour government of Ramsay MacDonald asked J.R. Fisher, Craig's private nominee, according to G. J. Hand a distant cousin of MacNeill who has made a detailed study of the Boundary Commission, to be the Northern representative. His acceptance two weeks later meant the work of the Boundary Commission could begin.

The terms of reference of the Boundary Commission had already been agreed. It is interesting in the light of subsequent developments that only the N.I. government wanted the decision of the Boundary Commission to be unanimous. During the summer of 1924 Britain supported the Irish Free State's demand that the Boundary Commission proceed by majority decision. The N.I. government's lack of enthusiasm for the boundary Commission reinforced the popular opinion, in the South that the N.I. state would suffer heavy losses.

An early meeting on 4/5th December 1924 dispelled any hope that Feetham was going to support the absorption of Northern Ireland into the Free State. "The new territory is to be 'Northern Ireland', and should be capable of maintaining a Parliament and Government," he asserted. "Readjustment of boundaries" only was the most that Feethan envisaged.

At the first meeting of the Boundary Commission on 6th November 1924 the Commissioners pledged themselves to strictest secrecy, "no Commissioner would consult any of the Governments concerned as to the work of the Commission or would make any statement as to such work either to any Government or any individual without first consulting his colleagues." While MacNeill was scrupulous about maintaining a wall of silence and put his duty to his fellow Commissioners before that due to his government colleagues, Fisher, a seventy-year-old lawyer from N.I. confided all to the wife of the leader of the Ulster Unionists at Westminster. In July 1925 when much of the work of the Commission was finished he wrote to her, "it will now be a matter of border town-lands... the result will, I think be a stronger and more compact territory" (for Northern Ireland). On 18th October 1925 when the proposed territorial transfers had been broadly agreed upon but before agreement on publication had been reached, Fisher once again breached the code of secrecy by writing to Carson, leader of the Ulster Unionist campaign against Home Rule 1912 - 1921 announcing triumphantly "the result... will not shift a stone or a tile of your enduring work for Ulster". Fisher's odd sense of confidentiality was revealed when he told Carson that he was writing to no one else but added that he had told the leader of the Ulster Unionist M.P.s that morning, adding "under seal of press secrecy for the present."

Press secrecy was not observed for very long. The English newspaper, the "Morning Post" of November 7th 1925 containing a full break-down complete with a map of all the Commission's findings. The accuracy of the account contrasted sharply with inaccurate speculation in British newspapers earlier and left nobody in any doubt that the information was leaked. Annoyance at the indiscretion of Fisher quickly gave way to anger as it was realised that only minor change was proposed. While the Irish Free State stood to gain more territory (approx. 180,000 acres against 50,000) and more people than N.I. (31,000 against 7,500) the knowledge that N.I. might gain Free State territory incensed a large body of opinion who believed that under the terms of the Treaty 1921 the Irish Free State should not lose any territory. "The Commission has no authority under the Treaty... to transfer any part of our territory to Northern Ireland", Cosgrave had asserted in February in 1925 when it was feared that large parts of Donegal were going to be given to N.I.

The furore was such over the "Morning Post" disclosures that on 18th November 1925 the "Irish Independent" reported thus, "not since partition was introduced has feeling run so high." MacNeill was recalled by Cosgrave in a manner reminiscent of de Valera's summoning of the Treaty signatories in December 1921. MacNeill, Minister for Education as well as Commissioner, was the only member of the Commission who was not a full-time Commissioner. He had to divide his time and attention between the department of education, the government, and the commission. He was also the only member of the Commission who was not a lawyer. He felt this acutely and had alluded to it in a letter to Cosgrave on 10th October 1925. On 19 November 1925 as Dáil deputies called for MacNeill's withdrawal from the

Commission, MacNeill took the boat back to England to inform the Commission of his resignation. Upon his return he resigned from the government. MacNeill, who, even before the Commission was set up had gloomily predicted his own political downfall, quoting the line from Shakespeare's "Richard II", "the ripest fruit first falls," was the Commission's first political victim.

After MacNeill's resignation the Cosgrave government was concerned to prevent publication of the majority report by the other two Commissioners. The only way this could be done was by a tripartite agreement between the three governments. Speed was of the essence because once the Commission's findings were placed before the respective governments they would have the force of law. A tripartite agreement between the three heads of government recommended itself strongly to the British Conservative Unionist government of the day. The British input into the Commission had been considerable. Not only had they appointed the chairman Justice Feetham but they also appointed and paid the salary of the N.I. Commissioner Fisher. In addition the secretary and Commission staff were all British. As soon as the British P.M. Baldwin realised that both Cosgrave and Craig were willing to come to London immediately in order to sign a "no change" border agreement in return for financial concessions to both the N.I. and Free State governments, the British government ordered that publication of the Commission's majority report be postponed.

A majority report was finally signed by Feetham and Fisher on 9th December 1925 six days after the tripartite agreement between Cosgrave, Craig and Baldwin had rendered it null and void. The commission's findings were finally made public in 1969 when civil unrest in the trouble-spots, Newry, South Armagh, Derry, Fermanagh and Tyrone, which were under discussion in 1925, threatened the very existence of the Northern Ireland state confirmed by the tripartite agreement of December 3rd 1925.

The tripartite agreement was historic in that for the first time, the signature of the N.I. Prime Minister Craig was appended to a part of the Treaty. The official title of the tripartite agreement was the Confirmation of Amending (of the Treaty) Agreement Bill. Its terms fell into three main categories. The existing boundary between N.I. and the Free State was to remain unchanged. The Council of Ireland provided for by the Treaty as means of bringing about Irish unity was effectively scrapped by transferring the powers of the Council relating to Northern Ireland to the N.I. government. The initiative was to be left with the two Irish governments who, it was hoped, would maintain regular contact. The next meeting of two Irish heads of government did not take place for forty years. The effect of the historic meetings between the N.I. P.M. O'Neill and Lemass, the Irish leader in 1965, was to shake Ulster Unionism to its foundations and to set in train the sequence of events which was eventually to lead to the suspension of the N.I. regime in 1972. Of immediate importance to both the Cosgrave and Craig governments in 1925 were the financial terms of the tripartite agreement. As early as September 1923 the "Morning Post" carried a story from an unnamed Dublin correspondent suggesting that Cosgrave wanted to set the boundary clause off against some of the onerous financial terms of the Treaty. The "carrot" for both Cosgrave and Craig was the agreement to release both states from their share of the British debt. Not only was Article XII of the Treaty amended, the Irish Free State was released from its financial obligations to the U.K. contained in Article V. Not for nothing was the Cosgrave government accused of having betrayed Griffith and Collins and of having sold out the Nationalists in N.I. for a handful of silver.

Yet the storm of protest in the Irish Free State was not as loud as might have been expected. The Confirmation of Amending Agreement Bill passed both houses of the Oireachtas on December 16th with only the Labour Party registering real protest. At no time were more than twenty votes recorded against the Government during the Boundary Crisis. The real political lesson of the affair was quickly learnt by de Valera, leader of abstentionist Sinn Féin. Within days of the signing of the tripartite agreement de Valera met the leader of the Labour Party with a view to "reuniting the people of all the parties... in effective opposition to partitioning of our motherland". Until, however, de Valera and his supporters abandoned abstentionism their political opposition remained ineffective. Within four months de Valera had broken from abstentionist Sinn Féin and announced in April 1926, "We are ourselves forming a new organisation" with no doctrinaire objection to the Dáil provided that the oath of allegiance was removed. The biggest political consequence of the Boundary Crisis was to call forth the Fianna Fail Republican Party which at the next general election in June 1927 ran the Government party close with 44 seats against Cumann na nGaedheal's 47. The electorate's verdict on the Boundary agreement and on other unpopular measures which included the Intoxicating Liquor Act which in the pre-election period took the unpopular step of limiting the numbers of public houses and of reducing their hours of opening, can be seen in the drop in Cumann na nGaedheal representation from 63 in 1923 to 47 in June 1927.

Law and Order

The June 1927 election results represented no immediate threat to Cosgrave's government as Fianna Fail, the largest opposition party, remained outside the Dail. The assassination of Vice-President O'Higgins on 10th July 1927 barely two weeks after the new Cosgrave administration had been formed, highlighted what had been the most serious chronic problem since the unofficial ending of the Civil War in 1923, i.e. the underlying threat of anarchy and the fear of a resumption of the Civil War. Fear of a total break down of Law and Order (between August 1923 and February 1924 there were 738 cases of arson and armed robbery) prompted the passing of further Public Safety Acts. The Public Safety (Emergency Powers) Act of 1923 had enabled any government minister to order the arrest and detention of any person deemed a danger to public safety. The 1924 Act renewed the powers of detention, imprisonment, flogging for armed robbery and arson, and in a country bedevilled by non-payment of debts, strengthened the powers of sheriffs in the legal recovery of debt. By the end of 1924 the government felt confident enough to release most of the internees including de Valera who had been arrested when he emerged from hiding in August 1923 to fight the general election of that year. Towards the end of 1926, however, a spate of IRA attacks on police stations resulting in the deaths of two unarmed Gardai made necessary the passing of a further Public Safety Act and the reintroduction of detention without trial.

The assassination in July 1927 of O'Higgins, called "the Irish Mussolini", because of his necessary close association as Minister for Justice with repressive public order measures, convinced Cosgrave that there could never be lasting peace until the main political opposition (Fianna Fail) was forced to accept the democratic process. Consequently, accompanying the customary Public Safety measures was an

Electoral Amendment Bill requiring every elected member to take the oath or to forfeit his seat. In addition, henceforth, every election candidate must declare his willingness to take the oath upon nomination of his candidature. Every loop-hole for Fianna Fail was closed when a Constitution Amendment Bill proposing the abolition of popular referendum was introduced. Faced with the stark choice: accept the parliamentary process by taking the oath and entering the Dail or put themselves outside parliamentary politics, Fianna Fail chose to enter the Dail one month after O'Higgins's assassination, declaring the oath to be "an empty political formula".

Cosgrave's decision to force Fianna Fáil to accept parliamentary democracy was almost political suicide. One of the first acts of Fianna Fáil as the biggest opposition party was to join with Labour deputies in a 'no confidence' motion on the government. The motion was defeated only by the casting vote of the Ceann Comhairle. The Dáil was dissolved and another general election was held within a month. Cumann na nGaedheal election posters attacked Fianna Fáil's recent "conversion" saying, "They took the Oath to save their party - they would not take it in 1922 to save the country from Civil War." Nonetheless the 13 seat increase for Fianna Fáil in the September 1927 election showed that the country endorsed the Fianna Fáil decision to enter the Dail. Cumann na nGaedheal representation also increased from 47 to 62 as sympathy for the government rose in the wake of the assassination of O'Higgins. Chief casualties of the second election in 1927 were the smaller parties. In 1927 a two-party political system with the two main parties dividing on the Treaty and Civil War emerged. The pattern for political life in the new state was set.

W. T. Cosgrave - forced Fianna Fáil to accept the democratic process in 1927.

Law and order continued, however, to be a major preoccupation. A draconian Public Safety Act of July 1927 declared the IRA and any other association aimed at the overthrow of the state illegal and set up military non-jury courts empowered to impose the death sentence for possession of firearms and related offences. Intimidation of jurymen after the repeal of the 1927 Public Safety Act at the end of 1928 meant that a Juries Protection Act had to be passed. The emergence of extremist

IRA splinter groups from 1929, in particular the socialist republican movement, Saor Eire, which hoped to overthrow not just the Treaty but also the whole capitalist system in Ireland enabled the government to exploit what they called the "Red Scare" and to enlist once again the support of the Church in their fight against the enemies of the state. A Constitution Amendment Act in October 1931 empowering the government to set up a military tribunal of five members to deal with political crime and allowing the government to declare unlawful any association and giving the police wide powers of arrest and detention was accompanied by a bishops' pastoral drawing attention to the "growing evidence of a campaign of revolution and communism which if allowed to run unchecked, must end in the ruin of Ireland, both soul and body." Two days later the government declared illegal 12 organisations, including the IRA, Saor Eire, and the Irish Communist party which was just emerging. The sympathy of de Valera and the Fianna Fáil party which described itself in 1928 as a "slightly constitutional party", for all radical republican movements, raised hopes that de Valera might be, if not an "Irish Lenin" at least an "Irish Kerensky", whose advent to power would pave the way for a Soviet revolution in Ireland in the same way as Kerensky's provisional government in post-Czarist Russia had led to Soviet seizure of power in 1917. Cumann na nGaedheal fought the 1932 general election on the same slogan of "the state in danger" as was used in 1927. One Cumann na nGaedheal election advertisement in 1932 asked a mainly conservative electorate, 'How will you vote tomorrow? The gunmen are voting for Fianna Fail. The communists are voting for Fianna Fail." Victory for Fianna Fail with 72 seats against only 56 for Cumann na nGaedheal was not the prelude to revolution. The democratic institutions of a capitalist state so firmly established and safeguarded by the Cosgrave administration 1922-32 were as steadfastly upheld by their successors.

The Economy: Agriculture

Without the industrial North the Irish Free State was almost exclusively agricultural. (The main industries, milling, brewing, distilling were agriculture-related and dependent.) In 1931 only 13.5% of workers were engaged in industry. Historian F.S.L. Lyons commented, "Upon the well-being of agriculture rested the well-being of the country at large." With this in mind responsibility for agriculture was given to extern minister Hogan, a solicitor by profession but from farming stock. As Minister for Agriculture between 1922 and 1932 Hogan became one of the outstanding ministers of the Cosgrave years.

The immediate concern in 1923 was to undo the ravages of the Civil War which had laid waste the countryside. The co-operative movement founded by Horace Plunkett in 1894 was encouraged to reorganise and co-operative creameries burned down during the Civil War were assisted to rebuild.

Land purchase had been a cornerstone of the Conservative policy of "killing home rule with kindness" during the period 1885-1906. The Birrell Land Act (1909) passed by a Liberal government was, however, the first compulsory land purchase scheme. It was to complete the work of compulsory land purchase that the Land Act of 1923 was passed enabling the Land Commission to take over all leasehold land and transfer it to tenants who became owner-occupiers. More than 450,000 acres were distributed to some 24,000 families by the Land Commission (1922-32). It was Hogan's hope to increase the size of small uneconomic holdings. The percentage of viable family farm units between 30 and 1000 acres increased from 38.5% in 1917 to 42.8% in 1931.

A trend away from farms under 15 acres and over 2000 acres in the period 1918-1958 pleased Hogan but he realised that unless farmers could gain access to attractive farming loans the quality and quantity of agricultural produce would not improve sufficiently to enable Irish farm produce to compete with high-quality international produce on the lucrative U.K. market. In 1927 the Agricultural Credit Act provided for the setting up of an Agricultural Credit Corporation to provide low-interest loans to farmers. By 1936 £1m. had been paid out in loans to 16,719 borrowers.

Just as Ireland had supplied British agricultural needs for centuries, Hogan was determined to establish the Free State as main exporter to Britain of Irish livestock. Knowing that quality was the key to success, the Livestock Breeding Act (1925) was passed licensing bulls and boars in order to improve the quality of herds for export. Similarly a series of Acts from 1924 to 1930 attempted to standarise butter, bacon and egg production and to regulate marketing of farm produce. In the marketing of farm produce the Irish Free State was 10 years ahead of Northern Ireland. Irish poultry's success story in the 1920s with the Free State supplying practically all of N.I.'s eggs by 1927 may well have prompted the Northern Ministry of agriculture to develop its own marketing schemes from the mid-1930's. A concentration on cattle farming, with the raising of livestock for export and dairy products for the home and U.K. markets in both N.I. and the British mainland, was therefore the main emphasis in Free State agriculture during the 1920s. Hogan was a firm advocate of free trade and resisted the move towards protection of home industries from the mid-1920s. Increasing specialisation in cattle meant, however, a consequent decline in tillage farming and increasing dependence upon imported foodstuffs. The fall-off in cereal production was somewhat compensated for by the introduction of a new cash crop, sugar-beet, which had the additional advantage of providing employment in the sugar-processing factories, the first of which was opened in Carlow in 1928. Figures for gross agricultural output reveal an increase until 1930 when the world slump brought about by the Wall Street Crash and the Great Depression from 1929 adversely affected Free State agriculture so dependent upon export. The value of agricultural exports (of which livestock and livestock produce accounted for 98%) fell from £35.8m in 1929 to under £14m. in 1935. By 1930 Irish agricultural exports which had enjoyed a virtual monopoly during World War I, were again firmly established on the British market although a post-war slump in British food prices in the early 1920s and the Great Depression after 1929 made such exports less profitable.

Industry

Whilst Irish agriculture wanted free trade to develop as an export industry, small scale Irish industry need protection in order to develop. The Cosgrave government divided into those like Hogan and O'Higgins who wanted free trade and those like McGilligan and his staff at the Department of Industry and Commerce who needed protection to develop infant Irish industries for the home market. Although there was no commitment to protection, a Tariff Commission was set up in 1926 to examine native industry with a view to recommending tariffs. Two years later an unenthusiastic Tariff Commission recommended tariffs on only two items, imported margarine and rosary beads. By 1930 factories were opened in mainly protected industries which included footwear, glass bottles (glass manufacture was revived in Waterford after a lapse of over 100 years), clothing and confectionery. The hundred new enterprises however, only created 13,000 new jobs. Family-based Irish industry remained small-scale.

E.S.B. Shannon Hydro-Electric Scheme

The greatest economic achievement of the 1920s, the Shannon Hydro-Electric Scheme, started in 1925 and in production by 1929, contained all the ingredients of large-scale successful enterprise in Ireland. Foreign skills, technology and assistance was provided by the German electrical engineering firm of Siemens. Public money was invested by the state which also set up the ESB by act of parliament in 1927. The largest of six semi-state bodies set up during the first decade of the state the ESB became the proto-type of semi-state organisations, fifty-five of which by the early 1960's were providing most of the large-scale enterprises in the country. The monitoring of industrial production, so essential for planned economic development from the Lemass era in the '60s, was also made possible through the Censuses of Industrial Production started in 1926 and held at five-yearly intervals. The foundations of future economic development were laid in the 1920s with enterprises such as the Shannon Hydro-electric Scheme which from the beginning provided the country's domestic and industrial needs for cheap electricity.

Radio: Censorship and the Catholic Church

Another lasting achievement of the 1920s and one which like the ESB marked the modernisation of the Free State was the advent of Irish radio. Douglas Hyde, founder of the Gaelic League and future first President of Ireland opened 2RN the first Irish radio station on January 1st 1926. The first football match to be broadcast in Europe was the 1926 hurling semi-final. The desire to preserve Ireland from outside influence which was generally perceived to be evil and destructive, prompted the passing of the Censorship of Films Act 1929 and ensured that Irish writers such as Sean O'Faolain and Austin Clarke became better know and appreciated outside of Ireland than within. Literary giants like James Joyce and Austin Clarke had already chosen to live abroad. Interestingly the relaxation of censorship by a new Censorship of Publications Act in 1967 which, by placing a 12-year prohibition restriction on books, released 5000 books at once, came after the launch of Irish television in 1961. Censorship was welcomed by the Catholic Church whose support Cosgrave was anxious to retain. For the same reason Cosgrave gave assurances in 1924 to those who feared that the secular Constitution of the Free State might permit divorce, "there are no real grounds for any apprehension regarding divorce bills passing into law".

Whilst the economic foundations of the state were laid during the 1920s economic growth was slow. Agricultural output rose from £57.8m, in 1926-7 to only £61.4m. in 1930. Thereafter the Irish economy suffered as did the economies of all the states of the western world affected by the Wall St. Crash in the U.S. in 1929. Figures for gross industrial output were even less impressive £23m. in 1926, £25m. in 1931. Unemployment 130,000 at the end of the Civil War, remained high throughout the decade. Hardship and grinding poverty were the lot of many families not eligible for the inadequate social welfare benefits available to the limited few. Unemployment insurance was only available to industrial and service workers and benefit was paid only for six months.

While it is estimated, in the absence of reliable figures until 1932, that unemployment never fell below 6% during the decade 1922-'32, in 1928 only 11,000 workers and their families qualified for unemployment benefit. Government preoccupation with financial orthodoxy, the need to balance the budget and seeming insensitivity to the needs of the poor and dependent in society, led to 10% cuts in 50p per week Old Age pensions in 1924. This single measure proved so unpopular that, in 1928, after disappointing election results in 1927, the 5p cut was restored. Cuts in salaries of teachers, civil servants and the Gardai in the late 1920s were also unpopular. De Valera's eve of election promises in 1932 to "tackle the unemployment and housing problems" and introduce pensions for widows and orphans sealed the fate of Cosgrave and Cumann na nGaedheal's chances as Labour, which had "pleaded in vain" according to Labour leader Norton for ten years for a better social policy, transferred its allegiance to de Valera and Fianna Fáil. Labour Deputy Morrissey who joined Cumann na nGaedheal in 1933 put it thus in an RTE interview in 1978, "the Cosgrave government were so busy trying to be statesmen and building the state that they forgot the people especially the poor."

External Affairs

Although Cosgrave in June 1922 expressed the view that "our Foreign Affairs, other than commercial, would be a matter of no importance" he was determined as president of the Executive Council to establish the right of the new state to have an external policy independent of either British or Commonwealth control. Consequently on 1st September 1922 while the Civil War was still raging the Irish Free State applied to join the League of Nations. Upon admission a year later on 10th September 1923 the Cosgrave administration had won within one year of its formation the international recognition vainly sought after since 1917 by de Valera and Sinn Féin Republicans. Registration of the Anglo-Irish Treaty as an international agreement with the League in July 1924 was secured in the face of British opposition. Both British and Commonwealth opposition did not deter the Cosgrave administration from seeking recognition from individual foreign powers. The appointment of the first Irish minister plenipotentiary to the U.S. government on 7th October 1924 was a real diplomatic coup for the Irish Free State and a body blow to the Anti-Treaty Republican cause in the U.S. Irish legations were also accepted in France, Germany and the Vatican by 1928-'29. Before the end of the decade the Irish Free State was a respected member of the international family and had already formulated the independent defence policy of neutrality which has governed the Irish state ever since. As early as 1925 a comprehensive memorandum prepared by the then Minister for Defence, Hughes, identified potential aggressors as three or four unnamed powers who might seek to exploit Ireland's "geographical position... as the aerial and submarine key to England" and stressed "the necessity for taking effective steps to maintain our neutrality".

Relations with Britain

While determined to assert the independence of the Irish Free State in relation to other states, the Cosgrave administration was anxious to demonstrate utter good faith with regard to its obligations to Britain under the Treaty. The establishment of a friendly working relationship of mutual trust and respect with successive British governments became the objective of the Cosgrave administration 1922-32. In 1923 the Cosgrave government agreed to pay land annuities due to Britain under the terms of the land purchase schemes made available by British land legislation 1891-1909. Cosgrave hoped that the prospect of a tripartite Boundary Agreement in 1925 would afford an opportunity to review, more favourably, the Treaty's financial obligations. Article 2 of the Boundary Agreement did indeed release the Irish Free State from its obligation to contribute an unspecified amount to the Public Debt of the U.K. and to the payment of war pensions of British personnel forced to retire from administrative posts in Ireland during and after the War of Independence. The financial concessions thus gained were however more than cancelled out by Articles 3 and 4 of the same Boundary Agreement whereby the Government of the Irish Free State assumed 'all liability undertaken by the British Government in respect of malicious damage done since the 21st January 1919" and further committed the Government to "repay the British Government... moneys already paid by the British Government in respect of such damage or liable to be so paid under obligations already incurred." In addition Article 4 committed the Irish government to increase by 10% the measure of compensation in respect of malicious damage done between 11th July 1921, the end of the War of Independence, and the end of the Civil War in 1923. The Labour Party, chief opponent of the Boundary Agreement, could well point out the "entirely one-sided indebtedness" acknowledged by a Free State government which had always maintained that, instead of paying Britain anything, the Irish people were entitled to receive a large sum from Britain as restitution for overtaxation. Three months later in March 1926 the Cosgrave government entered into what was called the Ultimate Financial Settlement. It reiterated the commitment of February 1923 to pay the full amount of the land annuities due. It further obliged the government to pay before the end of the month £550,000 being the amount withheld by the Irish government to date in respect of income tax on annuities. Future repayments were to be made without deduction. The Irish Free State agreed to discharge all its financial obligations to Britain including an agreement to pay 75% of the pensions and compensation due to ex-members of the RIC. The total bill amounted to £5m. per annum. The stipulation about RIC pensions actually reversed the pensions exemption of Article 2 of the Boundary Agreement. The terms of the Ultimate Financial Agreement were kept secret by the Cosgrave administration and came as a genuine shock to de Valera in 1932.

Commonwealth Conferences

The seeming capitulation of the Cosgrave administration to the financial demands of successive British governments contrasted sharply with its determination to win maximum independence from Britain under the terms of the Treaty. Cosgrave was determined to use Commonwealth Conferences to enlist the help of fellow progressive dominion states in their struggle for total independence both in internal and external affairs. The Irish Free State was fortunate in that no rigid constitution had been laid down for dominion states within the Commonwealth. Commonwealth Conferences held at regular intervals were regarded as opportunities for dissatisfied dominion states to progress further along the road to full independence. At the Conference in 1921 General Smuts from South Africa had called for a definition of dominion status and warned prophetically that, "...unless dominion status was quickly solved in a way that would satisfy the aspirations of these young nations, separatist movements were to be expected in the Commonwealth". At the 1923 Conference the Irish delegation were surprised and encouraged by the freedom given to dominion delegates who were treated as equals with the British delegates. In 1926 O'Higgins led a well-briefed Irish delegation which joined with the South African delegation led by its Prime Minister Hertzog and the Canadians in extracting from the British presiding chairman, Arthur Balfour a former Conservative Chief Secretary in Ireland, the "Balfour Declaration" of co-equality. Great Britain and the dominion states were defined as "autonomous communities within the British Empire, equal in status, in no way subordinate one to another in any aspect of their domestic or external affairs". The logical sequel to acceptance of the concept of co-equality was the Statute of Westminster which followed the Commonwealth Conference of 1930.

The Statute of Westminster 1931

The Statute of Westminster passed by the British parliament in December 1931 stated that, in future, legislation by the British government would apply to dominions only at their request and with their consent. Henceforward the dominion parliament would legislate in areas previously regulated by legislation of the U.K. parliament. Of greatest relevance to the Irish Free State however, was the clause permitting the dominion parliament to repeal laws previously passed for them in Britain. Winston Churchill who had played a prominent role in securing agreement on the Treaty in 1921 was among the first to point out that the Statute of Westminster empowered the Irish government to repeal every provision of the Treaty. Only the timely intervention of Cosgrave forestalled an amendment to prevent such an eventuality. Cosgrave's assurance that "the Treaty is an agreement which can only be altered by consent" and warning that, any attempt to safeguard the Treaty by legislation might have the opposite effect to that intended, persuaded the British government to rely upon the goodwill built up with the Cosgrave government since 1922 to preserve the Treaty rather than to shatter that trust by restrictive legislation. Thus the trust and goodwill fostered by Cosgrave since 1922 saved the Irish Free State from restrictions on its legislative process which would have made impossible the dismantling of the Treaty by the de Valera government from 1932. De Valera was gracious enough to acknowledge the role of Cosgrave in ensuring an unamended Statute of Westminster leaving the Irish Parliament under de Valera free to dismantle the Treaty. Conor Cruise O'Brien who has written extensively on Anglo-Irish relations, said of this first decade in an essay entitled "Ireland in International Affairs", "in these ten years the Irish state played a more momentous and influential part in international affairs than it was ever to play again. It had speeded up the process which may be called either the evolution of the commonwealth concept or the peaceful disintegration of the empire".

In Opposition

The smooth and peaceful transfer of power to political enemies in 1932, who just ten years before had been military adversaries, was as much due to the common sense of Cosgrave and his government colleagues as to the determination of de Valera to respect the democratic institutions set up by the Cosgrave administration during the decade after the Civil War. Indeed even before the February 1932 general election, Cosgrave, who was ever a realist and expected defeat in 1932, made representation on behalf of an incoming Fianna Fail government with the British. Through the Irish High Commissioner in London he let it be known on 18th January 1932 "that from all points of view it would be most unwise for the British government to adopt too aggressive an attitude or iron hand methods towards a government made up of the Fianna Fail Party". Such magnanimous gestures were characteristic of a man who had no personal ambition for power. The guns which some Fianna Fail deputies allegedly carried into the Dáil on the day that Fianna Fail took office were totally unnecessary.

Cosgrave and the Cumann na nGaedheal party, however, found that they needed protection. One of the first actions of the Fianna Fail government was to release prominent IRA men some of whom had been in jail since the Civil War. Rumours that the IRA were drilling and recruiting led to Cumann na nGaedheal seeking protection from their own private army. Ex-army men who had fought for the government during the Civil War were naturally attracted to Cumann na nGaedheal. When it became clear that the IRA were determined upon "no free speech for traitors" Cumann na nGaedheal was happy during the run-up to the January 1933 election to accept the protection of the Army Comrades Association formed in February 1932 and by late summer a formidable disciplined body 30,000 strong and led by T. F. O'Higgins brother of assassinated Kevin O'Higgins.

Cumann na nGaedheal and indeed Cosgrave's, singular failure to gain a majority share of the vote in any election since the foundation of the state did not go unnoticed by those who opposed government policies but who felt that Cumann na nGaedheal was unable to provide effective opposition. Cosgrave's lack of charisma as Opposition leader was an obvious drawback. It is significant that although Cumann na nGaedheal opposed the "economic war" caused by the non-payment of land annuities and although Cumann na nGaedheal was regarded "the party of the large farmers", beleaguered farmers who suffered most from the "economic war" rallied not to Cumann na nGaedheal but to the new party, the National Centre party led by dynamic and articulate spokesmen, McDermot and James Dillon son of the last leader of the Irish Parliamentary Party which collapsed and disappeared after the December 1918 general election. Historian F. S. L. Lyons described Dillon as "a striking figure with some claim to to be considered the only real parliamentary orator produced by any party since the setting up of the Free State. "It was however the colourful and controversial ex-Garda Commissioner, O'Duffy, dismissed in early 1933 when Fianna Fail had secured an overall majority, who stole the limelight in 1933/'34.

Although Cosgrave was happy with the fusion of Cumann na nGaedheal and the National Centre Party in September 1933 he was apprehensive about the association of the new political party with the reorganised A.C.A. which under O'Duffy had become a fascist-style Blueshirted National Guard. Cosgrave was particularly unhappy that O'Duffy's National Guard had been outlawed following the banned August 1933 Blueshirt parade through Dublin. Cosgrave, the great constitutionalist of the 1920s, did not want association with an illegal movement forced to change its name in order to retain legality. Even after the unconstitutional speeches and actions of the unpredictable O'Duffy had forced him to relinquish leadership of Fine Gael in September 1934, Cosgrave declined to assume leadership of Fine Gael until spring 1935 hoping that the passage of time would distance the parliamentary party, Fine Gael, from the extra-parliamentary Blueshirt movement.

Cosgrave and his fellow-ministers were once described by Kevin O'Higgins as "the most conservative-minded of revolutionaries". If this was true of Cosgrave in government it was equally true of him in opposition. The ending of the "economic war" in 1938 robbed Fine Gael of one of its main opposition policies. At the outbreak of World War II Cosgrave, committed to Irish neutrality since the mid-1920's, found himself in happy agreement with de Valera's war-time policies and persuaded Fine Gael, to lend whole-hearted support to neutrality. One of the positive political developments of the war was the sinking of old grievances and the common desire of all political parties to overcome the common external enemy. While de Valera would not contemplate a coalition government, a degree of inter-party co-operation was achieved which ten years before no one would have thought possible. A consultative defence council was set up during the critical summer of 1940 consisting of three members of government, three Fine Gael, and two Labour members. The breaking of the ice between Cosgrave and de Valera, who for years had not communicated at any level, was in itself an achievement. As late as November 1939 Cosgrave had complained "…that the Government's practice is not merely to turn a deaf ear to such advice but even to resent it."

Endorsing government policy is not however the way for oppositions to win general elections. If Cumann na nGaedheal failed to perform at elections its successor Fine Gael, which 10 years after its foundation still lacked a central organisation, fared no better. In the 1937 election Fine Gael managed to retain the 48 seats won by Cumann na nGaedheal in 1933. This figure however, represented a drop from 57 secured in 1932. In 1938 the Fine Gael figure dropped from 48 to 45. Two war-time elections saw further collapse to 32 in 1943 and to the lowest ever, 30 in 1944. In January 1944 before the crushing electoral defeat of that year, Cosgrave, who never secured an overall majority at the polls and whose party had not won an election since 1927 but had in fact lost seats steadily at every election since 1927, resigned from leadership of the party and subsequently from the Dáil.

In retirement Cosgrave indulged a life-long interest in horses and horse-racing, becoming Chairman of the Irish Racing Board for long periods. He died on 16th November 1965. Tributes poured in to the first statesman of the Irish Free State from both sides of the Civil War divide. De Valera, his adversary and political opponent for over forty years, mourned the passing of his colleague from the First Dáil and attended the state funeral accorded to Cosgrave.

Appraisal

Cosgrave's greatest years were the ten first years of the Irish Free State 1922 - 1932, the most critical in the history of modern Ireland. Churchill described Cosgrave as "a quiet potent figure" who more than filled the void left by the deaths of Griffith and Collins. Cosgrave inherited a situation not of his making. Always a "reluctant politician" he assumed leadership during the Civil War. Within a year he had secured peace, and had set up the democratic institutions of state which, despite another constitution, have, with only minor amendments, remained the institutions of state. Although it meant his own political downfall, he forced Fianna Fáil to accept the democratic process in 1927 and ensured the survival of the parliamentary process. Not content with securing the political foundations of the state, the Cosgrave government also took steps to establish the economic foundations of modern Ireland. Cosgrave was particularly enthusiastic about the Shannon Hydro-electric scheme. Indeed the economic policies of free trade, limited state intervention and encouragement of foreign assistance foreshadowed the economic policies of the Lemass era of expansion in the 1960s. In the field of diplomacy, Cosgrave achieved for Ireland international recognition and acceptance denied to Dáil Eireann without incurring the wrath of the British government. At the risk of being dubbed "pro-British" and "west-British" Cosgrave fostered good relations with Britain and N.I. While the Boundary Agreement of 1925 was not seen as a triumph it did have the beneficial effect of removing the border as an issue of serious tension and conflict for almost thirty years. Cosgrave's greatest diplomatic achievements were the imperial concessions wrested from Britain not by attempted force of arms but by reasoned negotiations. Cosgrave's quiet work on behalf of the Irish Free State and other dominion states during the 1920s made possible the achievements of the 1930s. Cosgrave's style of government has been described as 'scientific and objective". His cold unemotional approach to all issues was exactly what was needed in the emotion-charged aftermath of the Civil War and ensured peace and stability after a decade of turbulence. These are the lasting attainments of an under-rated, almost forgotten, first statesman.

Landmarks in Cosgrave's Life (1880 - 1965)

1880	Born in Dublin.
1909	Sinn Féin councillor on Dublin Corporation.
1916	Sentenced to death for his part in the Easter Rising; Death sentence commuted.
1917	*August* Elected Sinn Féin abstentionist MP for Kilkenny.
1918	Elected Sinn Féin M.P. for North Kilkenny.
1919	*April* Minister for Local Government in First Dáil Government.
1922	*August* Succeeded Griffith and Collins as Pro-Treaty leader.
1922	*December 5th* Constitution of the Irish Free State enacted.
1923	*April* Formation of Pro-Treaty Cumann na nGaedheal Party.
1923	*August* First elections to a Free State Parliament. Cumann na nGaedheal 63 Abstentionist Sinn Féin 44.

1924	*March* "Army Mutiny".
1924	*November - 1925* Boundary Commission.
1925	*December* Boundary Agreement.
1927	*June* General election - Cumann na nGaedheal 47, Fianna Fáil 44.
1927	*July 10th* Assassination of O'Higgins.
1927	*July* Electoral Amendment Act forced Fianna Fail to take the oath and enter the Dáil.
1927	*September* Second general election. Cumann na nGaedheal 62, Fianna Fáil 57.
1931	Commonwealth Conferences 1923, 1926 and 1930 led to Statute of Westminster 1931.
1931	*October 1931* Special Powers Act.
1932	*February* Cumann na nGaedheal defeated. Cumann na nGaedheal 56, Fianna Fáil 72.
1944	*January* Resignation as Fine Gael leader.
1965	*November 16th* Death of Cosgrave.

6. De Valera

Early Years

De Valera, arguably the most outstanding political leader of modern Ireland, was born on October 14th 1882 in New York, the son of an Irish immigrant mother and a Spanish father. Christened Edward de Valera the young boy left the United States in 1885 following the death of his father and returned to his mother's home in Bruree Co. Limerick where he was reared by his grandmother and Uncle Pat in a simple labourer's cottage. De Valera adopted his mother's family name Coll, and was known as Eddie Coll while at the local national school in Bruree between 1888 and 1896. In 1895 his grandmother died. De Valera, uncertain of his future in Ireland, requested permission to return to the United States. It was decided, however, to send him to the Christian Brothers secondary school in Charleville Co. Cork. Two years later in 1898 he won a three year scholarship to Blackrock College, Dublin. His favourite school subject was mathematics. At twenty-one years de Valera became a teacher of mathematics at Rockwell College in Co. Tipperary. There, de Valera was shortened to Dev. the name by which close acquaintances knew him for the rest of his life. De Valera maintained a life-long interest in mathematics and science. As a student he started collecting mathematical books. At the time of his death in 1975 his library of scientific books numbered 1,200 in all.

De Valera in Volunteer uniform in 1917

De Valera and the Gaelic League

Irish was not de Valera's mother tongue. His love and knowledge of Irish stemmed from association with the Gaelic League which he joined in 1908. Upon joining he changed his christian name from Edward to Eamon. Pearse, editor of the Gaelic League newspaper, *An Claidheamh Solais*, and Eoin MacNeill, a professor of early Irish history and a founding member of the Gaelic League in 1893, became important influences in his life. By far the biggest influence however was exercised by one of his Irish teachers, Sinéad Flanagan whom he married in 1910. The revival of the Irish language was for de Valera a cherished but largely unfulfilled dream.

De Valera and the Irish Volunteers

Although more interested in Gaelic culture and the Irish language than in Irish Politics at this stage, de Valera welcomed the passing by the House of Commons of the Third Home Rule bill in 1912. He viewed with apprehension however, the formation of the Ulster Volunteer force in January 1913, a private army prepared to fight if necessary in order to prevent Home Rule from becoming law. Eoin MacNeill's article in *An Claidheamh Solais*, "The North Began", calling for a Volunteer body, similar to that in Ulster, in order to ensure that Home Rule was enforced when it became law in 1914, was welcomed by de Valera. He was among the three thousand who attended the first meeting of the Irish Volunteer Force in the Rotunda on November 25th 1913 and enrolled at the inaugural meeting. In March 1915, in preparation for the Rising, Dublin Volunteers were divided into four battalions. De Valera was appointed commandant of the third battalion in the south-east of the city. Despite his lack of previous military experience, de Valera wrote on request a military drill manual used by the Volunteers.

The indefinite suspension of Home Rule (the Third Home Rule bill had finally become law on September 18th 1914 but its enforcement was postponed for the duration of the Great War and even more significantly until amendments acceptable to Ulster Unionists could be agreed upon), convinced de Valera that home rule would be won "not by ballots but by bullets". The speech by Redmond, leader of the Irish Parliamentary Party, at Woodenbridge, Co.Wicklow on September 20th 1914 urging the 170,000 strong Volunteer Force to fight "not only in Ireland itself but wherever the firing line extends in defence of right, freedom and religion in this war" was to de Valera an unforgivable betrayal. He regretted the split in the Volunteers but threw himself whole-heartedly into the rebuilding of his Donnybrook company which at one stage dwindled to just seven members in the aftermath of the National/Irish Volunteers split in 1914.

Until the Easter Rising 1916, however, de Valera remained a full-time teacher of mathematics and was a member of A.S.T.I, the first trade union for secondary teachers, since its formation in 1909. De Valera sought to excuse his political obstinacy on occasion thus, "You will bear with me, won't you? You know I am an old schoolmaster."

De Valera and the Easter Rising 1916

De Valera was not a member of the Military Council formed in May 1915 in order to plan the rebellion. Reluctantly, in 1915 he joined the IRB, a secret oath-bound organisation of which de Valera did not wholly approve. He did not attend IRB meetings. He joined the IRB to ensure that he was as fully informed of developments as were Volunteers under his command who were also members of the IRB. The IRB were masterminding the Republican struggle.

De Valera saw his role in the events of 1916 as being that of the soldier-revolutionary. He played no part in the intrigue and deceptions of Holy Week 1916. On Wednesday, the day on which MacNeill the leader of the Volunteers was shown the forged "Castle Document" containing "government" instructions for his arrest and the suppression of the Volunteers, De Valera received instructions for an Easter Sunday Rising. De Valera learned of the cancellation of "all orders for special action" on Easter Sunday while on an emergency visit that morning to a dentist for acute dental treatment. A disappointed de Valera returned to his battalion headquarters, Bolands Mills, and anxiously awaited the outcome of the Military Council's special meeting in Liberty Hall, headquarters of Connolly's Irish Citizen Army, on Easter Sunday morning. About 5 pm. on Easter Sunday de Valera learned that a Dublin Rising had been fixed for noon on Easter Monday.

De Valera knew that his biggest problem would be mustering a full-strength battalion. In the event only 120/140 of his 500-strong battalion turned up for active service on Easter Monday. Of the 5,000 Volunteers throughout Dublin only 1600 answered the call to arms on Easter Monday. Such was the effect of MacNeill's cancellation order, addressed to each Volunteer and published in the Sunday Independent 23rd April 1916. De Valera's primary military objective was to place under surveillance the British army garrison at Beggar's Bush. De Valera knew that military success would depend upon the prevention of British reinforcements from entering Dublin. At the beginning of Easter week British military strength in Dublin was less than 2,000 troops. On Wednesday morning the first British reinforcements started landing at Kingstown (Dun Laoghaire). De Valera's men lay between the newly-arrived Sherwood Foresters and the city centre. For nine hours on Wednesday 26th April 1916 men of the third battalion under Commandant de Valera held up the Sherwood Foresters and prevented their reaching that day their destination at Trinity College. The battle of Mount Street bridge, resulting in 234 British officers and men killed and wounded and just 4 Volunteers killed, was the Volunteers', most spectacular military achievement, accounting for almost half of the total British casualties during the whole week. Despite heavy counter-attack on Thursday de Valera's main defences remained intact. De Valera had the distinction of being the last Commandant to surrender at 1 pm on Sunday April 30th 1916, almost 24 hours after the official unconditional surrender at 4 pm. on the previous day. De Valera, relatively unknown before Easter Week 1916, rapidly became one of the heroes of the Easter Rising.

De Valera firmly believed that his execution would follow his court-martial on 8th May 1916. The executions of not just the "ringleaders", but of minor revolutionary figures such as Willie Pearse and the eighteen-year-old Con Colbert caused a wave of revulsion to sweep through Ireland. Public opinion in the United States and even in Britain was turning against the executions. Britain was reluctant to offend the U.S. a potential ally in the Great War (the U.S. joined the Allies, Britain and France, in April 1917) by executing the American-born de Valera. The British government, in response to an Irish Parliamentary Party appeal for clemency, was reviewing its "military solution" in Ireland. The death sentence on non-American Commandant Ashe was also commuted to life imprisonment. The arrival of Asquith the British P.M. in Dublin on May 13th 1916 stopped the executions. The final executions of the two remaining signatories to the Proclamation of the Irish Republic, MacDermott and the wounded Connolly, took place on the previous day 12th May 1916. All seven signatories to the 1916 Proclamation, Clarke, Ceannt, Connolly, MacDermott, MacDonagh, Pearse, and Plunkett were executed. The fifteen executions between 3rd-12th May removed the leaders. With the death of Ashe while on hunger strike in 1917 de Valera was the only commandant to have taken part in the Rising and to survive.

Political and Military Leader from 1917

As senior surviving officer after the Revolution de Valera quickly became leader and spokesman of the 1,841 Irish prisoners who were sent to English jails throughout the summer of 1916. De Valera used his influence with the imprisoned Volunteers to heal the divisions created by MacNeill's last minute cancellation of Volunteer plans for an insurrection. The decision to arrest and imprison Volunteers, irrespective of whether they had been "active" or not during Easter week, meant that Eoin MacNeill, who, as Chief-of-Staff of the Irish Volunteers, had done all in his power to prevent the Rising, eventually found himself in Dartmoor prison with de Valera. Upon learning of MacNeill's arrival de Valera insisted, upon pain of prison punishment, on Volunteers forming a guard of honour and saluting their respected founder leader. Through such conciliatory gestures de Valera acted as a healing force throughout 1916/17. The reward for his untiring work for unity among the Volunteers came at the annual Volunteer Convention on 26th October 1917, when de Valera, released in June 1917, was elected President of a united Volunteer association.

De Valera leader of a "transformed" Sinn Féin 1917

The most significant political development of the post-Rising period was the transformation of Sinn Féin, the political alternative for the Nationalists to the Irish Parliamentary Party. By wrongly attributing the Easter Rising to Sinn Féin, Britain had hoped to discredit and suppress Sinn Féin as well as the IRB and the Volunteers. British government policy enabled Sinn Féin to take credit for having organised the Easter Rising.

Sinn Féin was both willing and able to provide an attractive alternative for disillusioned nationalist voters. Impressive by-election victories in 1917 showed the strength of the reorganised Sinn Féin Party, (by the end of 1917 there were 1,200 Sinn Féin clubs throughout the country) and demonstrated to the "rebel" prisoners that Sinn Féin was the ticket to political power. Although de Valera was initially opposed to prisoners seeking election, the success of Volunteer prisoner MacGuinness in the South Longford by-election in May 1917 made de Valera accept the Sinn Féin candidature for a by-election in East Clare on the very day in June 1917 that he was released from Pentonville prison.

De Valera's release from prison in 1917 marked the beginning of a long political and public career. One of his first acts after a tumultuous reception in Dublin in which he was hailed as "the hero of the hour... the accepted leader of the men of Easter week", was to draft a letter to the President and Congress of the United States which in April 1917 had entered the Great War against Germany in order to make the world "safe for democracy". De Valera, Eoin MacNeill and twenty-four other released prisoners reminded President Wilson that he had also stated that the U.S. was fighting "for the liberty, self-government and undictated development of all peoples", and that "no people must be forced under a sovereignty under which it does not wish to live." International recognition of an independent Ireland became de Valera's primary political objective. In this he was in happy agreement with the first elected abstentionist Sinn Féin M.P. Count Plunkett, father of one of the executed signatories, and the founder leader of Sinn Féin, Arthur Griffith.

East Clare By-Election Victory July 1917

The death of Willie Redmond, Nationalist M.P. for East Clare and brother of the Irish Parliamentary Party leader John Redmond, in the trenches in France in June 1917, gave de Valera his first experience of electioneering.

Although strong Redmondite territory and although his I.P.P. opponent was a popular local man Patrick Lynch, de Valera's election victory on July 12th 1917 victory was a resounding one, "(de Valera 5,010, Lynch 2,035) which impressed Griffith who recognised and admired de Valera's leadership qualities.

De Valera knew that the union of the political (Sinn Féin) and the military (Volunteers) wings of the independence movement would make for a formidable force in Ireland. It was also essential to prevent a military dictatorship in a liberated country. De Valera carefully preserved unity within the Volunteers by insisting that MacNeill accompany him during the East Clare by-election campaign. By involving Volunteers, drawn from all over the country, in every aspect of his election campaign de Valera secured their on-going support and loyalty.

The political aims and aspirations of de Valera and the Volunteers happily coincided. De Valera was determined during the autumn of 1917 to find a political formula which would enable him to harmonise the diverse strands of political opinion represented by the umbrella organisation Sinn Féin which once again included views ranging from Griffith's dual monarchy to republicanism. De Valera wholly agreed with the Sinn Féin boycott of the Irish Convention July 1917 - April 1918, the last attempt to secure peaceful agreement on a form of Home Rule acceptable to both Unionists and Nationalists. He could not accept, however, Griffith's concept of a dual monarchy. For de Valera the monarchy could play no role in an independent Ireland. De Valera, hailed by the press as early as July 1917, as the "real leader of Sinn Féin" set about restating Sinn Féin aims. In mid October 1917 he announced, "Sinn Féin aims at securing the international recognition of Ireland as an independent Irish Republic". Then, in order to make it more palatable to non-Republicans, he added, "having achieved that status, the Irish people may, by referendum, freely choose their own government". One week before the Sinn Féin Árd Fheis on October 25th 1917 de Valera and Griffith agreed over coffee in a restaurant near the top of Grafton Street that "It is as an Irish Republic that we have a chance of getting international recognition." Next day de Valera's draft for a new constitution for Sinn Féin was proposed and accepted. Griffith, outgoing President, proposed de Valera whom he described as a statesman as well as a soldier as President. De Valera was elected unopposed. Next day he consolidated his victory by being elected President of the Volunteers. Most of the delegates present had, like de Valera, come straight from the Sinn Féin Árd Fheis. The two movements were united. De Valera's immediate objective had been achieved. It was a measure of de Valera's political and diplomatic skills that he remained the undisputed leader of the separatist movement for the next four years and that he preserved the unity of Sinn Féin until the Treaty hopelessly divided them on e the very issues which had united them in 1917.

De Valera and the Conscription Crisis

De Valera's first political test as leader of the "new" Sinn Féin came during the anti-conscription campaign which swept the country during the spring of 1918. The German offensive on the Western Front plus the slow arrival of U.S. troops seemed to make imperative the extension of conscription, in force in Britain since January 1916. De Valera knew that opposition to conscription was one issue on which he could unite the Irish people. Dillon, the new leader of the Irish Parliamentary Party upon Redmond's death in March 1918, vainly warned the British government, "All Ireland will rise against you."

De Valera was determined that Sinn Féin would dominate the anti-conscription campaign throughout Ireland. A Mansion House Conference called by the Dublin Lord Mayor "to arrange for a united opposition to conscription, and to consider the advisability of establishing an all-Ireland Covenant on the subject", accepted an anti-conscription pledge drafted by de Valera, "Denying the right of the British Government to enforce compulsory service in this country, we pledge ourselves solemnly to one another to resist conscription by the most effective means at our disposal." De Valera scored another triumph when the Catholic bishops approved of the pledge and arranged for collections for an anti-conscription fund to be made after masses on the following Sunday. De Valera was anxious to win the support of the all-influential Catholic Church for his leadership and had shed his tenuous links with the IRB, proscribed by the Catholic church as a secret society.

De Valera's great success at this time was to present conscription as a constitutional issue. The pledge, for which he secured agreement from all shades of Irish opinion including the Church (but excluding the Unionists, who had been invited but had declined to attend the Mansion House Conference), questioned the right of the British government, or any external authority to impose compulsory service in Ireland against the clearly expressed will of the Irish people."

Alarmed at the extent and intensity of the anti-conscription campaign and fearful of Sinn Féin "swallowing up" (to paraphrase Dillon's own words on the subject) the Irish Parliamentary Party, which had adopted Sinn Féin tactics of withdrawal from Westminster upon the passing of the Conscription Bill in April 1918, the British Government decided to shelve the implementation of conscription in Ireland, (the ending of World War I on November 11th 1918 meant that conscription was never enforced in Ireland). It also resolved to remove the powerful Sinn Féin leaders from the political scene. The so-called "German Plot" of May 1918 was the pretext for arresting 73 leading Sinn Féin activists, including de Valera and holding them without trial for almost a year in British jails. By attempting to make martyrs of Sinn Féin the British government repeated the mistakes of 1916. Sinn Féin doubled its membership and romped to victory in the first general election after the war. The December 1918 general election results, Sinn Féin 73, I.P.P. 6, Unionists 26, marked the demise of the Irish Parliamentary Party and enabled Sinn Féin to translate its dream of an elected independent assembly into reality.

The First Dáil

De Valera was not present on January 21st 1919 to share in the triumph of the opening of the First Dáil, still regarded by Republicans as "one of the foundation stones of Irish Republicanism". He was languishing in Lincoln jail hoping that efforts to release him would be successful. De Valera's successful escape on February 3rd 1919 and evasion of capture, gave international publicity and prominence to the First Dáil. The first meeting had been held just one day after the opening of the Paris Peace Conference on January 20th 1919. It further enhanced the hero-image of de Valera who was the obvious choice for Príomh-Aire (Prime Minister) when the Dáil reconvened in April.

The release of the remaining prisoners in March 1919 enabled 52 members to attend the second meeting of the first Dáil on April 1st 1919. De Valera's first government included Griffith, Minister for Home Affairs, Michael Collins, Minister for Finance, W.T. Cosgrave, Minister for Local Government, Barton, Minister for

Agriculture, Cathal Brugha, Minister for Defence, Count Plunkett, Minister for Foreign Affairs, Eoin MacNeill, Minister for Industry and Countess Markievicz, Minister for Labour and first woman government minister in Europe. Despite their lack of administrative experience, the First Dáil became an alternative government to many people in Ireland 1919-21.

De Valera knew, however, that British recognition of the Dáil could only come through international pressure. Although ten of the fourteen points peace plan drawn up by U.S. President Wilson as the basis of the post-war peace settlements dealt with the right of every nation to self-determination, U.S. President Wilson refused to offend his war-time ally, Britain. The Irish delegation was refused admission to the Paris Peace Conference. The Irish question remained an internal affair of the British government and outside the scope of the international conference. Notwithstanding on May 17th 1919, de Valera and Griffith wrote to the French Premier, Clemenceau, President of the Peace Conference, denying the right of the British representative, Lloyd George, to sign any treaty binding Ireland. Although the draft terms of the Versailles Treaty were already published, de Valera insisted on Ireland's formal claim for recognition as an independent sovereign state being recorded on May 26th 1919.

The diplomatic rebuff at Paris plus the worsening War of Independence, the first shots of which were fired at Soloheadbeg in Tipperary on 21st January 1919, the day on which the Dáil first met, made de Valera's trip to the United States (June 1919 - December 1920) imperative. Ireland must appeal directly, through the American people, to the U.S. government for recognition.

De Valera's American Mission

De Valera's main aims during his eighteen-month stay in the U.S. were threefold
(1) to secured official recognition of the new Irish state
(2) to secure the support and the funds of the Irish-American organisations for the First Dáil
(3) to raise an American loan in order to finance the Dáil government and the Volunteer war effort.

All three objectives were almost placed in jeopardy by the intransigence of some of the Irish-American leaders. Even Devoy, the respected old Fenian and founder member of Clan na Gael, refused to believe that the Dáil could survive and was reluctant to commit Irish-American money to a doomed project in Ireland. Despite initial opposition from Irish-American leaders to the issuing of bonds in the name of a Republic not yet recognised, de Valera's fund-raising activities in the U.S. raised 5m. dollars of which 4m. were spent in Ireland. De Valera was less successful in his primary objective of securing official recognition for the independent Irish state. While de Valera adopted the title, President, upon arrival in the U.S. and was pleased to be known as "President of the Irish Republic" he failed in all his efforts to gain recognition for Irish independence from President Wilson or either of the main political parties, the Republicans and the Democrats, who in 1920, were preparing for the forthcoming presidential elections.

Two incidents prompted de Valera to return to Ireland in December 1920. One was undoubtedly the arrest of Griffith, his deputy, in November 1920. The other was the faint hope that, as public opinion turned everywhere against the atrocities that were happening during the War of Independence in Ireland, an arranged truce might be possible.

De Valera's trip to the U.S. while not gaining recognition for an Irish Republic, certainly brought the idea of an Irish Republic firmly to the forefront. In August 1921 deputies of the Second Dáil, returned unopposed after May 1921 elections, took an oath, "to bear true faith and allegiance", not just to Dáil Éireann but to the Irish Republic, of which de Valera was President. One of the visible legacies of de Valera's visit to the U.S. was the setting up of a new Irish-American organisation, the American Association for Recognition of the Irish Republic, which, within a year, had a membership of half a million and threatened to supplant existing Irish-American movements.

De Valera and the War of Independence

De Valera's greatest virtue in the eyes of the British was that for the greater part of the Independence struggle he was absent from Ireland. Upon his return in December 1920 de Valera was anxious to reassert the political authority of the Dáil. Since the Dáil had been declared illegal in September 1919 the initiative had passed to the military. De Valera insisted on the Dáil meeting in January 1921 to commemorate its first meeting in January 1919. In March 1921 he declared that the Dáil was assuming full responsibility for the activities of the IRA which he called "the national army of defence". De Valera, although anxious for peace, approved the daring attack on the Customs House in May 1921. The operation went badly wrong. The search for an unconditional ceasefire became even more imperative.

Peace negotiations had begun before de Valera returned from the U.S. All negotiations, however, had foundered upon the British insistence on pre-conditions, such as the refusal to include Collins and the "Murder Squad" in a general amnesty or the insistence upon surrender of rebel arms. King George V's impassioned plea for peace at the opening of the Northern Ireland Parliament on June 22nd 1921 paved the way for Lloyd George's invitation just two days later to de Valera "as the chosen leader of the great majority in Southern Ireland" to a peace conference in London. When the offer was accompanied on July 4th 1921 by a promise of an unconditional truce in which both sides could keep their arms, de Valera eagerly accepted. On July 11th 1921 the truce ending the War of Independence cam into effect. Next day de Valera was on his way to London for direct talks with Lloyd George, head of the British government.

Treaty Negotiations I: de Valera -v- Lloyd George

De Valera, accompanied by the recently released Griffith, had the first of four meetings with Lloyd George on July 14th 1921. At the outset de Valera made it clear that the Dáil would be free to consider "without prejudice" any British offer made. The proposals made on 20th July 1921 offering limited dominion status to just 26 counties and insisting upon "full recognition of the existing powers and privileges of the parliament of Northern Ireland which cannot be abrogated except by their own consent" were totally unacceptable. Quoting an Indian proverb
"Fool me once, shame on you
Fool me twice, shame on me."
de Valera vowed, "The Irish people are not going to be fooled this time" and, upon his return to Ireland, urged "amicable but absolute separation" from Britain.

Nonetheless, he put the proposals before his fellow ministers and the Second Dáil immediately upon his return.

The Second Dáil, pledged to bear true faith and allegiance "to the Irish Republic, rejected both Lloyd George's proposed settlement and de Valera's compromise proposal of external association, in which an independent Irish state would be outside the British Empire, but would recognise a special relationship with it in all matters relating to the dominion states. External association was rejected by the British, by the Ulster Unionists, "the present dissenting minority to meet whose sentiment alone this step could be contemplated" (de Valera on August 6th 1921) and, most significantly, by die-hard republicans who rejected all association with Britain or the British Empire.

Treaty Negotiations II: Irish delegation -v- British Delegation

The issue of the form of association with the British Empire kept the line of communication open between Dublin and London. At the end of September Lloyd George found a formula upon which an Irish delegation could meet a British delegation.

A conference was arranged to begin on October 11th 1921. The decision as to who should represent Ireland was taken by the Dáil cabinet and ratified by the Dáil. From the outset de Valera made it clear that he did not want to be a member of the delegation. It was generally agreed that Griffith who had accompanied de Valera on the first round of talks in July 1921 should lead the delegation. Collins was a more reluctant delegate. The other members of the delegation were Barton to represent the republican view, Gavan Duffy and Duggan (legal experts), and Erskine Childers, Secretary and generally regarded as de Valera's watchdog on proceedings.

In retrospect, de Valera's decision not to lead the delegation personally, can be seen as his biggest political mistake. At the time, however, it was not so regarded. The Dáil endorsed his decision not to attend. De Valera, it was agreed, had already negotiated and failed. His inclusion in the Irish delegation might in itself be an obstacle to a peace settlement. An important consideration was the need to prepare "doctrinaire republicans" for the inevitable compromise. Assuming that external association could be presented by the Irish delegation in a form acceptable to the British then it would be up to de Valera to persuade republican opinion at home to accept the settlement. Some commentators feel that de Valera regarded the political battle at home as more important than that being waged across the conference table in London. De Valera gave as his chief reason for not going, the desirability of avoiding snap decisions under pressure. His remaining in Dublin meant that all proposals would have to be referred back to him and the cabinet before a carefully-considered decision was given.

This thinking underlay the "qualified" plenipotentiary powers bestowed upon the Irish delegates. Along with their credentials as plenipotentiaries, empowered "to negotiate and conclude... a treaty or treaties of settlement," de Valera gave explicit written instructions "before decisions are finally reached... a dispatch notifying the intention to make these decisions will be sent to members of the Cabinet in Dublin, and that a reply will be awaited by the Plenipotentiaries before a final decision is made". These instructions were renewed when Griffith and the Irish delegation returned to Dublin on December 3rd with Britain's final proposals. De Valera has gone on record as saying, "I probably would have gone nevertheless, had not Griffith given an express undertaking that he would not sign a document accepting allegiance but would bring it back and refer the matter to Dáil Éireann. This made us all satisfied".

Treaty Debates

De Valera's initial reaction to the news that a treaty had been signed on December 6th 1921 was one of joy and surprise. The only possible explanation was that the terms were so obviously favourable to Ireland that prior consultation was deemed unnecessary. When the full truth became known and it was learned that the text of the settlement was to be published without seeking Dublin approval, de Valera called it "an act of disloyalty to their President and to their colleagues in the Cabinet... probably without parallel in history".

The delegates were recalled peremptorily from London. On December 8th 1921 the Cabinet debate on the Treaty marked the first of a series of Treaty debates which fellow Cabinet member, Cathal Brugha, said would "split Ireland from top to bottom".

Treaty Debates: Cabinet Debates:

The cabinet debate on December 8th 1921 was long and bitter, revealing deep divisions acknowledged by de Valera in his proclamation to the Irish people the next day, "There is a definite constitutional way of resolving our political differences". Despite de Valera's resolute stand against the Treaty which he attacked as bringing "neither unity nor sovereignty", his cabinet voted for the Treaty with four of the seven cabinet members voting for acceptance. This cabinet defeat represented the first serious political defeat of de Valera. De Valera announced that he was not going to recommend acceptance either to Dáil Eireann or to the country. He was prepared to stake his political future on the Treaty debates.

Dáil Debate

The debate on the Treaty was the most momentous and most controversial in the history of the Second Dáil. De Valera dominated the proceedings, intervening at least 250 times during the thirteen days of public and private debate. De Valera's main objections to the treaty as outlined in a letter to a friend were, "They meant... Dominion status nominally, with an oath of allegiance to the British King as an organic part of the Irish Constitution and a recognition of him as head of the Irish state." Document No.2, de Valera's alternative to the Treaty, was essentially a restatement of external association and the proposals made and rejected in July by Lloyd George. It was rejected equally by pro-Treatyites and extreme republicans. Pro-treatyites argued that the differences between the Treaty and Document No.2 were so slight (the clauses on Ulster were the same as the Treaty provisions) that they were not worth risking war. To extreme republicans external association was "going into the British Empire sideways." De Valera felt every attack upon Document No. 2. as an attack on his integrity and sought to resign as President even before the Dáil vote was taken on January 7th, 1922.

Most commentators agree that the Christmas recess December 22nd - January 3rd was crucial in swinging support for the Treaty. Dáil deputies were given a clear

Pro-Treaty message for peace from Church and country. Not even emotive anti-Treaty appeals from the widows and relatives of Ireland's Republican dead could influence their decision. One Dáil deputy, Drohan, was forced to resign by his constituents because he refused to vote for the Treaty. The Dáil vote was taken on January 7th 1922, 64 voted for 57 against. Two days later de Valera resigned as President of the Dáil. A proposal for his re-election made by the widow of the executed signatory of the 1916 Proclamation, Thomas Clarke, was narrowly defeated. It was a measure of the esteem in which de Valera was held that two of those who had voted for the Treaty actually voted for de Valera. Although defeated by only two votes, de Valera and the anti-Treatyites found themselves in opposition and in a political wilderness for the next ten years.

De Valera and the Civil War

De Valera was still President of Sinn Féin. As such he had considerable political influence in the months before the Civil war. Painfully aware that a general election would probably go against the anti-Treatyites, his first objective was to secure a postponement of elections until June 1922. In March 1922 de Valera drew the anti-Treaty supporters together into a political party Cumann na Poblachta under his leadership. Although designed as a political initiative the introductory speeches were so war-like e.g. "It was only by Civil War after this that they could get their independence" that de Valera knew that Cumann na Poblachta would not appeal to voters who regarded a vote for the Pro-Treatyites as a vote for peace. Consequently de Valera sought to make an election "pact" with Collins and the pro-Treatyites on 20th May 1922 in the vain hope of taking the Treaty out of the election. When the "pact" was abandoned on the eve of the election by Collins calling on the people "to vote for the candidates you think best of ", the anti-Treatyites were decisively defeated, 58 Pro-Treatyites, 35 anti-Treatyites. De Valera knew that the initiative would pass to the military. The decision to hold an IRA convention in March 1922, banned at the last moment by the Collins government who feared an anti-Treaty army victory, was taken at the headquarters of de Valera's Cumann na Poblachta Party. Notwithstanding, de Valera had little influence over the military developments which resulted in the Civil War: viz. the formation of an anti-Treaty army among the IRA majority against the Treaty at the banned Army Convention on 26th March 1922, the seizure of the Four Courts in April, and the kidnapping of the Deputy commander of the Pro-Treaty National Army, General "Ginger" O'Connell on June 26th 1922.

When the attack on the Four Courts began on the morning of June 28th 1922 de Valera described the men of the Four Courts garrison as, "the best and bravest of our Nation". He went off to rejoin his old Volunteer battalion, re-enlisting as a private in the same house as he had first enrolled in November 1913. His heart however was not in the military struggle. Defeat in Dublin and the fall of the "Munster Republic" before the end of August 1922 told de Valera that the war had been lost. Although de Valera was elected President of the Republic by the anti-Treatyites in October 1922, when the Dáil passed the Irish Free State Constitution bill bringing the Free State into being in December 1922, he was unable to persuade fanatical military leaders of the need to surrender. His frustration at his inability to influence the struggle was expressed in a letter thus, "I have been condemned to view the tragedy... as through a wall of glass, powerless to intervene effectively". It was only after the death, in April

1923, of Liam Lynch, commander of the anti-treaty Irregulars who had sworn never to surrender, that de Valera's cease-fire appeal on May 24th 1923 to "Soldiers of the Republic Legion of the Rearguard" was finally listened to. The cease-fire involved no surrender of arms nor government amnesty of prisoners. De Valera was once again "on the run".

The prospect of fresh elections in August 1923 brought de Valera out of hiding. Amid a blaze of publicity, which to some extent protected him against unofficial assassination, de Valera prepared to address an election rally in Ennis on August 15th 1923. As predicted he was arrested and held without trial until July 16th 1924. While in prison he learned with satisfaction of his election victory over Eoin MacNeill, the rival Free State candidate.

De Valera and the Founding of Fianna Fáil

Although elected, de Valera and the 44 Sinn Féin anti-Treaty TDs refused to take their seats and provide a parliamentary opposition to the ruling Cumann na nGaedheal party in the Free State Dáil. De Valera was, however, one of the first to realise the political ineffectiveness of the shadow "republican government" which, in imitation of the First Dáil, formed a republican parliament. The success of the First Dáil one-party assembly and government was not to be repeated.

The failure of the Boundary Commission 1924-1925, and the treachery of the tripartite agreement of December 1925 between the three heads of government Cosgrave, Craig, and Baldwin, Conservative Unionist P.M. of Britain, called by de Valera an "ignominious bargain permitting the dismemberment of the country", made de Valera determined to return to effective political action. The Dáil vote on the Boundary agreement had been 71 for, 20 against. The Labour Party was the only political party to register officially its opposition in the Dáil to the permanent partitioning of Ireland in 1925.

The special meeting of the Sinn Féin Árd Fheis in March 1926 revealed deep divisions between de Valera and other members of the Standing Committee. While de Valera's only objection to entering the Dáil was the taking of the oath which de Valera in 1921 had said "crystallised in itself the main things we objected to - inclusion in the Empire, the British King as King of Ireland, chief executive of the Irish state and the source from which all authority in Ireland must be derived". Sinn Féin, however, was opposed in principle to sending representatives into "any usurping legislature set up by English law in Ireland." De Valera put to the Árd Fheis "that once the admission oath of the 26 County and Six County assemblies is removed, it becomes a question not of principle but of policy whether or not Republican representatives should attend these assemblies." When an amendment insisting upon abstention from "any usurping legislature set up by English law" was passed, de Valera resigned as President of Sinn Féin, a position which he had held since 1917. Earlier de Valera had cut his connection with the I.R.A. or rather, the I.R.A. had rejected de Valera at its army convention in November 1925, because of his announced intention to consider entering the Dáil if the oath was removed. De Valera had shed the two movements which had launched his political career. It was time for a fresh start.

In April 1926 de Valera announced the formation of a new Republican Party, Fianna Fáil and outlined its aims thus:
(1) Securing the political independence of a united Ireland as a republic.
(2) The restoration of the Irish language and the development of a native Irish

culture.

(3) The development of a social system in which, as far as possible, equal opportunity will be afforded to every Irish citizen to live a noble and useful Christian life.

(4) The distribution of the land of Ireland so as to get the greatest number possible of Irish families rooted in the soil of Ireland.

(5) The making of Ireland an economic unit, as self-contained and self-sufficient as possible, with a proper balance between agriculture and the other essential industries.

On May 16th 1926, the inaugural meeting of the Fianna Fáil party was held in La Scala Threatre beside the G.P.O. the rebel headquarters during the Easter Rising 1916. The attendance included many of de Valera's trusted Sinn Féin colleagues. Money and support flowed in from Irish-American organisations delighted to see de Valera and the republicans back in the political arena. The first Árd-Fheis of Fianna Fáil was held on November 24th 1926, the fourth anniversary of the execution of Erskine Childers convicted for possession of an illegal gun during the Civil War. The first political challenge for the new party was the general election 1927. De Valera, unanimously elected President of the new party, saw the first task as being the setting up of a national party with Fianna Fáil Cumainn in every constituency.

The results of the 1927 general election, (Cumann na nGaedheal 47 seats, Fianna Fáil 44) demonstrated, the growing popularity of the new party and increasing disenchantment with the Cumann na nGaedheal government. There was however no immediate threat to the Cosgrave government as de Valera and the Fianna Fail TDs refused steadfastly to take the oath. The situation was, however, dramatically changed by the assassination of Kevin O'Higgins, Minister for Home Affairs during the Civil War and Vice-President, Minister for Justice, and Minister for External Affairs in the new Cosgrave government.

Assassination of Kevin O'Higgins

De Valera called the assassination of O'Higgins inexcusable murder, "a crime that cuts at the root of representative government". The response of the Cosgrave government included two measures directed specifically against the Fianna Fáil party. An Electoral Amendment Act demanded of every Dáil candidate an undertaking to take the oath within two months of election or forfeit his seat. De Valera's hopes of removing article 4 of the Anglo-Irish Treaty dealing with the oath of allegiance, by calling a referendum on the issue, were dashed by another government measure restricting the right to initiate constitutional referenda to sitting Dáil deputies. De Valera was faced with, either taking the oath and becoming leader of the parliamentary opposition, or condemning his new party to political extinction. Two former members had already taken the oath and had entered the Dáil. On August 11th 1927, de Valera and the elected Fianna Fail deputies went through what de Valera called, the "empty formality" of taking the oath, and entered the Dáil. By doing so de Valera had chosen the path of parliamentary democracy and had turned away from unconstitutional violence.

The entry of the 44 Fianna Fáil deputies into the Dáil in August 1927 precipitated a government crisis. On August 16th the government nearly lost a confidence vote proposed by the leader of the Labour Party who hoped, in coalition with Fianna Fail, to defeat the Cosgrave government. Realising that government was impossible with such a formidable opposition, Cosgrave called a snap election. The September 1927 election results reflected popular sympathy for the government in the wake of the O'Higgins assassination. Cumann na nGaedheal won 67 seats. Fianna Fail won 57 seats which showed that the country endorsed their decision to enter parliament. Cumann na nGaedheal was able, with the help of the Farmers' Party and Independents, to stay in power for another four and a half years. De Valera had to be content with Leader of the Opposition and prepare for the next general election.

De Valera and the Irish Press
It was widely believed that one of the reasons why the anti-Treaty case had met with so little success was because national newspapers in both Britain and Ireland favoured the pro-Treaty case. A comment by Ernest Blythe, Minister for Finance in the first Free State government in 1929 that the Free State government was a happy member of the British Commonwealth prompted de Valera to retort, "If we had a daily paper at this moment I believe that Blythe's statement could be used to waken up the nation." Two years later at the height of a world depression the Fianna Fáil newspaper, the "Irish Press" was launched. De Valera maintained a lively interest in the fortunes of the Irish Press over the years commenting on one occasion that, if it came to a choice between leading the party and running the paper he believed that he would choose the latter.

Victory in the 1932 general election:
The Irish Press provided a much-needed mouthpiece for de Valera and the Fianna Fáil Party in the run-up to the 1932 general election. The Fianna Fail election manifesto, a comprehensive 8-point programme proclaimed as priorities the removal of the oath and the retention of land annuities in Ireland. The Irish Press gained popular notoriety on the eve of the election. The editor of the Irish Press was prosecuted for seditious libel before a mititary tribunal set up by the Public Safety Act of October 1931. The much-publicised trial had enormous propaganda value for Fianna Fail and won for it much public sympathy. The February 1932 general election gave Fianna Fail 72 seats. With the support of 7 Labour deputies and three Independents, de Valera was able to form a government. Ten years after his resignation as head of government, de Valera was back as government leader for an unprecedented 16-year period.

De Valera in Power 1932-48
The transition to power, from the men who had won the Civil War to those who were generally seen as having caused it, was smooth, although some Fianna Fáil deputies entered the Dáil on March 9 1932 with revolvers in their pockets.

Dismantling the Treaty
De Valera's primary objective upon taking office was to fulfil his election pledge to remove Article 17 of the Free State's Constitution requiring members of the Irish Parliament to take an oath of "true faith and allegiance" to the Constitution of the Irish Free State, the head of which was the British monarch. The achievements of the much-maligned Cosgrave administration 1923-32, in particular the Statute of Westminster 1931, permitting repeal of existing British legislation affecting the

dominions, cleared the way for the constitutional changes which characterised the early years of the de Valera regime.

The removal of the oath, described by de Valera as "an intolerable burden to the people of this state" and the studied contempt shown to the office of governor-general, the king's representative in Ireland, caused relations between the British and de Valera governments to be strained from the outset.

The conflict between the governor-general and the government reached a climax during the Eucharistic Congress in June 1932. Governor-General James MacNeill brother of Eoin MacNeill, was deliberately kept in the background while de Valera took his place welcoming the church dignitaries and the Papal Legate to Ireland and presiding over state functions held in their honour. The Governor-General was stung into action. Failing to receive apology or redress from the government, MacNeill published his grievances in the British press. De Valera's response was to demand the termination of MacNeill's appointment as Governor-General. De Valera believed that he had won an important round in his constitutional "war" with Britain when King George V agreed to MacNeill's removal on November 1st 1932 and ultimately agreed to de Valera's nomination of O'Buachalla, 1916 veteran, Irish language enthusiast and follower of de Valera. O'Buachalla, further demeaned the office of governor-general by refusing to live in the Viceregal Lodge and performed no official functions other than signing acts of the Irish parliament.

De Valera's hand was considerably strengthened in his quarrel with Britain by a decisive victory in January 1933. A snap election gave Fianna Fáil 77 seats and an overall majority of one in the Dáil. Fianna Fáil had been given a mandate for its policy of dismantling the Treaty.

One of the election promises of Fianna Fáil had been to abolish the Senate" as at present constituted". De Valera had never been happy with the Senate, the upper house of the Free State Parliament. Southern Unionist representation in a Senate dominated by Cumann na nGael had made the Senate appear a legislative obstacle to constitutional change in Ireland. The Senate successfully obstructed (until May 1933) the passage of the Removal of the Oath bill passed by the Dáil in May 1932. A bill to abolish the Senate was duly passed by the Dáil but was delayed as long as was legally possible by the Senate. On May 28th 1936 the abolition of the Senate came into effect. In June 1936 de Valera formally announced his intention of drawing up a new constitution. At the same time a commission was set up to examine the whole question of a second house of parliament.

By 1936 the Constitution of the Irish Free State had been subjected to so many amendments since its enactment in December 1922 that de Valera no longer regarded it "a fit document". November 1933 saw a further reduction in the powers of the governor-general who could no longer withhold assent to bills. A further act removed the right of appeal from the Supreme Court (the highest Irish court) to a Judical Committee of the Privy Council in London. The Judicial Committee found in favour of the Irish Free State in 1935 when it decided that the Statute of Westminster 1931 had indeed empowered the Irish Free State Parliament to amend or repeal the Treaty. Encouraged by this British judgement for his constitutional reforms, de Valera rushed through parliament the Irish Nationality and Citizenship Act defining Irish citizenship. An accompanying Aliens Act annoyed Britain by defining the British living in Ireland as aliens. A third bill allowed for British subjects while still aliens to be treated specially as Irish citizens. De Valera's concept of external association and special relationship with Britain mooted as his alternative to dominion status in 1921, was beginning to assume reality.

Abdication of Edward VIII 1936

One of de Valera's political strengths was his ability to seize an opportunity, e.g. the Eucharistic Congress in 1932, and exploit an unexpected situation or development to Ireland's advantage. One such situation was the constitutional crisis provoked in Britain by the abdication of Edward VIII on December 10th 1936. On the same day the Dáil was summoned "for the purpose of considering, in connection with the proposed abdication of His Majesty King Edward VIII, proposals for the amendment of the Constitution." A Constitution Bill (Amendment No. 27) removed all references to the king and his representative, the governor-general, in the internal government of the state. An External Relations Act, passed with the Constitution Bill within 24 hours of their introduction as there was no Senate to block them, legalised external association. The External Relations Act determined Anglo-Irish constitutional relations until the Republic of Ireland Act 1949. Significantly de Valera never took the ultimate step of declaring a republic. De Valera's constitution 1937 did not affect the External Relations Act. Professor Mansergh has explained the Anglo-Irish constitutional relationship thus "Relations with Britain and the Commonwealth had been taken out of the Constitution and had become matters of external policy for the government of the day. This was the most significant development in the whole period."

The Irish Constitution 1937

As early as May 1935 de Valera had given instructions to a legal advisor to prepare a draft of the heads of a new constitution for the State. The draft Constitution was ready two years later in May 1937. The "Irish Independent", regarded as the main Opposition newspaper commented favourably, "It is at least to his credit that he has produced a Constitution in regard to which there will be no serious division of opinion." The Dáil approved the Constitution on June 14th 1937. De Valera, however, was determined that the authority for the Constitution would come from the people. The Dáil was dissolved and a referendum on the Constitution was held on the same day as a general election, July 1st 1937. That the referendum was considered not just an election issue was reflected in the results. The voting on the referendum was close, 685,105 for the Constitution 526,945 against. Total first preference votes cast for Fianna Fail were, however, only 599,040. Fianna Fáil representation dropped to 68 seats and Fianna Fail relied once more on Labour support to govern.

The title of the Constitution was Bunreacht na hEireann. The opening preamble gave a new name to the Irish state, Eire, Ireland.
Article 1 proclaimed the "inalienable indefeasible and sovereign right of the Irish nation to choose its own form of government.
Article 2 claimed jurisdiction over the whole island of Ireland.
Article 3, however, acknowledged the reality of a separate six-county state and that, "pending the re-integration of the national territory", laws enacted by the parliament to be set up under the Constitution would have the same "area and extent of application as laws of Saorstat Eireann." (The Irish Free State)

As early as 1933 de Valera had stated his policy thus: "let us remove these forms one by one so that this State that we control may be a Republic in fact". Yet the word "republic" was not used in the Constitution. A President popularly elected over a seven-year period, once renewable, was to be the formal head of state. His duties were largely ceremonial though the Constitution has given him four special powers. After consultation with an advisory Council of State the President can refer a bill to the Supreme Court in order to decide its constitutionality. In certain circumstances the President may decline to sign a bill and insist upon a referendum on the issue. The President can in national emergency convene either or both houses of parliament. The President can also refuse to dissolve parliament upon the defeat of a Taoiseach or upon the Dáil's failure to nominate a Taoiseach and approve a government. The last of the powers was criticised on the basis that it might enable a popular President, such as de Valera, President 1959-73, to become a dictator. No Irish President, de Valera included, has shown any dictatorial ambitions. All, starting with the first, President Douglas Hyde 1938-45, Protestant, Irish Language enthusiast and founder of the Gaelic League in 1893, have deliberately removed themselves from the political arena.

Although de Valera had abolished the Senate, the Constitution restored a bicameral parliament with two houses, a Senate and Dáil. The system of government followed the British Parliamentary model with the Taoiseach, head of government, elevated "formally and in practice to the position of a strong British Prime Minister" according to Basil Chubb, Professor of Political Science. The Taoiseach not only appoints and dismisses government ministers but he also nominates 11 of the Senate's 60 members. Six represent the universities. The remaining 43 elected by TDs and county councillors represent vocational interests, the Arts, Literature, Education as well as Agriculture, Industry and Commerce. The Senate can delay the passage of bills for 90 days at most. It is no longer seen as the obstacle to legislative change that it was between 1932 and 1936.

Articles 40-44 have proved to be the most controversial. Article 40 entitled "Personal Rights" guarantees human and civil rights with the proviso that these are "subject to public order and morality." Articles 41, 42 and 43, dealing with the family, education and property reflect the teachings of the Catholic Church. The sanctity of marriage is upheld by the prohibition of divorce. Catholic thinking on the family, on education, recognising that "the primary and natural educator of the child is the family and, on the right to private ownership of property" predominates. The wording of the Constitution is heavily charged with religious phraseology. The opening words of the preamble are, "In the name of the Most Holy Trinity".... Article 44 recognised "the special position of the Holy Catholic Apostolic and Roman Church as the guardian of the Faith professed by the great majority of the citizens" but also recognised the other religious denominations "that existed in the community at the time of the enactment" and guaranteed "freedom of conscience and the free profession and practice of religion." De Valera, anxious to secure the approval and support of the Catholic Church for anti-Treaty Fianna Fáil, had sought and received the opinion of leading Churchmen including the Papal Nuncio, the Vatican (de Valera actually sent the Secretary to the Department of External Affairs to the Vatican to consult directly with Papal spokesmen) and the future Archbishop of Dublin, John Charles McQuaid. De Valera also consulted with the leaders of the

Protestant Churches and expressed the hope that recognition of the Protestant Churches "will produce considerable appeasement" ... "and may also lead to the desired political reunion of our country". Right-wing Catholics were disappointed that Article 44 did not go further and establish Catholicism as a "State Church". By 1969, however the Catholic Church's special position was seen as a barrier to ecumenism. A referendum, not opposed by the Catholic Church, removed the special position and the section according recognition to named religions only.

De Valera's Constitution was essentially conservative and Catholic in character. It can be seen as the successor of both the Constitution of the short-lived First Dáil (1919) and the Constitution of the Irish Free State (1922). All three constitutions reflect evolution not revolution from the British system of government.

Although the 1937 constitution provided a republic in all but name, the British government stated that the Constitution did not affect Irish membership of the Commonwealth. The Constitution in fact took the constitutional issue out of Anglo-Irish relations and, for the first time since 1916, enabled the Irish state to achieve stability. It did not help to reunite the country but over fifty years later, Bunreacht na hÈireann with minor amendments, remains the Irish Constitution.

The Economic War 1932-38

British acceptance of Bunreacht na hEireann emboldened de Valera in November 1937 to seek to resolve all other outstanding problems between Britain and Ireland, in particular to seek a satisfactory solution to the vexed question of payment of land annuities, non-payment of which had resulted in an "economic war", which was causing enormous damage to the economies of both countries.

Withholding of land annuities, annual repayments to Britain made by Irish farmers on loans advanced to enable them to buy out their farms under the terms of a series of Land Acts 1891-1909, had been one of de Valera's election promises in 1932. The first payment by the de Valera government was due on July 1st, 1932. When it was not forthcoming Britain responded by placing punitive 20% duties on Irish imports into Britain. The Irish government retaliated by placing like duties on British imports including machinery, iron, coal, and British steel, so important for Irish industry. Thus began the economic war. De Valera argued that the British-enacted Government of Ireland Act 1920 gave to each of the Irish Parliaments "the right to collect and retain the land annuities..." The Northern Ireland government was permitted to keep the land annuities as a "free gift."

De Valera proposed to do likewise. Much to the disappointment of many Irish farmers who hoped that non-payment would mean non-collection, the Land annuities still had to be paid by the farmers who suffered also from the restrictions placed on the export of live Irish cattle - Ireland's chief export. The British case for payment rested upon two financial agreements with the Cosgrave government which undertook in 1923 and again in 1926 to make direct payment of land annuities to Britain. Neither agreement had been ratified by either the British or the Free State Parliaments. Both were therefore, according to de Valera invalid.

A visit to Dublin by Thomas, the Dominions Secretary, in June 1932 and two visits by de Valera to London in 1932 produced no agreement and served to intensify the dispute as Britain sought to link the economic issue with the constitutional crisis between the two states. By 1934 the effects of the economic war were being felt in both Britain and Ireland. Cattle exports to Britain fell from 750,000 in 1930 to 500,000 in 1934. The value of agricultural exports was halved over the same period. Cattle farmers were encouraged to switch to tillage farming by the placing of subsidies on wheat. Although there was a dramatic increase in wheat production between 1931 and 1936 there was overall only a 10% increase in crop production. Although farmers where encouraged to produce their own animal feed and restrictions were placed on the import of flour, self-sufficiency in agriculture, de Valera's goal, was far from being realised in the Thirties. The slaughter of cattle and the distribution of free meat were also intended to discourage pasture farming. Such drastic measures however earned the resentment of cattle farmers in Leinster and Munster and drove many of them into the ranks of the discontented militant Blueshirts. In an effort to alleviate distress and remove grievances, land annuity charges were halved. Dissatisfaction however with Fianna Fáil policies was reflected in the election results of 1937 (F.F. 68 seats) c.f. 1933 results F.F. 77 seats.

The British publication "The Economist" acknowledged the damage that was being done to both economies in November 1934 when it observed, "The damage to Ireland is clearly large... The damage to great Britain is no less. Our best customer has fallen to fifth place". At the height of the Great Depression British industry could ill afford to lose its best customer. One disturbing effect of the economic war was to produce a spirit of economic nationalism in Ireland. This found expression in the government policy of economic self-sufficiency and protection of infant industry. It was also responsible for anti-British sentiment expressed in the popular slogan, "Burn everything British except their coal". Boycott of British goods reached comical proportions when a boycott of British beer resulted in a consignment of Bass Ale being dumped into the River Liffey in an incident reminiscent of the Boston Tea Party which had heralded American independence from Britain almost two centuries before.

A more serious and worrying aspect for Britain in 1934 was the active consideration Ireland was giving to the import of continental coal. If Irish industry made the necessary changes in order to adapt to German and Polish coal, the Irish market for British coal could be permanently lost. A sense of urgency about the situation in both countries led to the first easing in the economic war, the Coal-Cattle Pact in early 1935. Numerical quotas placed on live cattle imports were raised by a third. In return Ireland promised to take all coal imports from Britain. Duties however on coal and on other British imports were retained.

The worsening international situation from mid-1930's persuaded de Valera that with the threat of European war increasing daily, Irish neutrality in that war was of paramount importance. At the League of Nations in Geneva in July 1936 de Valera, who, as Minister for External Affairs represented Ireland at League Conferences, and who on his very first attendance found himself addressing the Assembly as President of the Council, affirmed Irish neutrality thus, "peace is dependent upon the will of the great states. All the small states can do ...is resolutely to determine that they will resist with whatever strength they may possess every attempt to force them into a war against their will".

The spectre of the Treaty 1921 was looming again. One of the less controversial articles in 1921 of the Anglo-Irish Treaty, Article 7, afforded Britain control of three Irish ports in the Irish Free State. In time of war the Treaty provisions were wider, allowing "such harbour and other facilities as the British government may require for the purposes of such defence". De Valera knew that return of the Treaty ports was absolutely essential to the securing of Irish neutrality.

De Valera hoped that the general policy of appeasement and a desire to preserve peace through removal of grievances which characterised British foreign policy through the Thirties, would permeate Anglo-Irish relations. From 1935 the signs were hopeful. In that year, Thomas, Dominions Secretary in 1932 who called de Valera "the Spanish onion in the Irish stew", was replaced by MacDonald, with whom de Valera had established friendly relations through frequent meetings in Geneva. By 1938 the British Prime Minister, Chamberlain was anxious for a peaceful solution of the Irish problem. In addition the American representatives in both Britain and Ireland were Irish-American. Joseph Kennedy, (father of future U.S. President Kennedy) recently appointed U.S. Ambassador to Britain was prepared to intervene at a crucial stage in the Anglo-Irish talks to put pressure on Britain to arrive at agreements favourable to the Irish state.

Anglo-Irish Agreement 1938

The Anglo-Irish talks which culminated in the trade agreement, April 1938 bringing to an end the economic war, were in many respects like the Anglo-Irish Treaty talks of 1921. An Irish delegation met a British delegation in a series of discussions over a fourteen-week period. There were, however, important differences. The Irish delegation this time consisted of the most senior government ministers led by de Valera who dominated the discussions. While war threatened, as in 1921, it was not to be a war waged by Britain on Ireland but rather a war which would threaten the existence of Britain.

Before attending the talks, de Valera made it clear that the topics on the agenda in order of importance were partition, defence and the disputed repayments. De Valera, urged on by the I.R.A. who were clamouring, not just for the return of the Treaty Ports but for the return of the Six Counties also, made partition the first topic of discussion. There was to be no agreement on partition. For de Valera the Ulster question was an Anglo-Irish issue to be settled by the British government putting pressure on the Northern government to accept reintegration with the rest of Ireland. For the British, partition was essentially a matter for amicable settlement between Ulster and the South. Britain has always held that, as long as a majority of people living in Northern Ireland wish to remain part of the United Kingdom, Britain will defend their right.

De Valera secured total victory in the unconditional return of the Treaty Ports. Articles 6 and 7 of the Anglo-Irish Treaty were revoked. De Valera announced to the Dáil on April 27th 1938, two days after the agreements had been signed, "the ports are handed over unconditionally and the effect of that agreement...is to hand over to the Irish State complete control of those defences; and it recognises and finally establishes Irish sovereignty over the Twenty-six Counties and the territorial seas." The financial arrangement which ended the economic war can also be regarded a victory for de Valera. Ten million pounds was all that Ireland had to pay as a final settlement of all outstanding debts between the two countries. Initially the British had demanded £104m. In addition a trade agreement removed all special duties imposed by both sides since 1932. Irish cattle, Irish food products and Irish manufactured goods could enter Britain again with few restrictions. The Free State could still however impose tariffs on British imports in order to protect industries "not fully established".

The economic war 1932-'38 demonstrated the close economic bonds between Ireland and Britain. Political independence may have been won in 1921 but Eire despite desperate efforts to gain alternative markets for Irish exports, was still sending over 90% of its exports to Britain in 1938.

At the time the settlement was hailed by the American ambassador to Eire as "a wonderful triumph for de Valera". The electorate was in happy agreement. A snap election in summer 1938 gave de Valera (77 seats). Fianna Fail had an overall majority of 16 seats. His hand was therefore considerably strengthened in dealing with the main remaining threats to the state viz. the internal threat posed by the I.R.A. and, within a year, the external threat posed by World War II.

De Valera's authorised biographers Longford and O'Neill called the Agreements "a qualified triumph". De Valera himself said, "Some may say that this is not a good agreement". He was disappointed that no progress had been made on partition and that, despite P.M. Chamberlain's private lack of enthusiasm for partition, he had failed to elicit a public statement to that effect. De Valera acknowledged however that "these agreements will remove from the field of dispute between Great Britain and ourselves all the major items now except that one" i.e. partition.

The return of Berehaven, Cobh and Lough Swilly in December 1938 marked the end of eight centuries of British occupation and made possible a new era of détente in Anglo-Irish relations.

Law and Order Under de Valera

One of the big question-marks hanging over de Valera's first years in power was his attitude to law and order. De Valera was popularly perceived as the political leader of those who had opposed the lawful government of the state during and immediately after the Civil War. Ten years later de Valera was leading the lawful government of the state.

The I.R.A. considered themselves old comrades-in-arms to some government ministers (e.g. Aiken, Minister for Defence in the first Fianna Fáil government had succeeded Liam Lynch as Commander of the Anti-Treaty Irregulars upon Lynch's death in April 1923 and was the first leader of the I.R.A. after the Civil War) and expected to find themselves in positions of power and authority under the new regime. The first signs were encouraging. On 9th March 1932, de Valera's first day in government, Aiken, Minister for Defence visited the I.R.A. leader in prison. Fianna Fáil had opposed the outlawing of the I.R.A. and the setting up of a military tribunal under the terms of the draconian Public Safety Act during the last months of the Cosgrave government. March 10th 1932 saw the release of 17 prisoners convicted by military tribunal. One week later the military tribunal was discontinued and the order outlawing the I.R.A. was allowed to lapse. Encouraged and emboldened by a "sympathetic" regime, the I.R.A. started making menacing gestures towards their enemies, Cosgrave and the former government ministers, who then formed the Opposition.

The Blueshirts

February 1932 saw the emergence of a new organisation, the Army Comrades Association. Composed of ex-servicemen its aims were uncontroversial at first, - to uphold the state and to honour dead comrades. By August 1932 the ACA had 30,000 members and had been taken over by T. F. O'Higgins, brother of the assassinated Kevin O'Higgins. Increasingly the ACA assumed the role of protector of the Opposition political party. ACA marshals stewarded Cumann na nGaedheal election rallies during the run-up to the January 1933 election. Running battles between the IRA and the ACA who policed Cumann na nGaedheal meetings were a sinister feature of the 1933 election campaign and seemed to mirror the Nazi-Communist disorders in Germany which accompanied the rise to power of Hitler at the same time.

Comparison with the Brownshirt movement in Nazi Germany and the Blackshirts in Mussolini's Italy became more pronounced during 1933 when the ACA adopted a Blueshirt uniform and acquired a new colourful leader in the recently-dismissed first Garda Commissioner, Eoin O'Duffy. Under General O'Duffy the Blueshirts adopted the straight-arm fascist salute and became the National Guard. O'Duffy planned to hold a huge rally and march past Leinster House on August 13th 1933 to commemorate the dead of the Irish Free State, Griffith, Collins and O'Higgins. The government fearing a Mussolini-type "march on Dublin" took decisive action. The controversial Public Safety Act of 1931 was restored. The Military Tribunal was reconvened. Guns held by members of the public, including those held by government ministers since the death of Kevin O'Higgins were withdrawn. Most important of all, the commemorative parade and rally of Sunday 13th August was banned. O'Duffy was placed in the same dilemma as that of Daniel O'Connell almost 100 years before when his monster meeting of the Repeal Association at Clontarf was banned at the last moment. Like O'Connell in 1843, O'Duffy in 1933 chose the constitutional path. The rally was cancelled but provincial parades were held one week later in defiance of a government ban. This led to the proscribing of the National Guard. Undeterred and, in imitation of O'Connell who in order to act within the letter of the law had changed the name of the proscribed Catholic Association to New Catholic Association during the 1820's, the National Guard became the Young Ireland Association. When this in turn was declared illegal it became the League of Youth, modelling itself on the Balilla, the Fascist youth movement in Italy and the Hitler Youth of Germany. O'Duffy drew his main support from the discontented young farmers, sons of cattle owners in the midland and southern counties who saw their livelihood wrecked by the economic war and who were delighted with his appeal in 1934 to all farmers to refuse to pay rates and land annuities. It was, however, O'Duffy's preference for unconstitutional methods which cost him the support of constitutionalists.

The political opposition was alarmed in 1933 by what they saw as the government's determination to prevent freedom of speech and association. It was particularly alarmed at the decision to set up an armed auxiliary police force, the Broy Harriers, so-called after the new Commissioner Broy. Cosgrave and the parliamentary opposition regarded the setting up of an armed police body as a means of legalising violence directed against them. Within a month of the August ban the main political parties, Cumann na nGaedheal, the National Centre Party which, under the leadership of James Dillon, son of the last leader of the Irish Parliamentary Party at Westminster in 1918, was championing the cause of the farmers, and the National Guard, came together as a new political force under the name Fine Gael. Although General O'Duffy was not a member of the Dáil he became the first leader of Fine Gael. O'Duffy's failure to gain election to the Dáil plus his provocative and unpredictable behaviour which included, not only encouragement for agrarian strife but also calls for a war with Britain to end partition, created problems. As the leader of a party pledged to a united Ireland within the Commonwealth this was unacceptable. Intellectuals within the movement, like Professor Hogan of University College Cork, attracted by the Blueshirts' opposition to Communism and O'Duffy's interest in a Mussolini-style corporate state, resigned in protest against O'Duffy's "destructive and hysterical leadership". On September 21st 1934 O'Duffy was obliged to resign the leadership of Fine Gael. Some loyal to O'Duffy left with him and the Blueshirt movement, hampered by a government ban on uniformed movements, was split. It was never again a force in Irish political life.

Two years later however O'Duffy was in the news again. Despite Irish neutrality in the Spanish Civil War and a prohibition on Irish citizens going to Spain during the War, O'Duffy trained and led an Irish Brigade into war-torn Spain. Glory and success eluded him in the field of battle also. In June 1937 the dispirited remnants of the war-weary Brigade voted to return to Ireland. O'Duffy himself said, "Our little unit did not... play a very prominent part in the Spanish Civil War but we ensured that our country was represented in the fight against World Communism".

De Valera and the IRA

The problem posed by the IRA was not destined to go away as had the Blueshirt threat. The "honeymoon" between the IRA and the Fianna Fáil government was prolonged because both saw the Blueshirts as a common enemy. IRA violence, which might have been directed against the state, was safely channelled against a legitimate target. Even before the Blueshirt threat receded, however, from 1934, there were ominous signs that the IRA were not going to be satisfied with anything less than a united thirty-two county Irish republic. An IRA convention in 1933 expressed dissatisfaction at the piece-meal dismantling of the Treaty. Many IRA extremists could see little difference between de Valera's gradual progress towards independence in the Thirties and the "stepping stones to freedom" theory advocated by Collins during the Treaty debates of 1921/22 and rejected equally by both de Valera and the IRA.

At first de Valera tried to woo the IRA from unconstitutional activity by allowing ex-IRA men to join the auxiliary armed police force (Broy Harriers) and by providing pensions for IRA men who had fought during the Civil War. A series of brutal murders culminating in the murder in March 1936 of a 72 year-old retired British navy admiral prompted de Valera to take the same coercive action against the IRA as he had condemned some five years previously under the Cosgrave administration. On the occasion of the banning of the IRA in June 1936 de Valera said in the Dáil "if any other body than the State relied on physical force to advance any of their ideas, it would, in the first place necessarily mean a civil war". In an obvious reference to a possible twin threat posed by opposing private armies, Blueshirts and IRA, he stated in August 1936, "if one section of the community could claim the right to build up a political army so could another and it would not be very long before this country would be rent asunder by rival military factions." To the amazement of those who remembered de Valera's pre-election statement in 1922 that, there were "rights which a minority may justly uphold even by arms against a majority" de Valera fourteen years later was saying, "if a minority tries to have its way by force against the will of the majority it is inevitable that the majority will resist by force and this can only mean civil war". Not surprisingly attempts to get the IRA to voluntarily surrender their arms failed. One of the leaders of the IRA, Sean Russell, reminded de Valera that it had been on de Valera's instructions in 1923 that arms had not been surrendered at the end of the Civil War.

The Republican/Socialist split in the IRA in the mid-1930's weakened the movement somewhat and reduced the threat to the state as did the decision of some 200/300 IRA men to fight for the Republican/Socialist cause in the Spanish Civil War. Of the latter the best known was Frank Ryan, an avowed Communist who, having fought with valour on the Republican side, was arrested and imprisoned by Franco. He was released into Nazi Germany in 1940 where he died in 1944. Divisions in the IRA were welcomed by the government although internal feuds were in themselves a threat to law and order. Unseemly scuffles had broken out between warring factions at the annual commemorative parade to Wolfe Tone's grave in Bodenstown cemetery in 1934 and 1935. The lack of a unified command made government control difficult. The break-away groups tended to be fanatical. On 18th June 1936 the de Valera government took the ultimate step of declaring the IRA unlawful.

The effect of the banning of the IRA in 1936 was to remove the existing leadership. The IRA Chief-of-Staff Maurice Twomey was imprisoned in 1936. His place was briefly taken by MacBride who accepted the 1937 Constitution and left the IRA. MacBride was replaced in 1938 by Sean Russell who in January 1939, following the return of the Treaty ports sent an "ultimatum" to Britain demanding British withdrawal within four days from "every part of Ireland". This was followed by a bombing campaign in Britain culminating in the killing of five people in an explosion in a crowded street in Coventry in August 1939 just days from the outbreak of World War II.

Ireland during World War II - The Emergency

The IRA: De Valera understood all too well what major war would mean to the IRA - England's difficulty would once again be Ireland's opportunity. He was determined, however, that nothing would endanger the recently-won independence of the Irish State. No IRA operation either inside or outside the state would be permitted to excuse either British or German intervention in Ireland.

In June 1939 anti-IRA legislation was strengthened with an Offences against the State Act providing for internment without trial. In late August over seventy leading activists were arrested. Constitutional loopholes in the Offences against the State Act led to the subsequent release of many of the first internees but amendments and fresh legislation, including an Emergency Powers Act in January 1940, resulted in fresh internment swoops and the opening of Curragh military detention camp for war "criminals". Over a thousand Irish Volunteers spent the greater part of World War II behind bars.

The Treason Act of June 1939 provided the death penalty for crimes of treason. In all, nine men were executed during the war years. The most emotive issue of the early war period was a hunger-strike organised by internees in protest at being detained after deportation from Britain. In November 1939, having stated the government's determination "not to release the prisoners," de Valera relented and ordered the release of one of the hunger-strikers, Patrick McGrath, when told his death was imminent. The man recovered, however, and the following August two detectives were shot dead when they attempted to rearrest McGrath and a colleague. Both men were executed. De Valera, as spokesman for prisoners in British jails in the aftermath of the Easter Rising 1916 had, for a brief period, considered using the hunger-strike weapon to extract better conditions for political prisoners. His attitude to hunger-strikers, however, had hardened. In April 1940 two hunger-strikers died. De Valera felt that his gesture of clemency to McGrath in November 1939 had resulted in six unnecessary deaths altogether.

Likewise, released internees were held responsible for a daring raid on the Phoenix Park arms depot in late December 1939. The subsequent search was so thorough that more than the million rounds of ammunition stolen was uncovered. De Valera had given his word at an early stage in the negotiations that led to the Anglo-Irish Agreements of 1938 that the Irish State would not be used as a base for attacks upon British territory. Although five IRA men died in gun-battles with police on both sides of the border, the "threatened" IRA invasion of the North did not materialise. By 1943 repressive measures on both sides of the border, plus strict censorship, depriving the IRA of publicity and public sympathy, had rendered the IRA a spent force. It was to remain so for the next ten years.

German Spies

A real nightmare for de Valera in the early war years was the prospect of a German-assisted IRA invasion of Northern Ireland. In 1940 his greatest fear was that Ireland would become a "cock-pit" of war between Britain and Germany. "If we let one country in, that inevitably would provoke the other to attack" he observed in an interview with an American journalist in July 1940. With this in mind de Valera warned in a radio broadcast of 8th May 1940, "Danger threatens now from within as well as from without". This was an obvious allusion to the growing IRA danger (the previous day an attack on two detectives escorting mail to the Department of External Affairs marked a sinister escalation in IRA terrorism and had prompted de Valera's radio broadcast). In the same month, the first evidence of a German spy, Goertz, at large and making contact with the IRA, came to light. Goertz, a trained spy who had worked for German espionage in England for six years was undoubtedly the most important of fourteen German spies landed in Ireland. He evaded capture for many months and made contact with both the German Ambassador Hempel and the IRA. With the latter he was most unimpressed. He urged them to end their "war" on the south and to concentrate instead on waging a guerilla war on the North. About the IRA he is reputed to have said, "you know how to die for Ireland, but how to fight for it you have not the slightest idea". The German spy threat was taken very seriously. Hempel was forced at the height of the invasion scare in both Britain and Ireland during the summer of 1940 to give an assurance that in no circumstances would Germany invade Ireland. Goertz's Irish radio operator was sentenced to ten years imprisonment while Goertz himself was held until 1947. Although de Valera promised political asylum to Germans in Ireland after the war, arrangements were made to return Goertz into Allied custody in Occupied Germany. Rather than return, Goertz committed suicide on May 23rd 1947.

It is a measure of the skill and expertise of the Irish intelligence service, ably assisted by British intelligence, that all the other generally ill-informed ill-equipped German spies were picked up within 24 hours of their arrival. Military intelligence managed to crack secret German codes including the coded messages sent by Goertz from prison back to Germany. The German spy scare of 1940/41 bred a distrust and suspicion of strangers as all were urged in a special radio broadcast of 8th May 1940, "to be the eyes and the ears of the national defence."

Neutrality during the "Emergency"

During the sixteen years of Fianna Fáil rule (1932-1948) de Valera held the post of Minister for External Affairs and took responsibility for foreign policy. Ever since the first tentative overtures to the U.S. in 1917, his quest for international recognition of Irish independence had been ongoing.

Neutrality was proof of independence and became the ultimate objective of all political parties after 1922. De Valera used Ireland's membership of the League of Nations to exhort fellow small states not to "become the tools of any great power and to "resist with whatever strength they may possess every attempt to force them into a war against their will". Insistence upon neutrality led to a stated policy of non-involvement in the Spanish Civil War. (July 1936-39)

Neutrality in the Spanish Civil War presented no major problem for the Irish Free State as Britain had also opted for non-involvement. Neutrality in a British war however, would not be possible without the return of the Treaty ports. De Valera regarded the Anglo-Irish Agreements of 1938, providing for the handing-over of the British naval bases at Cobh, Berehaven and Lough Swilly by 31st December 1938, as his greatest political achievement. For the first time in centuries Ireland was free to adopt a neutral stand in a war in which Britain was involved.

On September 2nd 1939 (before the official declaration of war by Britain and France on Germany on September 3rd 1939) the Dáil met to enact legislation affirming the neutrality of the Irish state for the duration of the "Emergency" as the war years became known in neutral Ireland.

Dáil support for neutrality was almost unanimous. The only dissenting voice was that of Fine Gael member, James Dillon. Dillon, like his father in World War I advocated active support of the Allies and resigned from the Fine Gael party in 1941 over the issue. World War II brought political benefit. It enabled the political parties to sink their differences over the Treaty and to unite in a common cause which was universally popular throughout the state - Irish neutrality. De Valera helped the healing process by setting up a Consultative Defence Conference in summer 1940, drawn from representatives of the three main parties, Fianna Fáil, Fine Gael and Labour, to advise on defence issues and to demonstrate national solidarity in the face of external threat.

De Valera warned in the Dáil on September 2nd 1939 that neutrality would not be easy and spoke of "problems much more delicate and much more difficult of solution even than the problems that arise for a belligerent".

The German Threat

The possibility of a German invasion posed a double threat for Ireland, the attack by Germany itself and the prospect of a British invasion either to forestall the Germans or to drive them out. In an effort to prevent a pre-emptive strike by the British, de Valera gave assurances to Britain that British assistance would be sought in the event of a German attack. Detailed planning for a war-time British occupation included the designation of the Grand Hotel in Malahide, Co. Dublin as HQ for a British commander, who would co-ordinate a joint Anglo-Irish defence in the event of a German invasion. Other contingency plans included the relocation of the Irish government at a secret location outside Dublin. Fortunately neither emergency measure had to be implemented.

The time of greatest danger for Ireland came after the fall of France in June 1940. "Operation Green" was Germany's secret plan for the occupation of Ireland as part of "Operation Sealion", code name for the German plan for the invasion of Britain. German plans drawn up in September 1940 reveal that Dublin was to be one of six administrative headquarters after both islands had been taken. S.S. documents uncovered after the war showed S.S. plans to deport 5,000 Irish Jews after Nazi occupation. Hempel, the German Minister in Ireland, had however given a guarantee in June 1940 that in no circumstances would the Germans invade Ireland. Whilst victory in "Operation Sealion" may well have changed everything, Germany's defeat in the Battle of Britain lessened the threat of German invasion. Although Hitler is reputed to have said as late as December 1940 that, "possession of Ireland could have the effect of ending the war", his military advisers judged that German occupation of the island of Ireland was impossible without an accompanying all out war between Britain and Ireland.

Ironically, one major German air-raid, the North Strand bombing of 31st May 1941, killing 29 people and leaving 25 families in North Dublin homeless, occurred at a time when the Germans were turning their military machine eastwards on Russia. "Operation Barbarossa" in June 1941 saved both Britain and Ireland.

The British Threat

In the early stages of the war, however, Eire saw its neutrality threatened more by Britain than by Germany. Whilst Germany gave verbal assurance through the German Minister in Ireland, Hempel, that Irish neutrality would not be violated, at no time during the war did Britain give an assurance to respect Irish neutrality.

The need to establish formal diplomatic relations with Britain (Britain had refused to allow the appointment of a British ambassador to Eire as this might be interpreted as formal recognition of Irish independence) led to the appointment of Sir John Maffey as U.K. Representative to Eire. Henceforth direct governmental contact and consultation, which could be construed as an abuse of neutrality, could be cut to a minimum.

In October 1939 the first demands for the use of at least Berehaven were made and rejected by the de Valera government. Churchill, then First Lord of the Admiralty, urged the seizure of the Irish ports described by him as "the sentinel towers of the western approaches". In 1938 Churchill, from the Opposition benches, had warned against the return of the Treaty ports, "in a war against an enemy possessing a numerous and powerful fleet of submarines these are the essential bases". Chamberlain, British P.M. in 1939, did not press the issue.

Relations, however, between Britain and Ireland sharply deteriorated when Churchill became Prime Minister on May 10th 1940. From 1938 de Valera had maintained that the one obstacle to Irish alliance with Britain was the continuation of partition. In an interview to a London newspaper in 1938 he warned, "no Irish leader will ever be able to get Irish people to co-operate with Great Britain while partition remains". Churchill took this to mean that de Valera would be willing to trade Irish neutrality for the ending of partition. In June 1940 after the fall of France a six-point proposal was made to the Irish government. In return for a U.K. government declaration to accept the principle of a united Ireland, Eire would enter the war on the side of the U.K. forthwith and allow Britain the use of ports and military facilities in Eire. A joint administrative body with representatives from both the Northern and Southern government would work towards the Union of Ireland while a joint Defence Council assisted by Britain would organise the defence of the whole island. For de Valera neither the ending of partition nor Irish neutrality was a bargaining factor. Union of Ireland would have to come first. A united Ireland could consider declaring war on Germany. In his rejection of the proposals on July 4th 1940, de Valera warned that a united Ireland would probably vote against entering the war. The similarity with the promise on Home Rule given to Redmond in 1914 was striking, but de Valera was determined not to fall into the trap as Redmond had during World War I.

Although the strategic value of the Southern ports declined after the Fall of France, when British convoys had of necessity to be re-routed around the North of Ireland because the Southern coast was too exposed to attack, Churchill again made a blistering attack in November 1940. "The fact that we cannot use the south and west coasts of Ireland to refuel our flotilla and aircraft and thus protect the trade by which Ireland as well as Great Britain lives, is a most heavy and grievous burden..." Churchill followed this up by ending abruptly in December 1940 the shipping arrangements entered into earlier whereby Britain agreed to supply 400,000 tons of foodstuffs, fertilisers and essential goods to Ireland.

The subsequent economic hardship was severe. De Valera complained in a radio broadcast to America on St. Patrick's Day 1941 "both sides in blockading each other are blockading us". Notwithstanding this, de Valera had resisted the offer of a German shipping arrangement in August 1940, when the Germans had announced a total blockade of Britain which included the seas around Ireland. De Valera never wavered from the attitude stated to an American on the eve of war in 1939, "We are desirous of being helpful... short of actual participation in the war".

"Friendly" Neutrality

De Valera's achievement during the war years was that Ireland succeeded in being "helpful beyond the strict definition of neutrality" in the opinion of Maffey the British representative to Eire, without seriously compromising the official policy of neutrality. Help to the Allies included exchange of information with British intelligence regarding all aliens (including Germans) living in Ireland. Military collaboration included right of pursuit and attack to the British navy in Irish territorial waters. Meteorological reports were secretly released to the British navy although public transmission of weather forecasting was curtailed in case of breach of strict neutrality. German pilots who crashed were interned for the duration of the war and their aircraft impounded. In 1943, however, 24 interned British airmen were released en bloc and thereafter Allied airmen were free to return to Northern Ireland and arrangements were frequently made for the salvage of damaged aircraft. In addition "non-operational" flights were permitted over Irish air-space. By 1944 in practice this meant all Allied flights. In February 1945 the British war cabinet recognised fourteen different areas in which the Southern Irish government afforded assistance to the Allies, and acknowledged "in general the Southern Irish Government has been willing to accord us any facilities which would not be regarded as overtly prejudicing their attitude of neutrality".

Despite Churchill's hostility to Irish neutrality, Britain benefited considerably from Ireland's "friendly" neutrality. For the first time in modern history nationalist Ireland was prepared to defend itself against Britain's enemy. Although the fear of British invasion was kept alive by Churchill's hostile speeches, the British military authorities, as well as the German, by the end of 1940 had ruled out invasion and occupation of Ireland. The British war effort would have been seriously hampered by having to keep an army of occupation in a hostile Ireland. Far from being hostile, upwards on 50,000 Irish people joined the British armed forces. Unlike other neutral countries Ireland imposed no ban on foreign enlistment nor were steps taken against 4,000 Irish soldiers who effectively deserted from the Irish Army in order to join the British Army. In addition over 100,000 Irish men and women sought work in war-time Britain. Irish employment exchanges advertised job opportunities in Britain during the war. "Friendly" Ireland was therefore a useful source of manpower for Britain during the war-years.

The American Threat

As the threat from both Britain and Germany receded in 1941, neutral Ireland came under verbal attack from the U.S. who, although neutral until December 1941, showed little sympathy for, or patience with, Irish neutrality. A Gallup poll early in 1941 revealed that 63% of Americans felt that Britain should be allowed to use Irish ports. A direct appeal, for economic aid resulted in two ships being offered for sale but a request for American arms was denied. American weapons could only be given to those "actively waging war on behalf of the maintenance of democracy."

De Valera and the Irish State experienced the full brunt of American hostility upon U.S. entry into the war, on December 7th 1941. Gray the American Minister in Ireland, unlike the British Representative Maffey and the German Minister Hempel, made little effort to win the goodwill of the Irish. In vain, de Valera protested in 1942 at the use by U.S. marines of a base in Derry. As part of the national territory de Valera demanded unsuccessfully that he be consulted about U.S. intentions. De Valera resisted diplomatic pressure repeatedly applied by Gray throughout 1944, to close the German and Japanese embassies in Dublin. He risked international opprobrium when, on the death of Hitler on 30th April 1945, de Valera called personally on the German Minister to offer formal condolences. No other single incident aroused such indignation among the Allies as this controversial visit at the moment of Germany's defeat. It called forth a scathing attack from Churchill on Irish neutrality in a victory broadcast of May 13th 1945 and ensured that Irish neutrality during World War II was followed by Irish isolation on the international scene.

Consequences of Neutrality

Churchill's speech, castigating de Valera, contrasted the "loyalty and friendship of Northern Ireland" with the seeming apathy of the rest of Ireland..."if it had not been for the loyalty and friendship of Northern Ireland we should have been forced to come to close quarters with de Valera or perish forever from the earth". De Valera's response on 17th May 1945 compared British aggression to Ireland over several hundred years with the much-deplored fascist aggression of the war years.

The war taught both Britain and the U.S. the strategic value of partition and a Northern Ireland state happy to be linked to Britain. During the first years of partition (the 1920s) De Valera believed that Britain was the chief instigator of partition. In Chamberlain, De Valera believed he had found a British Prime Minister who had no strong commitment to a divided Ireland. De Valera hoped in 1938 that, with a disinterested British government and a sympathetic U.S. administration, partition would be ended quickly. Irish neutrality in World War II, however, made both Britain and the U.S. firm advocates of partition.

Neutrality for DeValera was the highest expression of national independence. It was never intended to bring with it isolation. Diplomatic isolation was however one of the painful consequences of neutrality. In August 1946 Ireland's application for membership of the United Nations was rejected. The Soviet Union's stated reason for vetoing Ireland's membership was that Ireland had failed to help the Allies and had maintained cordial relations with the enemy while refusing to open diplomatic relations with the U.S.S.R. De Valera was in opposition in 1955 when Ireland was finally admitted to the U.N.

Although Ireland was not anxious to enter into military commitments and did not become a member of N.A.T.O. in 1949, De Valera was determined that Ireland should share in the American programme for post-war economic recovery in Europe, Marshall Aid. De Valera personally attended the Conference on European Economic Co-operation in Paris in 1947. Ireland became a founder member of both the Organisation for European Economic Co-operation and the Council of Europe. De Valera thus initiated a process of closer co-operation with Europe which was to result in Ireland becoming a member of the E.E.C. in 1973, the last year of De Valera's presidency of the Irish Republic.

"Life in Ireland during the Emergency"
Defence

Neutrality presupposes an ability to defend oneself. Yet Ireland's military resources at the beginning of the war were so meagre that Norton, the Irish Labour leader, spoke in 1940 of Ireland's "hopeless unpreparedness". An ill-equipped army of 7,000 regulars and 14,000 reserves, in uniforms strikingly similar to those of the German army, stood between the Irish people and the triple threat from Germany, Britain and the I.R.A.

A mass all-party drive in the summer of 1940 doubled the size of the regular army. A local Defence Force was formed along the lines of the British Local Defence Force. Among its youngest recruits was future Taoiseach, Garret Fitzgerald who joined in 1942 aged 15 years. The L.D.F. reached 100,000 members. By the end of the war Eire could boast a fighting force 250,000 strong. The rapid growth in the armed services accentuated the acute military shortages. A military consequence of neutrality was the virtual inability of the Irish state to get arms. Limited military co-operation with the Allies from 1941 ensured limited military assistance. At the height of the invasion scare in 1940 all that could be spared were 20,000 American rifles, given by the British, to demonstrate Irish military dependence upon Britain.

Black-out and the hasty construction of do-it-yourself air-raid shelters were the first visible effects of the war. Both were a precaution against much-feared air warfare. The infant army air-corps was expanded but was powerless to prevent sporadic air attacks. The first air-raid was on 26th August 1940 when three bombs fell on a creamery at Campile, Co. Wexford killing three girls. Three more people were killed when bombs fell at Borris Co. Carlow. The North Circular Road, Phoenix Park and Sandycove in Dublin were bomb-damaged but the real horror of air war-fare was experienced on May 31st 1941 when 29 people were killed, 45 injured and twenty-five houses completely destroyed in Dublin's North Strand. The Germans apologised, claiming that the raid was intended for Liverpool on the British mainland. Compensation was eventually paid by the West German government in 1958. Massive air-raids on "un-neutral" Belfast in April and May 1941 caused de Valera to ignore border frontiers and rush all available assistance to "our people". De Valera thus used the crisis to lay claim to the whole territory.

To counter the growing menace of air warfare gas-masks were issued to the civilian population and public air-raid shelters were constructed in urban centres. As the threat of air attack receded from 1941 these were never used.

Censorship

The 1937 Constitution provided for censorship of press, radio and films. This Constitutional provision, much criticised by contemporary Irish literary figures, enabled the government to exercise the strictest censorship on the written and spoken word during the war-years. Aiken as Minister for the Co-Ordination of Defensive Measures, a new government post created by the Emergency, was responsible for censorship which was so wide-ranging that it monitored not only radio news bulletins and press accounts of war "news" but also censored a bishop's pastoral letter because it condemned German bombing of civilians. Farmers and fishermen were severely disadvantaged throughout the war because of inadequate weather forecasting in order not to appear to give assistance to air or naval forces of either side. At the same time, weather reports were being secretly transmitted to the Allies. Cinema-going was the most popular form of entertainment at this time. Yet films, especially British and American propaganda films, were heavily censored. Despite a strict censorship Irish people managed to get both sides of the war-story through the biased and also censored broadcasts of the B.B.C. and the nightly German-propaganda broadcasts of Irishman William Joyce, "Lord Haw-Haw" from the German war capital, Berlin. Joyce was captured and executed as a traitor in the Tower of London at the end of the war.

Rationing

The parody on the music-hall song
> "Bless 'em all,
> Bless 'em all,
> The long and the short and the tall,
> Bless De Valera and Sean MacEntee,
> For their dirty brown bread and their half ounce of tea."

summed up the national attitude to rationing; the most long-term and most universally felt consequence of the war-years. Emergency measures at the outbreak of war in September 1939 included the setting up of a new government department of Supplies under the former Minister for Industry and Commerce, Sean Lemass. The new Minister for Supplies immediately introduced petrol rationing and set an example to all by cycling to work. The supply situation was the most critical issue of the war-years. Ireland had no merchant navy and relied on British merchant ships to carry Irish imports and exports. An informal arrangement at the start of the war enabled Britain to charter neutral shipping without competition from Ireland in return for an informal undertaking to supply Ireland's requirements. The abrupt termination of this arrangement in December 1940 led to the setting up of an Irish merchant shipping fleet, Irish Shipping, in 1941. Shortages of essential goods, however, became acute. The tea ration fell to 1/4 ounce per week per person. Citrus fruits, oranges and bananas were unobtainable, while by 1942 bread and clothes were among items rationed. Rationing and shortages of essential goods were generally seen as being more severe in Ireland than in Britain. As the termination of British shipping arrangements was seen as being largely responsible for Irish hardship, food shortages engendered much anti-British feeling in Ireland from 1941. The high casualties inflicted on Irish merchant ships, (up to 20 unarmed merchant ships of the Irish Shipping Co. were sunk and 138 Irish seamen killed during the war) highlighted the dangers to all ships in German-blockaded British and Irish waters and threw into sharp focus the inadequacy of naval protection from a small but growing Irish marine service.

By 1943 Ireland was getting no domestic coal from Britain. Home-produced turf became an unpopular substitute. Electricity and gas were also strictly rationed. Gas inspectors known as "glimmer men" were appointed to monitor domestic gas consumption. In 1942 petrol supplies for private motoring ceased. Public transport was limited and difficult as turf-burning trains took up to twelve hours to travel from Dublin to Cork. The fact that shortages and rationing continued after the war was over was a major cause of discontent. This was reflected in the first post-war general election in 1948 when defeat ended sixteen years of Fianna Fáil rule. The decision in January 1947 to continue the state of emergency in force since September 1939 with the warning, "the position regarding supplies essential to the life of the community is in some respects worse than at any time since 1939," and the gloomy prediction, "the possibility is that a period of even greater difficulty may occur" was not calculated to win votes in the February 1948 election, just 12 months later.

Economic Policy
Pre-war frugal self-sufficiency

Fianna Fáil's economic policy, 1932-1948, put to the test the Sinn Féin philosophy of economic nationalism as expounded by its founder, Arthur Griffith. As early as 1928 Sean Lemass, who as Minister for Industry and Commerce until 1939 and thereafter Minister for Supplies, was largely responsible for economic policy during the de Valera era, said "We believe that Ireland can be a self-contained unit, providing all the necessities of living in adequate quantities for the people residing in this island". In the economic climate of the Thirties when the Great Depression forced even free trade advocates such as Britain to impose protective tariffs and when self-sufficiency was the stated economic goal of fascist Italy and Germany, protectionism seemed to be the only prudent economic course open to the young Irish economy.

The "economic war" 1932/38 afforded an excellent opportunity to begin the change-over to tillage farming so essential for self-sufficiency in agriculture. A 'battle for wheat" not unlike that being waged by Mussolini in Italy at the same time, resulted in a dramatic increase in the acreage under wheat from 21,000 acres in 1931 to 225,000 acres in 1936. The increase in subsidised wheat production, however, was at the expense of other crops cheaper to grow and more suited to the Irish climate, such as barley. The ending of the "economic war" in 1938 and the removal of the restrictive tariffs imposed since 1932 caused a return to more profitable pasture farming. By 1939 tillage levels had slipped back to 1931 levels. The government was compelled to introduce compulsory tillage in 1940. Despite this and despite the drive for agricultural self-sufficiency during the Thirties, bread rationing had to be imposed in 1942 and was continued after the war was over.

The effects of the "economic war" was not confined to agriculture. The reduction of farmers' incomes meant a reduction in spending power among the biggest sector of the population. This was to have disastrous consequences for the whole range of small "home" industries Fianna Fáil was determined to develop behind a wall of protective tariffs. The Control of Manufacturers' Acts 1932-1934 ensured that Irish industry would be Irish-owned. The biggest obstacle to the development of small-scale Irish industry was the lack of private capital for investment in industry. The Industrial Credit Corporation was set up in 1933 to provide attractive loans to industrialists. The ICC was the industrial counterpart of the ACC set up in 1927 to help farmers. In many respects Fianna Fáil economic policy of the 1930's was an extension of the Cumann na nGaedheal policies of the 1920s. State sponsorship of industry continued. Nineteen state-sponsored bodies in all were set up between 1927 and 1939. These included the Irish Sugar Company, Aer Lingus, Aer Rianta, Bord Fáilte and the Hospital Trust Board. State sponsorship provided public capital for large scale enterprises not forthcoming from the private sector.

The value of net industrial output rose during the period 1931-38 from £25.6m to £36m. Industrial employment increased from 111,000 to 166,000. The Housing Act of 1932 released state funds for local authority housing. The building of 132,000 houses in the ten years after 1932 provided much needed employment in a decade when job opportunities in industrially-depressed Britain and the U.S. dropped sharply. For the first time in decades emigration from Ireland slowed down. When, however, preparations for war opened up job opportunities abroad again the rate of emigration accelerated. Domestic demand for home-produced goods declined accordingly. Whilst there were some successes in the small industries sector (the manufacture of shoes and related leather goods meant a four-fold increase in employment in the leather industry) the lack of competition from imports (by 1936 over 1,000 imports had prohibitive tariffs placed upon them) meant home industries had little incentive to improve quality or price. Over-concentration on the home market was at the expense of the old-established export industries, brewing, distilling and biscuit-making, which also suffered as a result of the economic war. The real weaknesses of Irish industry were exposed during the war when shortages of imported raw materials, machinery and most important of all, imported fuel and energy sources on which all industry depended, cancelled out the advances of the previous years and demonstrated that industrial self-sufficiency in Ireland was a myth. Self-sufficiency during the Thirties meant in the words of Sean O'Faolain, contemporary writer and critic, "frugal sufficiency for all". The war years saw more frugality and even less sufficiency.

War Years: Economic Survival

The benefits of the quest for agricultural self-sufficiency during the Thirties were appreciated during the war. Ireland's dependence upon imported flour had been reduced from over 3m. cwt. in 1931 to just 100,000 cwt. of imported flour in 1938. Compulsory tillage however had to be introduced in 1940. By 1944 it was obligatory to till 3/8 of arable land on each holding. Notwithstanding this, strict bread rationing had to be introduced in 1942. Whilst the acreage under wheat had risen from 250,000 acres in 1939 to record levels of 662,000 acres in 1945, shortages of imported fertilisers and farm machinery meant that yield per acre fell sharply. The exhaustion of the soil during the war years had an adverse effect on tillage farming in Ireland for many years after the war.

An outbreak of foot-and-mouth disease among cattle, plus strict price control in war-time Britain ensured that there would be no repeat of the World War I war-time boom for Irish farmers. In 1944 food prices in Britain were lower than pre-war prices. Churchill, in announcing the embargo on British shipping to Ireland in December 1940 stated, "we do not need the food which Eire has been sending us". Irish agriculture, in particular the cattle industry, had not recovered from the effects of the economic war when it was faced with the double crisis, the war and disease which seriously threatened Ireland's main export - live cattle and meat products.

By far the greatest threat to the Irish economy during the war years was the refusal of British merchant ships to supply Ireland from December 1940. The government response was to set up Irish Shipping with unwanted British and American ships. Thus Ireland emerged from World War II with its own infant merchant shipping company, which, from 1942, when British trade with Ireland virtually ceased, had provided the trickle of goods necessary for economic survival.

In anticipation of severe shortages of essential goods a Department of Supplies was set up in September 1939. Shortages of imported fuel and petrol were particularly worrying. It was argued that Irish Shipping itself would suffer due to petrol shortages. The use of peat as an Irish alternative to imported fuel for both domestic and industrial purposes was considered extremely important in a country poor in mineral resources. Even the army was deployed harvesting turf on occasion. In 1946 the setting up of Bord na Mona transformed turf production into a major industry which might never have been developed but for the "Emergency".

The war years saw the beginning of longer-term economic planning with the setting up of an economic subcommittee of the cabinet to chart economic development. Economic survival, however, was the keynote of the war years. Living standards fell as rigid wage controls imposed by the government kept wages down but shortages caused prices to rise. Industrial output fell but emigration to war-time Britain on an average of 18,000 per annum cushioned the economy against the worst effects of unemployment. The end of the war was universally welcomed. The effects of the war on the Irish economy were however to be felt for many years.

Post-war Stagnation

The war-time decline in agricultural exports reached its lowest level in 1947, the bleakest year yet for the Irish economy. A wet summer seriously reduced the grain and peat harvest. An exceptionally severe winter caused widespread hardship made worse by continued bread rationing and a fuel crisis. Food subsidies and social welfare measures which included unemployment assistance from 1933, widows' and orphans' pensions in 1935 and children's allowances in 1944 did little to alleviate hardship. A seven-months strike over pay by primary teachers, members of the Irish National Teachers' Organisation in 1946, showed that workers were not going to be "satisfied with frugal comfort" of which de Valera spoke in the Ireland of his dreams in 1943. Emigration became a major political issue. Norton, the Labour leader condemned F.F. economic policy thus, "The cattle boats are leaving empty, the emigrant ships are full". The emergence of a new republican party, Clann na Poblachta, under the leadership of a former chief of the IRA Sean MacBride, robbed Fianna Fáil of much of its support. Two war-time elections had shown a drop in Fianna Fáil's popularity. In the 1943 general election Fianna Fáil lost 10 seats. A snap election in 1944 enabled F.F. to win back nine seats. With 76 seats in 1944 they had a comfortable margin over the next biggest party in the Dáil, Fine Gael, who in 1944 held only 30 seats. Fianna Fáil strength from 1944, however, depended upon a weak fragmented opposition. In the first general election after the war the political parties came together, ironically using the slogan de Valera had used sixteen years before to gain power, "Put them out". After the election Fianna Fáil was still the biggest party in the Dáil but a coalition of the Opposition forced Fianna Fáil out of office and ended de Valera's sixteen-year rule.

Prelude to Presidency

The political instability of the Fifties was in marked contrast to the stability of the de Valera years. The collapse of the Coalition government in 1951 brought de Valera back. The general election however gave Fianna Fail just one seat more (69) than it had won in 1948. De Valera was forced to lead a minority government ruling with the help of Independents and former government minister Noel Browne whose controversial Mother and Child scheme had helped bring down the coalition government. Although Fianna Fáil were only in power for three uncertain years they tackled many of the social issues left unsolved by their predecessors. A Health Act, passed in 1953 was the basis of health services until 1970. The Social Welfare Act of 1952 brought together all previous social welfare legislation and aimed to provide a co-ordinated system of social welfare such as was emerging in post-war Britain.

Failure to tackle the pressing economic problems of chronic unemployment and emigration led to defeat in 1954 when Fianna Fáil won only 65 seats, its lowest number since 1927. In 1957 de Valera was back when Fianna Fáil won its largest number of seats yet (78) and embarked on a further sixteen-year rule. De Valera was convinced that the reason for the political instability of the Fifties was the proportional representation method of voting. P.R. could, however, only be changed by referendum. De Valera was seventy-five years old in 1957. He decided to resign as Taoiseach and contest the presidential election in 1959. As in 1937 when the referendum on the constitution coincided with a general election, de Valera decided to combine a constitutional referendum on P.R. with the presidential election. The Fianna Fáil slogan in 1959 was "Vote yes and de Valera". The electorate voted "No" on the abolition of P.R. and "Yes" on de Valera for President.

President of the Irish Republic
De Valera's double term as President (1959-73) was a fitting climax to a lifetime of public service. On New Year's Eve, 31st December 1961 his was the first voice to be heard over Ireland's first television channel Telefis Èireann.

During his fourteen years as President, de Valera was host to a stream of state visitors to Ireland. Among the most important of these was J.F. Kennedy, the Irish-American President of the U.S.A. in 1963. The warmth of the reception accorded to President Kennedy during his visit, the depth of the sorrow expressed at his assassination just a few months later and the welcome given to de Valera on the occasion of his state visit to the U.S. in 1965, showed that the coolness of the war years was forgotten as the common bond of friendship and kinship between the two peoples were rekindled. De Valera's return to the land of his birth as President of the Irish Republic was particularly satisfying as he recalled the period he had spent in the U.S. in 1919-20 as President of a Republic vainly seeking recognition.

President de Valera with U.S. President J.F. Kennedy in Dublin in 1963.

It was fitting that de Valera should be President during the Sixties, the decade of golden jubilees of the events which had brought about modern Ireland. In November 1963 he celebrated the fiftieth anniversary of the formation of the Irish Volunteers. "Some of the great events of our time were" he said, "the founding of the Gaelic League, the founding of the Irish Volunteers, the uprising of Easter Week, the establishment of Dáil Eireann and the Declaration of Independence."

The return of the remains of Roger Casement in 1965, executed in August 1916 for plotting with the Germans, was regarded as a triumph on the eve of the golden jubilee celebrations of the Easter Rising in 1966. De Valera was present at most of the commemorative events and paid tribute at the G.P.O. on Easter Monday to the "singlemindedness and unselfishness" of those who gave their lives in the struggle for independence. He gave the commemorative address to Dáil Eireann and the Senate on the occasion of the golden jubilee of the founding of the First Dáil on 21st January 1969 paying particular tribute to the twelve members of the First Dáil, himself among them, who were still alive.

Ireland became a member of the E.E.C. in 1973, de Valera's last year as President of the Irish Republic. Although de Valera had expressed the opinion in

1957 that "the nations of Europe could not lend much ear to our problems" Ireland's membership alongside Britain and Denmark in the European Community was the kind of international recognition which de Valera had made his primary political objective.

De Valera made his last St. Patrick's Day message to the Irish people in 1973. Upon termination of his second presidential term in 1973 he retired to a private nursing home where two years later on 29th August 1975 he died aged 93 years.

Appraisal

"Of American-Irish Spanish race" was how de Valera was introduced to the Irish electorate in June 1917. Virtually unknown before the Easter Rising, he dominated Irish political and public life for over half a century. He was described by Yeats as "a living argument". Lloyd George described negotiating with him as being like "picking up mercury with a fork".

In retrospect, de Valera's most unfortunate decision was his refusal to lead the Irish delegation at the Treaty Talks in London between October and December 1921. Ironically, de Valera, in dismantling the Treaty during his first years in power, was really carrying to fruition the aspiration of his political opponents, Michael Collins and the pro-Treatyites, that the Treaty would be a "Stepping Stone" to full freedom.

The Constitution, Bunreacht na hEireann 1937, laid the constitutional foundation of the Irish Republic and is de Valera's most enduring legacy to the Irish people. The Anglo-Irish Agreements of 1938 were hailed as being the victory which was denied in 1921. Neutrality in World War II demonstrated to the world the sovereignty of the Irish state. De Valera's successful stewardship of Ireland during the war has been described as his "finest hour".

Yet one reviewer upon de Valera's death wrote "By his own stated ambitions", the revival of the Gaelic language and the ending of partition, "he was a failure". De Valera is reputed to have said that he would prefer a Department of Irish to a Department of Education. Yet insistence upon compulsory Irish had killed love of the language while the depopulation of Gaeltacht areas through emigration had resulted in a steady decline of the Irish-speaking population. It was not until 1956 under the inter-party coalition goverment of Costello that a geographical definition of Gaeltacht areas was finally arrived at and a special department for the Gaeltacht set up. De Valera's concern for a Gaelic Catholic Ireland did not translate itself into material benefit for impoverished Gaeltacht areas, which continued to decline unchecked during the de Valera years. In 1938 de Valera said "until I die, partition will be the first thing in my mind". De Valera also said that "he would consider his career a failure" if during his life-time Ireland was not united.

It is, however, historian John A. Murphy's view that throughout his career de Valera promoted what he considered to be the interests of the 26 county state above theoretical considerations of unity. De Valera's one great weakness has been seen as his stubborn "not an inch" attitude to Northern Unionists and his insistence upon seeing partition as a matter to be resolved by the British and Irish governments without reference to the Unionist majority in Northern Ireland.

At the height of the Dáil debate on the Treaty de Valera declared "whenever I wanted to know what the Irish people wanted I had only to examine my own heart and it told me straight off". The regularity with which the Irish people voted for de

Valera in the period 1926-66, is a measure of the trust which the electorate placed in him.

Therein lay the success of his long political career spanning the formative years of the new Irish state. For his role in shaping the Ireland of the Twentieth Century de Valera can be truly called a Maker of Modern Ireland.

Landmarks in de Valera's Life (1882 - 1975)

1882	*October 14th* Born in New York.
1908	Member of Gaelic League.
1913	Founder member of Irish Volunteers.
1916	Commandant of the Boland's Mills garrison during Easter Rising.
1916	*May* Death sentence commuted to life imprisonment.
1917	*June* Release from Pentonville prison.
1917	*July* East Clare by-election victory.
1917	*October 25th* De Valera President of Sinn Féin.
1917	*October 26th* De Valera President of Volunteers.
1918	*May* "German Plot" de Valera rearrested.
1919	*February 1919* Escape from Lincoln Jail.
1919	*April 1* De Valera Priomh Aire of First Dáil.
1919	*June - December 1920* American trip.
1921	*July 11th* Truce ended War of Independence.
1921	*July 14th* De Valera opened the Treaty Negotiation in London.
1921	*December 6th* Anglo-Irish Treaty.
1921	*December 8th* De Valera voted against the Treaty in the Cabinet debate.
1922	*January 9th* Resignation as President of the Dáil
1922	*June 28-May 1923* Civil War. De Valera anti-Treaty President of the Irish Republic.

1923	*May 1923* His cease-fire appeal ended the Civil War.
1923	*August - July 1924* Imprisonment in Irish Free State.
1926	*March* De Valera resigned as President of Sinn Féin.
1926	*April* Launch of new Republican Party Fianna Fáil.
1927	*August 11th* De Valera signed the Oath of Allegiance following the assassination of O'Higgins and entered the Dáil.
1931	Launch of Fianna Fáil newspaper, the "Irish Press".
1932	Fianna Fáil election victory.
1932	*March - February 1948* The de Valera Years.
1932 - 38	The "economic war".
1937	The Constitution *Bunreacht na hÈireann*.
1938	*April* Anglo-Irish agreements.
1939 - 45	"Friendly" Neutrality in World War II.
1948	Election defeat.
1951- 54	Leader of minority government.
1957	Biggest electoral victory ever.
1959 - 73	President of Ireland for two terms.
1975	*August 29th* Death of de Valera.

7. Brookeborough

Early Influences

Basil Stanlake Brooke, Northern Ireland's longest ruling Premier (1943-63), was born on the Colebrooke estate in Co. Fermanagh on 9th June 1888. The 30,000 acre estate had been in the hands of the Brooke plantation family for almost 250 years. Basil Brooke, the eldest of five children, was given the education befitting a future member of the landed gentry. Private school in France was followed by attendance at an English public school in preparation for entry into the Royal Military Academy at Sandhurst. Brooke was an indifferent student and excelled only in marksmanship, becoming the best shot in Winchester public school between 1903 and 1905.

Brooke graduated from Sandhurst Military College in 1908 as a second lieutenant and served as a junior officer in the Indian sub-continent until mid-1912. He was back in Ulster during the stirring summer of 1912 when support for Carson and Craig's Ulster Unionist campaign seemed to be the only way to preserve the ascendancy of the Protestant landed gentry such as the Brookes of Colebrooke. On the 18th September 1912, he was one of the welcoming party who received Carson in Enniskillen at the start of the Covenant Campaign. Ten days later Brooke signed the Solemn League and Covenant at Colebrooke, appropriately one of the signing centres throughout the province. In mid-December 1912, he was appointed by the Orange Order to a sub-committee authorised to organise the formation and training of Ulster Volunteers. Colebrooke became a UVF stronghold. After the "Larne gun-running" of April 1914, one quarter of the arms in Unionist hands were held at Colebrooke which had the biggest armoury in Co. Fermanagh.

Basil Brooke (1888-1973)

Brooke was forced to abandon illegal military activity in 1913, however, and to return to official military duty firstly in South Africa and then in France upon the outbreak of World War I. The horror of trench warfare on the Western Front and the nightmare of the British withdrawal from Gallipoli filled Brooke with a healthy hatred of war. In response to the increased militancy in Ireland, which culminated in the Easter Rising 1916, Brooke wrote from the war front, "of the two evils, civil war or home rule, the former is the worse for Ireland." Brooke was at home on leave when the Easter Rising occurred. Predictably he condemned the Rising as a treasonous "stab in the back" in Britain's hour of need. He himself returned to the war front after receiving the Military Cross "for gallantry and devotion to duty in the field" at Gallipoli in 1915. Brooke rose to the rank of captain during the war but resigned officially from the army in March 1919 and returned to the family estate at Colebrooke which he had inherited outright in 1913. Upon the death of his father in 1907, Brooke inherited the baronetcy and became Sir Basil Brooke.

The Formation of the Ulster Special Constabulary

A short stay in Dublin from March to May 1920 upon the birth of his son (in 1919 Brooke had married an English girl) convinced Brooke of the need to set up an armed civilian force in Fermanagh in order to prevent what he described as, "the anarchy that had taken over the city" in the throes of the War of Independence. In June 1920, Brooke formed the first Fermanagh vigilante group consisting of fourteen men from his own estate. His wife, Lady Brooke, described the vigilantes in her diary thus, "an arrangement for mutual protection against Sinn Féin, in which two men from each townland do sentry duty one night per week." The success of the Fermanagh vigilante groups in preserving relative peace in Fermanagh (up to the 10th November 1920 of thirty-three police barracks attacked in Ulster only three were in Fermanagh) went a long way towards persuading the Lloyd George government to allow Unionists to assume responsibility for law and order in the six counties of Northern Ireland. On 8th September 1920, the decision was taken to form an Ulster Special Constabulary (USC) an armed locally-recruited paramilitary police force of upwards of 50,000 recruits divided into three categories, "A" whole-time paid officers serving with the regular police force, "B" part-time and paid and popularly known as "B" Specials and "C" an unpaid reserve force. Although Brooke was only "one of the originators" of the USC, his recommendation that the "B" Specials copy the command structure within the Fermanagh Vigilantes was adopted.

As with the Vigilantes, a chain of command within the "B" Specials left control of units within the hands of townland leaders who had a thorough knowledge of the people and area designated to them. Brooke, however, was not first choice for county commandant of the Fermanagh USC Brooke's close association with the illegal armed civilian force, the Fermanagh Vigilantes, initially damaged his prospects. Brooke's military record, however, best suited him for the full-time organisational post and, on 18th November 1920, just seven days after enrolment for 230 "A" and 2,500 "B" Specials in Fermanagh started, Brooke became county commandant. By mid-March 1921, Fermanagh was the only area within the Six Counties, apart from neighbouring Tyrone, to reach its recruitment quotas.

Brooke, in recalling the "troubles" of 1920-22, wrote "I had thought that my soldiering days were over . . . I was to become a soldier of a very different sort . . . defending my own birthplace." Brooke always considered that the greatest threat to Unionist Fermanagh came not from the small Nationalist majority within (the 1911 census showed that 52.6% of the Fermanagh population was Catholic) but from the largely Nationalist hostile bordering counties, Monaghan, Donegal and Cavan whose populations were over 75% Catholic and who were destined to form part of the Irish Free State. A spate of attacks by IRA flying columns based in Monaghan on isolated Unionist enclaves along the Monaghan/Fermanagh border between January and June 1921 drove large numbers of Loyalists, who lived in remote areas and saw the force as their only protection, into the ranks of the "B" Specials. The strategic vulnerability of Fermanagh surrounded by hostile Nationalist territory led to the decision in April 1921 to increase "B" Special strength from 2,500 to 3,000. The response to the "call to arms" was such, especially in remote border areas, — 1/3 of the total complement of "B" Specials in Fermanagh came from the border areas — that, by July 1921, "B" Special strength in Fermanagh was 2,620.

The truce on July 11th 1921 ending the War of Independence, suspended "B" Special activity and an uneasy peace descended on Fermanagh as on the rest of the country. Brooke, who had been awarded a C. B. E. on the occasion of the opening of the Northern Ireland Parliament on June 22nd 1921, toyed with the idea of becoming a N.I. Senator and therefore, of resigning from his position as County Commandant of the USC. Brooke, however, resigned from the Senate in February 1922 in order to resume full-time leadership of the USC as his native county plunged from relative peace to the brink of civil war in the immediate wake of the Anglo-Irish Treaty. Article 12 of the Anglo-Irish Treaty of 6th December 1921 allowing for a Boundary Commission to decide the border between Unionist Northern Ireland and the Irish Free State was greeted with dismay by Fermanagh Unionists and with rejoicing by Fermanagh Nationalists who hoped that boundary changes would bring Fermanagh into the Irish Free State. (A "rebel" Sinn Féin Fermanagh Co. Council had already, in November 1921, declared its non-recognition of the N.I. government and was subsequently dissolved).

Two spectacular border incidents in February 1922 were the mass kidnapping of over forty prominent Unionists along the Fermanagh-Tyrone border with Monaghan on the night of 7/8th February 1922 and the "battle of Clones" on 11th February 1922 when the IRA attacked a party of "A" category constables who had violated Free State jurisdiction by crossing the border at Clones on their way from Newtownards to Enniskillen. In the ensuing gun-battle four "A" Specials died as did the IRA commandant. There was deliberate and dramatic exaggeration of both these events in the Unionist press with such sensational headlines as "War on Ulster" in the Belfast "Newsletter" and "Murders, Woundings and Wholesale Kidnappings" in the "Tyrone Constitution" which grossly exaggerated the kidnappings by reporting "Two hundred prominent Protestants, Orangemen and Special Police were kidnapped and taken across the border." The outbreak of actual civil war in the Free State plus the introduction of repressive Special Powers legislation in N.I., making possible the internment of over fifty leading Fermanagh Nationalists including the future Westminister M.P. Cahir Healy, saved Fermanagh and Northern Ireland from civil war. By mid-1922 there were 3,500 "A" and "B" Specials in Fermanagh in addition to recently formed RUC which, from June 1922, replaced the RIC as the armed police-force of Northern Ireland. The successful defence of the border areas in the early years ensured that although the "A" and "C" categories were disbanded in 1925, the "B" Specials remained the primary defenders of the border until their replacement by the British-controlled Ulster Defence Regiment in 1969. Although Brooke resigned as County Commandant in May 1929 upon election to Stormont, he always spoke with fondness of "his" "B" Specials. The "B" Specials were always hated and dreaded by their Catholic/Nationalist neighbours. Amid mounting criticism in the Sixties before their dissolution, Lord Brookeborough (Sir Basil Brooke had become Lord Brookeborough in 1952) came out of retirement to speak of his pride in still being an honorary commandant and spoke of "the reassuring effect of having a properly organised and strictly disciplined force on the roads."

Rise to Political Prominence

Brooke wrote in July 1920, "I am not a politician . . ." but he added, "I know what is being thought by the people here." His involvement with the USC had brought him to the notice of Craig, N.I.'s first Prime Minister. On a visit to Colebrooke in January 1924, Craig described Brooke as "one of the finest leaders in Ulster today." Brooke decided to contest the local government elections in 1924. The abolition of PR and the redrawing of local government electoral constituencies enabled the Unionists to take control of councils in Nationalist areas. The Nationalist newspaper, the "Irish News" described the local elections as "a farce". Nationalists refused to contest a single seat in Fermanagh and Tyrone and Brooke had no difficulty in being returned as Unionist councillor for the newly-created local government district of Brookeborough. In the absence of Sinn Féin representation, Brooke was one of the fourteen Unionist councillors to put the Unionist case for retention of the existing border to the Boundary Commission when submissions were invited from the "borderline" county of Fermanagh. Healy, local Nationalist leader, whose internment prevented him from presenting a Nationalist case for revision, dismissed Brooke's arguments for retention as based on "land, bullocks and poor rates . . . not the will of human beings." The successful outcome of the Boundary issue enhanced Brooke's political reputation. In 1928, he became chairman of Fermanagh county council. Next year, he was returned unopposed as Unionist member for the N.I. parliament for Lisnaskea, one of the new single-member seats created in March 1929 under the Redistribution Act of 1928.

From his first day in Parliament, Brooke was a junior member of government. As a Unionist whip and assistant parliamentary secretary to the Minister of Finance, Brooke was an uncritical government supporter. From 1932, he took an increasing interest in the activities of the Ministry of Agriculture and Fisheries. Upon the resignation of the 80-year old Minister of Agriculture, fellow Fermanagh man, Archdale, in November 1933, Brooke succeeded to the key government post of agriculture in December 1933.

Before Brooke became a senior member of government, he made, on 12th July 1933, at an Orange Order demonstration in the mainly Nationalist Fermanagh village of Newtownbutler, the most controversial speech of his political career. In a speech which was otherwise moderate in tone and unremarkable in content, he launched into a tirade of abuse against Catholics declaring that they were "out with all their force and might to destroy the power and constitution of Ulster. There was a definite plot to overpower the vote of Unionists in the north." Announcing that "he had not a Roman Catholic about his own place" he appealed to loyalists "wherever possible to employ protestant lads and lassies." Such a provocative speech at the height of the Great Depression exacerbated sectarian divisions. Amid escalating sectarian violence and, in the face of mounting criticism from Nationalists led by Fermanagh MP Healy, Brooke refused to retract one word. PM Craig, although acknowledging that he spoke "entirely on his own when he made the speech", added "there is not one of my colleagues who does not entirely agree with him and I would not ask him to withdraw one word." Brooke's sectarian outburst in 1933, contrasted sharply with statements made in 1922 when he is on record as saying "it did not matter what his religion was so long as he was a good man and knew his job". Brooke, however, was convinced that Catholic farm labourers from the Free State working for prosperous Protestant farmers were contributing to the increasing Catholic population in Fermanagh. Brooke remained unrepentant. In an interview given in 1968 after his retirement, Lord Brookeborough was still referring to Roman Catholics as the enemy "out to destroy Northern Ireland."

Minister for Agriculture

The "Fermanagh Times" of August 1939 reported Brooke as saying that he was "more interested in agriculture than in politics." Describing himself as "drain-cleaner in chief" Brooke retained an active and abiding interest in agriculture throughout his public life. His first-hand knowledge of the needs and problems of the North's farmers, stemming from membership of Ulster Farmers' Union and membership of the Fermanagh Farming Society, made him an ideal choice for the prestigious post of Minister of Agriculture. The permanent decline of the old-established ship-building and linen industries upon which Unionist Ulster had built its prosperity and its economic argument for the Union during the years before World War I, gave a new significance to agriculture, N.I.'s largest single industry. Upon Brooke's appointment in December 1933 PM Craig described agriculture as undergoing "one of the greatest revolutions in the history of our country." The greater revolution, however, was taking place in Britain which had finally moved from free-trade to a programme of protection which included, as well as tariffs and import quotas, subsidies and marketing legislation. This had the double advantage for agricultural products of both raising standards and guaranteeing prices. Brooke was determined to secure similar assistance for N.I.'s producers.

The cornerstone of Brooke's agricultural policy was laid in a measure passed before he took office. The Agricultural Marketing Act of 1933 enabled the setting up of boards, similar to those already functioning in Britain, for the marketing of a range of farm produce. Brooke's agricultural achievements between 1933 and 1939 have been described as a triumph of "adaptability". While not innovating policy, Brooke extracted optimum benefit for N.I. farmers from schemes and subsidies introduced in Britain.

Both the quality and quantity of agricultural produce improved dramatically under the strict marketing control provided by marketing boards from 1934. Northern Ireland's small farm units were particularly suited to pig production. Yet in the late 1920's almost 40% of pigs slaughtered for bacon were imported from the Free State. Stable rising prices for pig products assured by the Pig Marketing Board from 1934 encouraged small farmers to turn to profitable pig production. By the late 1930's, N.I. accounted for 1/4 of all U.K. pig production. Milk subsidies provided by Britain and price and quality control by the newly-formed Joint Milk Council gave the N.I. consumer "by far the cheapest milk supply in the United Kingdom" according to Brooke in 1936. An egg marketing scheme introduced in 1936 was described by Brooke as "an innovation without parallel in Great Britain." Attempts to popularise tillage farming, however, by subsidies on oats and barley, failed, largely due to the availability of cheap imported animal food in the pre-war years. Brooke's "progressive pre-war policy" acknowledged by the Unionist newspaper the "Northern Whig" in December 1940, had brought about what was described as a "veritable revolution in agriculture since the war" and enabled N.I. to take advantage of uniform guaranteed prices throughout war-time Britain and Northern Ireland. The war-time decision by the British government to buy directly from the N.I. farmer saved the N.I. farmer the costly transport costs to British mainland markets. Northern Ireland was able to supply one-fifth of all eggs consumed in the UK during the war. By the end of the war not only was N.I. able to supply its own milk requirements but it was also sending three million gallons to war-time Britain. The contrast with the relatively slow development of agriculture in Eire, both before and during the war years, prompted N.I.'s official historian of the war years, Blake, to make the exaggerated boast that to travel South from N.I. "was to be transported in a matter of minutes from the twentieth to the seventeenth century".

Brooke was described by the "Belfast Telegraph" at the beginning of the war as "Ulster's busiest minister." The dynamism of the Ministry of Agriculture contrasted sharply with the inertia of other government ministries. Government critics in the dying days of the Craig government in 1940 urged that Brooke, who, although fifty-two years old, was considered "a young virile able man" compared with his aged colleagues, be given new and increased ministerial responsibilities. Despite speculation that Brooke might succeed Craig and despite Brooke's own belief that Craig was "grooming" him for the leadership, Craig was succeeded by J.M. Andrews, like Craig a founding member of the N.I. state and just one year younger than Craig. Brooke had to wait for almost three years and to threaten resignation on at least three occasions between December 1940 and April 1943 before Andrews' resignation in May 1943 gave Brooke the opportunity to become N.I.'s longest ruling prime minister.

Brooke and World War II

Brooke was being described by the "Belfast Telegraph" as early as January 1940 as "The man the war made." Andrews, Craig's successor as PM, offered Brooke the senior government post of Minister of Finance. Brooke declined in favour of the less prestigious but, during war-time, more important post of Minister of Commerce. In 1941, Brooke took over a moribund junior ministry dealing with "odds and ends" and not fully responsible for either production or supply. The Ministry of Supply based in London controlled food rationing and decided petrol and fuel requirements for Northern Ireland as well as fixing prices and allocating raw materials to N.I.'s industries. Brooke noted with dissatisfaction that not one of the area supply officers in Northern Ireland had any connection with the Ministry of Commerce. One of Brooke's major achievements as Minister for Commerce was the setting up, in June 1941, of a Production Council chaired by himself and appointed by the Ministry of Commerce. Brooke agreed with critics that Northern Ireland was "only half in the war in the industrial sphere" but argued that his department could increase production "simply by personal contact and powers to deal on the spot with the constant union difficulties". Prohibition of strikes and lock-outs, from August 1940, did little to ease industrial unrest which frequently threatened to disrupt production in key industries such as Short Bros. and Harland aircraft production. As Minister for Commerce and Production from February 1942 Brooke earned the reputation of being the man of action who got things done. Unemployment was still rising in January 1941. By June 1941, it had fallen by 30,000. Although unemployment continued to fall, Brooke was unhappy that 5% of the insured population, 19,000, were still unemployed in April 1943 on the eve of his premiership. Brooke blamed the insufficient flow of work into Northern Ireland and made sixteen trips to London as Minister of Commerce and Production in order to gain vital war contracts for Northern Ireland.

World War II gave a new lease of life to the depressed shipbuilding and textile industries. Employment in shipbuilding almost trebled as 150 new ships were built during the war. Belfast's engineering industries benefited from the revived shipbuilding and from a rapidly growing aircraft industry. The Short Bros. aircraft factory had only started production in 1937. Its war-time output of bombers alone was 1,500 and employment quadrupled from 5,800 in 1938 to 23,500 in 1945. Even in the declining linen industry, hampered by chronic flax shortages, war contracts for uniforms and military supplies were met.

Not only was Brooke the "only effective minister" in an otherwise weak ineffective government, in the words of a contemporary Southern Unionist, he was also chairman of the Home Defence Executive. Brooke, two of whose sons were killed during the war, advocated conscription but accepted the British government decision not to extend conscription to N.I. and contented himself with the formation of an Ulster home guard drawn largely from the ranks of the trusted "B" Specials to deal with the twin threat of German invasion and German-supported IRA attaks. In addition, he was deputy Prime Minister and chairman of a government committee planning for post-war reconstruction.

Andrews' appointment as Prime Minister in November 1940 was "generally received with resignation rather than enthusiasm" according to Barton, Brookeborough's biographer. From the outset, Brooke urged Andrews to get rid of the old men in the government whose increasing incompetence over the years had brought the Craig government into disrepute. Andrews at almost seventy years, steadfastly refused to countenance change. A series of by-election defeats from March 1941 when the government suffered the humiliation of losing the safe North Down seat of the former PM Craig to an Independent Unionist showed that Unionist supporters were losing confidence in the government. Further defeats gave another safe seat to Labour and returned a Labour MP at a Westminster by-election in West Belfast.

The government came under severe criticism during the "blitz" of Belfast in April-May 1941. Fear of a sustained bombardment on vulnerable Belfast was a factor in British reluctance to award large war contracts to Northern Ireland during 1940/'41. Yet civil defence materials had been sent to Britain in the mistaken belief that N.I. would escape aerial bombardment. Consequently, when the bombs fell on 15/16 April 1941, resources were "completely inadequate to the task which faced them" in the view of Brigadier Watson, Commander of the Belfast area. PM Andrews was forced to make a public plea for outside help, answered with alacrity by the neighbouring de Valera government. Thirteen fire engines from Dublin, Drogheda and Dundalk helped quench the fires both in April and again in May, when fractured water mains threatened to hamper fire-fighting in the city until the arrival of fire units from the South with sufficiently long hoses to tap the waters of the River Lagan. Public despair was reflected in the thousands who nightly left the city and returned at dawn. For a brief period, the war bridged sectarian divides as Protestants and Catholics knelt together in silent homage to the 745 killed in the first wave of bombing. Border differences were set aside as representatives from the Eire government travelled to Belfast to discuss with their N.I. counterparts how best to alleviate the refugee problem. One hundred thousand had been left homeless. Good relations, however, were soured in 1942 by an upsurge in IRA violence. Although the threat of an IRA-led German invasion had receded, the shooting dead of N.I.'s first policeman in ten years in April 1942 resulted in N.I.'s first hanging of a convicted Republican terrorist in September 1942. Mass escapes in 1942 of IRA prisoners prompted serious questions about internal security and further undermined the government.

A decision in November 1942 to postpone a general election due in March 1943 was the signal for not just a backbenchers' revolt but also a revolt by junior ministers. Brooke supported the call for change, but Andrews was as obdurate in 1943 as he had been in 1940. On April 30th 1943, he resigned rather than change his cabinet. Brooke, aged 55 years, succeeded to the premiership on May 1st 1943.

Brooke's Premiership (1943 - 63)
Change without change

Brooke was generally perceived as the "new broom" who would bring about the sweeping changes which were so long overdue. Government ministers were warned at the first government meeting that "no one was to consider himself permanently in the job." Close inspection of his cabinet, however, reveals no clean sweep. Although one non-Unionist (former Labour M.P. Midgley whose by-election victory in 1941 had robbed Andrews of crucial support) was given cabinet rank and, although Brooke rewarded two "rebel" junior ministers who had helped bring about Andrews' downfall, five of the seven members of cabinet had been members of the previous government.

In his first address to Parliament as Prime Minister, Brooke defined his policies thus, "to continue to maintain the existing constitutional position of Northern Ireland, to bring the utmost vigour to the task of assisting the war effort . . . and to make further preparation for dealing with the problems of the post-war period." Brooke was lucky to take over the premiership in 1943 when allied victory in World War II was virtually assured, just as he had been lucky to become Minister of Agriculture in December 1933 when N.I. was about to reap the benefit of major policy changes evolving in Britain. Similarly, Brooke's transfer to Commerce in January 1941 came at a time when the N.I. economy was at last gearing itself to war-time production. Brooke retained Commerce and Production until 1945, a measure of the significance he attached to war-time production. Brooke was particularly anxious to meet every need of the American troops who, from early 1942, used Northern Ireland as a forward base for the planned Allied invasion of Occupied France in 1944. Brooke noted with pride, "we are the first to welcome American troops. I think it is a great honour." Although not then PM, he was happy to act as host to the Americans and extended the hospitality of his Colebrooke home and estate to them. Brooke fully appreciated the economic significance of the American military presence in Northern Ireland. The building of a US naval base at Derry employed three thousand local workers at peak construction. Stone production from local quarries rose from 400,000 tons per annum to 400,000 per month as a massive programme of airfield construction, supply depots and barracks got under way to meet the requirements of over 100,000 US combat troops.

Brooke's main concern from 1943 was to ensure sustained growth after the war. One positive aspect of the "blitz" in 1941 was to physically remove some of the worst slums in Belfast and to expose the evil of appalling living standards in working class areas. A long overdue review of housing revealed an immediate shortfall of 100,000 houses but recommended radical slum clearance which would require double that number. A N.I .Housing Act (1945) set up a government-sponsored N.I. Housing Trust. By 1963, the year of Brookeborough's resignation as Prime Minister, 112,383 new houses had been built, over half of which had been built by local authorities and the Housing Trust. Such houses were frequently allocated to unmarried Unionists by Unionist-dominated local councils. These local councils successfully resisted, both in 1946 and again in 1962, attempts to introduce "one man one vote" in local government elections. Conceded in Britain in 1948, "one man, one vote" was the burning issue central to the Civil Rights campaign of the late 1960's which was eventually to bring down the N.I. regime.

The Welfare State

The war years brought enormous change to Northern Ireland as well as to the rest of Europe. From the outset tight control was exercised from Westminster on "many matters which in peace would have come automatically under the jurisdiction of the parliament", observed N.I.'s official war historian, J. W. Blake. Further, Blake noted, "policy would be formulated . . . at Westminster in the light of broad strategic and national considerations often having little or no bearing on the special requirements of Northern Ireland." For the most part, the N.I. government was happy to go along with British policy, especially plans for social and economic development leading to a welfare state, envisaged in the Beveridge Report of 1942. The British Chancellor of the Exchequer reiterated the 1938 Simon Declaration of Parity and privately assured N. I. Prime Minister Andrews, in 1942, that not only would existing and new services advance "step by step" with services in Britain but where "leeway" had to be made up "the principle of parity requires us to do so". Northern Ireland looked forward to the introduction of a welfare state in Northern Ireland similar to that about to be set up in Britain. In anticipation of a state medical service, a ministry of health and local government was established in June 1944.

The foundation stones of the post-war welfare state were laid in the National Insurance Act 1946, the Industrial Injuries Act 1946, the Education Act 1947, the National Assistance Act 1948 and the National Health Service Act 1946, operational from July 1948. It was generally acknowledged that the cost of providing such welfare services could not be met by the N. I. exchequer. By the 1960s direct payment by the U.K. to Northern Ireland amounted to on average £45m. per annum. Growing economic dependence on Britain brought with it even greater loss of autonomy. In 1946 the annual NI budget and indeed all supplementary budgets had to be approved in advance by Westminster. One contemporary observer described the relationship thus, "Instead of managing our own house we were living in furnished lodgings under a benevolent landlord."

If the gulf between living standards in Northern Ireland and mainland Britain narrowed after the war, the gulf between living standards and expectations in N.I. and the rest of Ireland widened so dramatically as to render Irish unity economically impractical. It has been estimated that in 1968, in order to provide welfare standards throughout all of Ireland at levels provided in Northern Ireland by Britain in

1968/'69, taxation levels, already high in the Republic, would have had to be raised by a punitive 60%. Yet uneasiness and a defensive attitude both to the Southern Ireland government and to the Nationalist minority within Northern Ireland persisted. Nor did better living conditions under a British welfare state, whose provisions applied equally to all, irrespective of creed, foster gratitude or acceptance in the N.I. minority. Each new provision was jealously scrutinised for possible discrimination against the minority. An attempt by the N.I. government to deviate from the terms of the Westminster enacted Family Allowance and National Insurance Act of 1956, designed to give larger (generally Catholic) families proportionately more money than smaller (usually Protestant) families, was successfully resisted. The same payments were made in Northern Ireland as in Britain but the N.I. government's reputation for "fair and equal treatment" suffered. Equally the government's refusal to subsidise the Catholic Mater Hospital in Belfast, which refused to recognise the N.I. Hospital Authority, was seen as further discrimination against the minority.

In the field of education, however, the Brooke administration, while failing to end segregated education or bring Catholic schools into the state educational system, did provide free second and third level education to all on the basis of merit. The 1947 Education Act (N.I.) followed the main provisions of the Butler Act 1944 which provided competitive entry into second-level education at age 11 years and into grant-aided third-level education. By 1964, Northern Ireland with a population less than half that of the Republic had 95,000 students in second-level education compared with 85,000 in the Republic. Expenditure on third-level education was three times higher in Northern Ireland. Significantly, the 1925 and 1930 amendments requiring teachers to give compulsory Bible instruction were declared illegal. Despite opposition from Protestant pressure groups, a "conscience clause" allowed teachers to opt out of Bible teaching and opened up the possibility of Catholic teachers being appointed to teach Protestant children. In addition the state grant to voluntary schools was raised from 50% to 65% and the number of pupils in largely Catholic grant-aided schools increased from 213,211 to 295,855 between 1945 and 1963. An important consequence of the provision of free second and third-level education to all was to educate an articulate Catholic middle-class, whose sense of grievance at being excluded for religious reasons from public and professional jobs for which they were qualified, was acute. Middle-class Catholics and Catholic university students spearheaded the movement for reform in the 1960's which was eventually to bring about the downfall of the Stormont regime.

Relations with Britain

World War II was a watershed in the history of Northern Ireland. Social and economic change, undreamt of before the war, had transformed the lives of the people within ten years of the end of the war and at no additional cost to the N.I. state. Northern Ireland's loyal participation in the British war effort contrasted sharply with Eire's determined neutrality and drew from Churchill, British war leader, warm tributes both during the war and at war's end. In May 1943, when the war had still to be won, Churchill said, "the bonds of affection between Great Britain and the people of Northern Ireland have been tempered by fire and are now, I firmly believe, unbreakable." The strategic significance of N.I., especially after the fall of France in 1940, strengthened these bonds. Churchill's victory speech of 13th May 1945 acknowledged a new British awareness of Ulster's strategic value to Britain, "a strong loyal Ulster will always be vital to the security and well-being of our whole empire and commonwealth."

Yet the Unionist ascendancy had little cause for complacency as the war ended. Labour's landslide victory in the British post-war general election in July 1945 meant that a Labour government, not pledged to Unionist domination in Northern Ireland, ruled in Britain. Unionist representation at Westminster supported the Conservative Unionist opposition and frequently voted against the Labour government's welfare proposals which were bringing such benefit to Northern Ireland. Ironically, the Unionist Party, conservative, and drawing its support from predominantly the landed and propertied middle class, was ideologically opposed to the "creeping socialism" of the Labour government and to the increasing state intervention which marked the coming of the welfare state.

The British Labour Party numbered among its members some of the Unionist regime's most outspoken critics. A group of some thirty British Labour M.P.s called themselves "Friends of Ireland" and declared themselves sympathetic to the idea of a united Ireland. The Nationalist opposition expressed their satisfaction at the return of a Labour government at Westminster by returning en masse to both Stormont and Westminster Parliaments. Since 1937 only two Nationalist M.P.s from Belfast had attended Stormont with any regularity. In 1945, the two Nationalist M.P.s for Fermanagh and Tyrone took their seats at Stormont for the first time. Catholic businessmen throughout Northern Ireland and their Nationalist leaders hoped to capitalise on sympathy for Irish aspirations both in Britain and in Eire. The emergence there of a new republican party, Clann na Poblachta, in 1946 and its rapid growth between 1946 and the general election in 1948, when it won ten seats and contributed to the defeat of de Valera after sixteen years in power, encouraged Northern Nationalists. In November 1945 at a meeting at Dungannon, attended by 500 representatives of "nationally minded" groups, the Anti-Partition League was launched. Its aim was to mount a propaganda campaign against the border by holding anti-partition rallies not just throughout N.I. but also in Britain and the U.S.

Alarmed, Brooke's Unionist government went on the defensive. The Safeguarding of Employment Act of December 1947 restricted employment to N. I. residents and was aimed against Southern workers who had crossed the border during the war in search of war-time work. Fourteen years after his "employ no Catholics" speeches in 1933 Brooke was still haunted by the fear of an "invasion" of Southern workers who would boost the numbers of a growing Catholic nationalist minority. (Census figures revealed a small increase in the Catholic population of N.I. from 33.5% in 1926 to 34.9% in 1961).

The Ireland Act 1949

Alarm turned to anger and suspicion in 1948 when it became clear that the Inter-Party Coalition government of Costello intended to repeal the External Relations Act, Eire's last link with Britain and to pass a Republic of Ireland Act in December 1948. Brooke sought consultation with Attlee, the British Labour Prime Minister, in November 1948 but British government assurance to Northern Ireland did not come until June 1949, almost two months after the official declaration of the Irish Republic on Easter Monday 18th April 1949. The Ireland Act, whilst acknowledging that Eire had ceased to be a dominion state on 18th April 1949, declared "that Northern Ireland remains part of . . . the United Kingdom" and, most significantly for the Unionist-dominated N.I. parliament, "that in no event will Northern Ireland or any part thereof cease to be part of . . . the United Kingdom without the consent of the Parliament of Northern Ireland." This was the kind of statutory assurance of Northern Ireland's constitutional position which Unionists had always craved. That it should be made by a Labour government not previously committed to partition was an added triumph. In addition the Northern Ireland Labour Party, previously uncommitted on partition, announced its acceptance of the constitutional position of Northern Ireland in January 1949 and thereafter became a pro-partition party. Northern Ireland's constitutional position, although strengthened by the 1949 declaration, still recognised the supremacy of the Westminster parliament, which could at any time repeal either or both legislative measures, the Ireland Act of 1949 or the Goverment of Ireland Act of 1920, which had brought the Northern Ireland state into being.

Unionist Ulster chose to interpret the Republic of Ireland Act of 1949 as the cementing of partition in Ireland. The Unionist newspaper, the "Newsletter", greeted Costello's dramatic announcement in Canada of his government's intention to leave the Commonwealth with a reference to "the yawning gulf that separates Ulster from Eire." Brooke chose, in February 1949, to hold an election, the "Union Jack" election, declaring "Our country is in danger . . . we fight to defend our very existence and the heritage of our Ulster children . . . our determination to remain under the Union Jack should be immediately and overwhelmingly reaffirmed." The Unionists increased their majority by three seats to 37. Eleven Anti-partition candidates were returned however, nine of them Anti-Partition League candidates and the other two anti-partition Labour candidates who refused to accept the N.I.L.P.'s position on partition. Nonetheless, the visit of the future Queen Elizabeth to Northern Ireland in 1949 and Brooke's elevation to the peerage in 1952 as Lord Brookeborough were seen as further signs of approval of Unionist ascendancy in Northern Ireland. The return of a Conservative Unionist government in Britain in 1951 was further reassurance for Lord Brookeborough who looked forward to the 1950's with increased confidence.

I.R.A. terrorism : The "Border War" (1956 - 62)

Yet the 1950's brought little peace of mind. The Brookeborough government remained uneasy about the failure of successive British governments to treat Irish citizens in Britain as aliens. An upsurge of sectarian violence, sparked off by flag-waving and marching during the traditional summer marching season, resulted in a Public Order Act in 1951 empowering police to cancel or reroute parades. The Flags and Emblems Act of 1954 forbade all flags other than the Union Jack and was regarded as deliberately provocative by the Nationalist minority. Renewed terrorist activity, with raids on military barracks in a desperate search for arms and the emergence of an I.R.A. splinter group, Saor Uladh (Free Ulster) in 1952, led to the most serious outbreak of I.R.A. violence since the border war of the early 1920's. In December 1956, an I.R.A. manifesto proclaimed a border war. By March 1957, a sustained offensive on R.U.C. barracks and customs posts along the border was beginning to lose momentum but the "war" spluttered on for another six years and represented the most protracted I.R.A. military campaign against the state since its inception. The release of war-time activists on both sides of the border in the early 1950's had enabled the I.R.A. to regroup. The anti-partition campaign mounted by both government and opposition in the Irish Republic since 1949 had encouraged extremists.

Decisive action, however, especially by de Valera and the Fianna Fáil government which reintroduced internment in July 1957, dealt a serious blow to the insurgents. Internment of suspects without trial on both sides of the border, vigilant policing by R.U.C. and "B" Specials, with back-up by the British army where necessary, proved too powerful for a weak and divided I.R.A. leadership. Nonetheless, 600 terrorist incidents between 1956 and 1962 including, an abortive attack upon police barracks in Lord Brookeborough's own home town of Brookeborough resulted in nineteen deaths, six of whom were policemen, and in the internment of some 335 sympathisers in the north and 100 in the south. The N.I. government felt sufficiently confident about border security to release all internees before the official ending of the campaign in February 1962. The I.R.A. attributed their failure to the lack of local support especially among the Nationalist minority who showed no enthusiasm for unity brought about by violence. "Foremost among the factors responsible for the ending of the campaign has been the attitude of the general public" stated the I.R.A. manifesto of February 1962. The "Ulster Year Book 1965", the official record of these years, also acknowledged this, "By contrast with the state of affairs in the 1920's there was no civil strife." The border war 1956 - 62 served to reinforce partition. Firm decisive action by the Irish government showed that the Irish Republic was as opposed as N.I. was to the ending of partition by the use of force.

Lord Brookeborough - the longest ruling N.I. Premier (1943-63)

Disillusionment and Decline

In 1962, Lord Brookeborough, aged 74 years fought his last general election. Coming in the wake of the defeat of the I.R.A. it should have been a triumph for Unionism. For the first time since the foundation of the state, the border seemed safe. Unionist voters were able to concentrate on social and economic issues. The economic record of the post-war years was not as good as supporters of the N.I. regime had hoped. The election results of the 1950's reflect increasing dissatisfaction among Unionist voters. In 1953, Unionists had won 38 of the 52 seats in the N.I. parliament, in 1958 just 37 and in 1962 Unionist representation dropped to 34 with no Independent Unionists elected. On the two occasions on which Unionist representation had been lower, in 1945 when it was 33, and in 1925 when it was only 32, Independent Unionists had held two and four seats respectively. In 1962, the anti-Unionist Opposition numbered 18 the largest in the history of the N.I. Parliament. The most significant political development of the 1950's, the growth of the N.I. Labour Party, which in 1962 held the four seats they had won in 1958, mirrored dissatisfaction with the economic stagnation and decline of the last years of Brookeborough's rule.

Brookeborough knew that, in order to maintain the economic momentum of the war years, aid would have to be given to the heavy industries which had benefited from war-time demands but which went into irreversible decline during the post-war years. The fall in world shipping demands meant that over 7,000 shipyard jobs were lost in 1961. A government report on the economy of Northern Ireland, the Hall Report published in 1962, recommended that further resources should not be spent propping up uncompetitive outdated industries. Instead, N. I.'s industrial base must be broadened. A series of Industries Development Acts (1945-53) were designed both to assist the old ship-building and textile industries to adapt to a changed post-war world and to attract new industries. The government's record in attracting new, mainly British, industries was good. By 1962, eighty-four advance factories had been set up. New enterprises included Courtaulds rayon factory at Carrickfergus in 1950, an acrilan plant at Coleraine in 1959 and Standard Telephones and Cables outside Belfast in 1962. Discontented Nationalists noted, however, that only 10% of new jobs were sited in predominantly Nationalists areas west of the River Bann. In all, 42,000 jobs had been created since the war. Nonetheless, unemployment, which did not disappear even during the peak production years of the war, remained on average three to four times higher than other regional blackspots throughout the U.K. in the period 1956-62. The year 1958 recorded 50,000 job losses. Job losses were highest in the old industries, shipbuilding, linen, with the closure of one-third of linen plants between 1958 and 1964, and agriculture where mechanisation had replaced the agricultural labourer. An "Economic Survey of Northern Ireland" commissioned by the government in 1947, completed in 1955 and published in 1957, was critical of the government's economic record during the first decade after the war. While acknowledging "industrial handicaps" such as "climate, lack of fuel and other raw materials and the remoteness of the chief British markets" the survey concluded that "Northern Ireland is worse off economically than it would be if the Government of Ireland Act were repealed and the semblance of self government were thereby removed." Its startling conclusion "that provincial autonomy had been a doubtful privilege economically" was an indictment of Unionist administration in Northern Ireland. Northern Ireland still remained the poorest part of the United Kingdom.

The Brookeborough administration had, therefore, failed to live up to the promise of its early years. After twenty years, Brookeborough had become a tired old man (like Craig in 1940) whom younger ministers like Terence O'Neill, with conflicting ideological viewpoints such as conciliation of the Catholic minority in Northern Ireland and economic co-operation with the Republic, wanted to push aside. On March 25th, 1963 pleading ill-health as a reason, Lord Brookeborough in his seventy-fifth year resigned. Ten years later, Lord Brookeborough died on the 12th August 1973. One year before his death, he saw all that he had held dearly during his public life crumble as the Unionist regime came to a turbulent end with the imposition of direct rule from Westminster in March 1972.

Appraisal

Tributes paid to Lord Brookeborough at the time of his death in 1973 described him as "a leader and inspirer of the Ulster people" especially at times of crisis as during the 1920's and during World War II. The British newspaper "The Times" however, condemned his "refusal to bring the Roman Catholic minority into active participation in public affairs" as "a serious blemish on his political record." The sectarian strife, which at the time of his death, was tearing N.I. asunder was attributable, in the opinion of "The Times", to the "immobility imposed in his long period of political leadership." The most scathing condemnation came, however, from his successor, Prime Minister O'Neill who described Brookeborough as "a lazy man of limited ability". O'Neill wrote in his autobiography, "Those who met him imagined that he was relaxing away from his desk, what they didn't realise was that there was no desk." Listing as his only attribute his "immense personal charm" O'Neill commented, "The tragedy of his premiership was that he did not use his tremendous charm and his deep Orange roots to try to persuade his devoted followers to accept necessary reforms."

The Brookeborough Years have often been described as the locust years, the years of lost opportunity. Among Brookeborough's sins of omission were continued rejection of the minority, refusal to recognise N.I. trade unions which were affiliated to a Dublin based T.U.C. and his condemnation of long-term economic planning as being "a socialist menace." Although it was not realised at the time, Brookeborough presided over the final years of Unionist ascendancy. The golden age of Ulster Unionism 1945-65 coincided with the greatest period of change in the history of Northern Ireland. In the words of historian, F. S. L. Lyons "Within a decade Northern Ireland passed from the status of an exceptionally backward area to full membership of the welfare state." Visible signs of the province's prosperity included the opening of N.I.'s first motorway in July 1962. Yet it was a time of change without change. Increasing government control, a consequence of the welfare state, was seized upon as an opportunity to increase Unionist domination and to polarise even more N.I.'s divided society.

Throughout his premiership, Brookeborough remained what he always was, a Fermanagh squire ever influenced by the enemy from within, the Nationalist majority in Co. Fermanagh, and the enemy, from without, the Republic just across the Co. Fermanagh border. In defence of his own prejudices Brookeborough wrote in 1968, "it must be remembered that I lived through . . . the most troubled of times."

Landmarks in Brookeborough's Life   (1888 - 1973)

1888	*June 9th* — Born at Colebrooke, Co. Fermanagh.
1920	*November* — A founder of the Ulster Special Constabulary.
1929	*May* — Elected as Unionist MP for Lisnaskea, Co. Fermanagh.
1933	*July 12th* — Controversial "employ no Catholics" speech.
1933-41	*December-January* Minister of Agriculture.
1941-43	*January-April* Minister of Commerce and Production.
1943-63	*May 1- March 25* Premiership.
1949	Ireland Act.
1956- 62	Border War.
1963	*March* — Resignation.
1973	*August* — Death of Lord Brookeborough.

8. O'Neill

Early Influences

Terence Marne O'Neill, Lord Brookeborough's successor as Prime Minister, and arguably the most controversial of N.I.'s Prime Ministers, was born on 10th September 1914 in London. Born in England but descended on his father's side from one of the ancient Gaelic royal families, O'Neill was not cast in the mould of traditional Ulster Unionists. His birth in September 1914 coincided with the battle of the Marne, the first big battle of World War I, hence his second name Marne. Prime Minister O'Neill differed from his predecessors in having no personal memory of the Ulster Unionist Campaign against Home Rule, of the 1916 Rising, of the War of Independence or of the developments 1920-21 which led to the birth of the Northern Ireland state. Yet his father, Unionist M.P. for mid-Antrim since 1910 and the first soldier M.P. to be killed in World War I, had been a Carsonite and had helped to drill and train the U.V.F. in the pre-war period. Similarly, the ancestral home of the O'Neill family, Shane Castle on the shores of Lough Neagh was burned down in 1922 as part of the IRA campaign against the big houses of the landed Anglo-Irish gentry. O'Neill, however, referred to this incident in his autobiography thus: "I was always determined that this early event in my life should in no way influence my outlook on Irish affairs, and it never did."

Terence O'Neill, N.I. Premier (1963-69)

O'Neill was brought up as a typical young English gentleman. Attendance at a private school in Winchester was followed by public-school education at Eton, England's most prestigious public school. In 1922, O'Neills' English mother remarried a British Ambassador. The inter-war years were spent in areas as diverse as Abyssinia before the Italian conquest in 1935, and Austria before the Anschluss. School holidays were spent occasionally with relatives in Northern Ireland but O'Neill did not live there for a prolonged period of time until after World War II and can be said to have acquired a rich experience of life but in areas other than Northern

Ireland. O'Neill did not regard birth and upbringing outside Northern Ireland as a handicap to a political career within Northern Ireland. His greatest admiration was reserved for a Private Secretary Bloomfield, whose parents were English. O'Neill wrote of him thus, "his English origins made it possible for him to see things in a wider context."

O'Neill was in Australia when World War II broke out in September 1939. He hastened home to join the Irish Guards in May 1940, having completed an officer course at Sandhurst. As Captain O'Neill of the Irish Guards, he took part in Operation Overlord — the Allied landings in Normandy from June 6th 1944. He was wounded as the Irish Guards reached the Dutch frontier and had to return to England. By the time he was well enough to return to his unit in Spring 1945, the war in Europe was almost over. Before the end of 1945, O'Neill was demobilised and anxious to embark upon a political career in Northern Ireland.

World War II had an important and lasting effect on O'Neill. His brother, Brian, had been killed early in the war in the defence of Norway in 1940 just as his father had been killed during the first year of World War I. In 1944, before D-Day, he married an English girl. The most important effect, however, was the awakening of a political consciousness and an awareness of and admiration for Northern Ireland's heroic role during the war. Like so many of his contemporaries both in Britain and Northern Ireland, O'Neill contrasted the stubborn refusal of the South of Ireland to ally with Britain and the U.S. against, what he called, "the most vile tyranny the world has seen for centuries" with the courageous and enthusiastic participation of the N.I. state in the Allied war effort. O'Neill, in his autobiography, said that the Ireland Act of 1949, Britain's constitutional guarantee to Northern Ireland, "stemmed directly from Eire's policy of wartime neutrality." Even before the war was over, O'Neill was pondering the possibility of representing a N.I. constituency at Westminster or in the N.I. parliament at Stormont. It was not, however, until O'Neill had bought a home in Ahoghill, Co. Antrim, that his candidature for the Unionist nomination for the safe Unionist seat at Bannside was approved by the Unionist Association. O'Neill was returned unopposed as Unionist M.P. for Bannside in November 1946. Thereafter, he represented Bannside constituency in the N.I. parliament until his elevation to the House of Lords in 1970. On only one occasion, in February 1969, did O'Neill have to fight an election. Opposed by his arch-enemy and Protestant extremist, Paisley, Prime Minister O'Neill was narrowly elected just two months before his resignation as Premier.

Political Life in Northern Ireland 1946-63

O'Neill's maiden speech in the N.I. parliament in support of the N.I. Education Act 1947 set the tone for his whole political career. Speaking in favour of a proposal to raise the level of government assistance to voluntary, mainly Catholic, schools from 50% to 65%, he made a special appeal to die-hard Unionist opponents of concessions to Catholics to, "sink our differences, pull together and determine that it will be possible for a man or woman born in Ulster . . . to say with pride, 'I was educated in Ulster.'" In February 1948, O'Neill became Parliamentary Secretary to the Minister of Health. He remained in junior positions until 1956 when, within the space of six months, he moved from the senior government post of Minister of Home Affairs to the most senior cabinet post of Minister of Finance. In this position, O'Neill was second in seniority to Prime Minister, Lord Brookeborough, during the last six and a half years of his premiership. He subsequently became his most outspoken critic and did nothing to ease the pressure on Brookeborough whose resignation on 25th March 1963 paved the way for O'Neill's premiership.

Prime Minister during an era of change

At forty-eight years, O'Neill was the youngest Northern Ireland Prime Minister. Unionist Prime Ministers were not elected. They "emerged" after consultation with the Northern Ireland Governor, the British representative, who announced the appointment. Brookeborough was reputed to have said that his successor should be elected by a vote of the full parliamentary party. Many commentators feel that a vote would have returned Faulkner, the young, able Minister of Home Affairs whose firm decisive action against the IRA during the "Border War" in the late fifties had won the admiration of hard-line Right-wing Unionists. The speed and secrecy surrounding O'Neill's appointment which followed private meetings between Brookeborough, O'Neill and the Governor, Lord Wakehurst, meant that Prime Minister O'Neill always had critics within Unionist circles. Faulkner was in the U.S. on a business trip. Upon his return, O'Neill was already in command. Faulkner and his supporters were presented with a fait accompli. O'Neill could never be sure of the full support of key members of his cabinet including Faulkner who held the all-important post of Minister of Commerce and was Deputy Prime Minister. Faulkner and fellow minister West, who was dismissed as Minister of Agriculture in 1967 for breaching a business code drawn up by O'Neill which prevented government ministers from using their official position for private gain, were at the centre of leadership crises from 1966 which eventually forced O'Neill's resignation in April 1969. Before 1963, O'Neill's first year as premier, was over, N.I.'s former Attorney General, Warnock, was questioning O'Neill's right to office and suggesting Faulkner as a worthier choice. Not only had O'Neill to convince the public of the righteousness of his policies, he had also to persuade his conservative cabinet not only of the need to change but also of his right to leadership.

O'Neill's premiership came during a decade of change — political, social and economic, not just in both states in Ireland but throughout all of the western world. The accession of Lemass to power in the Irish Republic in 1959 meant that from 1963 government leaders in both parts of Ireland were anxious to break down the political and economic barriers which had kept the two states apart since 1925. Further, the economic revolution in the Southern Irish economy being brought about by planned Programmes for Economic Expansion (1959-63) and (1963-70) demanded a similar programme of long-term economic planning in order to transform the Northern economy.

Outside of Ireland, the spotlight fell on changes within the Catholic Church. The Second Vatican Council from 1962 to 1965 questioned traditional Catholic practices and attempted to break down religious barriers by fostering a spirit of ecumenism and co-operation between Christian churches. In the U.S. the first Catholic President, John F. Kennedy, proudly boasted of his Irish origins. His presidency marked an end to the war-time hostility between neutral Ireland and the U.S. Growing friendship between the Irish Republic and the most powerful state in the western world was sealed by President Kennedy's visit to Ireland in June 1963 just months before his assassination.

The winds of change both within Northern Ireland and without were recorded and analysed by press, radio and television in such a way that Northern Ireland could no longer insulate itself from outside influences nor prevent the television camera from telling both to the outside world and to the people of Northern Ireland the true story of events within Northern Ireland. Prime Minister O'Neill, was the first N.I. Prime Minister exposed to constant T.V. coverage. O'Neill, aware of the political impact of television, commented thus in 1966, "in an age of mass communications, the raucous sound of extremism is often heard much more loudly than the steady ground-swell of moderation." O'Neill's failure to win over the masses to his reforming policies meant the failure of his reforms and the destruction of the Northern Ireland state as extremists on both sides seized the initiative from the moderates.

Economic Planning under O'Neill

O'Neill's six and a half years as Minister of Finance (1956-63) had convinced him of the need for long-term economic planning in order to bring about sustained economic growth. In one of his first speeches as Prime Minister, O'Neill told the Ulster Unionist Council in April 1963 "Our task will be literally to transform Ulster." Government reports on the economy commissioned by the Brookeborough government — the Hall Report, which discouraged further subsidising of the old established but unproductive industries, ship-building and linen, and, a "Belfast Regional Survey and Plan", which recommended limiting the growth of Belfast in favour of a new city some thirty miles from Belfast — were adopted. As evidence of the "new technocratic Unionism" of O'Neill an economist Professor Wilson was appointed economic consultant to the government in October 1963. His report "Economic Development in Northern Ireland" became the blueprint of the government's economic policy.

A six-year plan accepted in principle by the government in February 1965 envisaged the building of 64,000 houses by 1970 and the creation of 65,000 new jobs in the same period. New growth areas outside of Belfast were designated. It was hoped to created some 5,000 new jobs in the construction industry in the creation of a new town and the extension of existing centres of population throughout the province. Thirty thousand jobs in manufacturing and thirty thousand more in service industries in not only the proposed new city but also in the Antrim/Ballymena, Bangor/Newtownards, Carrickfergus/Carnmoney areas and in the only area west of the Bann, Co. Derry, were projected. This ambitious development project envisaged £900m investment by 1970 of which half, it was hoped, would come from the private sector. The closure of unproductive railway lines, commenced under his predecessor, continued. Recognition, however, of the need for speedy road communications led to increased motorway construction. Road modernisation throughout the sixties was one of the visible signs of prosperity in the province.

Crucial to the implementation of Wilson's six-year economic plan was the setting up of an economic council similar to the regional development councils in mainland U.K. 1963 was productivity year everywhere throughout the U.K. except in Northern Ireland which had no productivity council. The steadfast refusal of Brookeborough to allow recognition of the Northern Committee of the Dublin-based Irish Congress of Trade Unions meant the non co-operation of northern trade unions affiliated to Irish trade unions. Co-operation of management and unions was necessary for the successful operation of an economic council. In August 1963, after "eighteen months of behind-the-scenes activity", according to O'Neill in his autobiography, the Northern Committee of the I.C.T.U. was recognised. The way was clear for the formation of the N.I. economic council set up before the end of the year under the chairmanship of Faulkner, Minister of Commerce, even though O'Neill felt that he had opposed the recognition.

The creation of a new Ministry of Development as part of a Cabinet reshuffle in July 1964 "the first major alterations to the structure of the Government since its inception" according to O'Neill, and the unveiling of the Wilson Plan "Economic Development in Northern Ireland" before the year's end, prompted the "Belfast News Letter" to assess the year thus, "For him (O'Neill) and for Ulster, history may yet record 1964 as a turning point, as a year of greatness."

The reality, however, did not quite live up to the promise. The six-year economic plan was sharply criticised for its preference for the already favoured eastern counties at the expense of the nationalist areas west of the River Bann which remained areas of heavy male unemployment. The decision to site the new city just thirty miles from Belfast was regarded as economically unsound by the first planner appointed to design the new city. His resignation in August 1964 from the whole project created a furore especially as he said that the site chosen was a poor one and that the expansion of Derry would have been economically more feasible. Accusing the government of blatant sectarian motives in preferring the Lurgan/Portadown centre to Catholic Derry the architect and professional town-planner had this to say, "Stormont on my brief but deep acquaintance has shown signs of a crisis-ridden regime — too busy looking over its shoulder to look outwards." The decision, less than a year later, to call the new town Craigavon was regarded by Catholics as evidence that little had changed. The "Father of Sectarianism" in Northern Ireland, Craigavon, was to be honoured by those who professed to deplore sectarian policies.

The government's record in attracting new firms to Ulster was impressive. Twenty-two American firms had set up in Northern Ireland by 1965. O'Neill and Faulkner ensured that incentives offered to industrial investors in N.I. rivalled those offered by the Lemass government in the Republic. A series of Ulster Weeks was launched in Nottingham in 1964. These trade exhibitions of N.I. goods, held twice yearly in British cities from Edinburgh to Southampton until Prime Minister O'Neill's resignation in April 1969, helped to promote Ulster goods at home and abroad. Economic achievements of the O'Neill years were the opening of an oil refinery outside Belfast in 1964 and the beginning of construction of a new Belfast airport to "match our position as the busiest air centre in Britain outside London" as O'Neill said in his book "Ulster at the Crossroads." Targets for house-building were reached by 1968 and the anticipated boom in the construction industry materialised. Twenty-nine thousand manufacturing jobs were created in the "new" industries, light engineering, electronics and synthetic fibres. Unfortunately the "old" industries, ship-building and aircraft manufacture, continued to contract. Allowing for closures and lay-offs the net gain in manufacturing was only 5,000 jobs. Northern Ireland's unemployment rates still stood at almost three times the British rate. In the south and west of the province, largely unassisted by the economic development plan, unemployment figures were seven times the U.K. figures. O'Neill estimated in 1962 that on average the manual worker in Northern Ireland earned £4 per week less than his British counterpart. In 1970 N.I. still had the lowest levels of earnings and the highest percentage of households in low income groups (with less than £20 total weekly income). Whatever the chances of sustained economic growth in Northern Ireland beforehand, the terrorist activity from 1966 shattered O'Neill's dream of creating an "Opportunity State" in which "every citizen will have the chance to realise his full potential" (O'Neill, May 1965).

Improved Community Relations

Co-operation became the key-note of O'Neill's premiership. Economic development and improved relations with the Catholic minority were interdependent. A strong and prosperous Ulster must also be a united Ulster was a constant theme running through Prime Minister O'Neill's public speeches. From his first year in office, Prime Minister O'Neill showed that, unlike his predecessors, he was going, by symbolic gesture and word at least, to extend the hand of friendship to transpose the Catholic minority. Thus the death of Pope John XXIII in June 1963, whose ecumenism offended many Protestants, was marked by a public message of condolence to the Catholic hierarchy and the flag was flown at half mast over the City Hall in Belfast in mourning. O'Neill commented in his autobiography that in twenty years as Prime Minister, his predecessor, Brookeborough, "never crossed the border, never visited a Catholic school and was never received or sought a civic reception from a Catholic town." Prime Minister O'Neill was to do all of these things. In April 1964, just one year after he had become Prime Minister, O'Neill took what he regarded as "my first step in the direction of improving community relations" by visiting a Catholic voluntary school.

For the majority of the Catholic population, however, such symbolic gestures were too little too late when set against the government decision in November 1963 to appoint a Committee on higher education, the Lockwood Committee, on which there was no Catholic representative. The decision by the Lockwood Committee to site a new university not in the Catholic university town of Derry (Magee College) but in a relatively small Protestant town without any academic tradition, Coleraine, was seen by most people as sectarian. Although an advocate of integrated education, O'Neill, as unable as his predecessors to persuade the Catholic hierarchy to accept non-denominational state education, was forced in 1968 to increase building grants to mainly Catholic voluntary schools from 65% to 80%, thereby subsidising segregated education which he always held to be a divisive force in the community. Likewise, encouragement of Civic Weeks, the N.I. parallel of the Ulster Weeks on mainland U.K. especially Civic Weeks in Nationalist Catholic towns like Newry where O'Neill was accorded a Civic reception in 1966, rang hollow when it was realised that the Northern Ireland Economic Council included no Catholic. Also, Catholic Nationalist areas west of the Bann did not in the main benefit from the economic development plan of the Sixties and remained areas of high unemployment and consequent discontent. As already noted, the decision to site a new city of 100,000 in the Unionist East of the province and to name it Craigavon was an acute disappointment for Catholics who hoped for expansion and industrialisation of the depressed Derry area. A development plan for Derry city drawn up in 1968 limited its growth to between 75,000 and 80,000 by 1970 and envisaged a disappointing additional 6,000 manufacturing jobs. Yet O'Neill acknowledged a correlation between sectarian unrest and economic discontent saying, just one month before his resignation in April 1969, "I have always believed that much of the unrest of recent months has essentially social and economic origins."

Despite conciliatory gestures to the Catholic minority, O'Neill was a member of the Orange Order refusing to break a Unionist tradition whereby the N.I. Prime Minister was a member of the avowedly anti-Catholic Orange Order. Of fifty-four N.I. government ministers between 1921 and 1969 fifty-one belonged to the Orange Order. The road to political advancement in Northern Ireland was via membership of the semi-secret ultra-Protestant Orange Order. Despite O'Neill's assertion in 1968 that "Unionism welcomes the support of all, whatever their background or affiliations, who seek through our link with Britain to build a better and prosperous Ulster," continued religious discrimination on public bodies, such as that set up to plan the new city on which there was only one Catholic among prominent Unionist businessmen, in the police force, where the percentage of Catholics had actually dropped since 1936, and above all, in the allocation of jobs and housing by Unionist-dominated local authorities, led Catholics to reject O'Neill's overtures as bland verbalising and to seek real reforms through the power of street politics in the Civil Rights campaign from 1968 which was to bring down not only O'Neill but also the N.I. state within four years.

Relations with the Irish Republic — O'Neill-Lemass Meetings

Improved relations with the neighbouring Irish state, the Irish Republic, became another objective during O'Neill's "new style" Unionist premiership. O'Neill in his autobiography claimed that a suggestion of the British Conservative Prime Minister Douglas-Home in November 1963 that O'Neill should meet his counterpart in the Irish Republic, Lemass, led eventually to O'Neill's invitation to the Irish Taoiseach to a historic meeting at Stormont Castle, seat of the N.I. government, in January 1965. O'Neill was anxious to capitalise on the friendlier attitude in Southern Ireland towards Northern Ireland evident since Lemass's accession to power in 1959. World Bank meetings attended by both Irish and Northern Irish government ministers from 1957 enabled personal contacts to be made between O'Neill's Private Secretary and the Northern-born Secretary of the Irish Department of Finance, Whitaker, whose report "Economic Development" had led to the highly-successful Programmes for Economic Expansion, blueprints of economic progress in Southern Ireland during the Sixties. A favourable speech made by Taoiseach Lemass in July 1963 acknowledging that "the Government and Parliament (of N.I.) exist with the support of the majority" prompted O'Neill to use his contacts with Whitaker to bring about in January 1965 the first meeting between two Irish leaders since 1925.

So worried were both leaders about possible reaction to the visit that news of the historic encounter was not released until after the meeting had taken place. Faulkner, Deputy Prime Minister, later accused the Prime Minister of secrecy over the whole affair and dated the beginning of what he called, "the slide away in support for O'Neill within the Unionist community" to the Lemass meeting. Yet O'Neill was able to claim that Lemass's trip to Stormont was Southern recognition of "the plain fact of our existence and our jurisdiction here." Not only had the Irish government accepted "in free agreement" the border in 1925 but also the existence of a legitimate Parliament and Government in Northern Ireland in 1965. Therefore, O'Neill argued, the constitutional authority of the N.I. state was consolidated by the Lemass visit.

The joint communiqué issued after the meeting stressed that the talks did not touch upon constitutional or political questions. Only matters of mutual economic interest were discussed. In this, the historic meeting was not revolutionary. Although Brookeborough had resolutely opposed high-level communication and co-operation, cross-border projects such as drainage of the River Erne, which flows across the border from Co. Fermanagh into Co. Donegal, and the Dublin-Belfast railway link had been undertaken during the post-war period. The emphasis both in the first and subsequent ministerial meetings was on economic co-operation. Faulkner the Northern Minister of Commerce met with the Republic's Minister for Industry and Commerce Jack Lynch and discussed the possibility of an electricity link-up. O'Neill's return visit to Dublin on February 9th and the hospitality accorded to the Northern Minister of Agriculture, West, at the Dublin home of the Irish Minister of Agriculture, Haughey, marked a new departure in North-South relations which made possible the creation of a joint North/South committee on tourism, the first practical expression of the new mood of détente.

The most important consequences of the Lemass-O'Neill meetings were, however, political. The most immediate political consequence was the decision by the Nationalist Party on February 2nd 1965 to assume, for the first time, the role of official opposition at Stormont. Catholic Nationalists were, thereby, indicating that they were prepared to work for change within the constitution. The hopes of Nationalists had already been raised by the return in October 1964 of a British Labour government, under Wilson, who condemned sectarianism and was known to be sympathetic to the idea of Irish Unity. By June 1965 Labour backbenchers and supporters had started a Campaign for Democracy in Ulster. Up to 100 Labour M.P.s in Britain were prepared to support demands for civil rights being made by pressure groups such as the Campaign for Social Justice in Northern Ireland which in 1965 affiliated to the powerful National Council for Civil Liberties in London and was the forerunner of the Northern Ireland Civil Rights Association of 1967.

Despite the misgivings of Conservative Unionists and the outright alarm voiced by extreme Protestants, O'Neill's policies got a resounding vote of confidence in a general election in November 1965. Under the slogan "Forward Ulster to Target 1970" O'Neill broke further new ground by canvassing in both Catholic and Protestant homes and wooing the Catholic vote with a manifesto which O'Neill claimed for the first time had "no sectarian overtones or undertones." Labour successes of 1958 and 1962 were reversed. The poll showed an average swing of 7% to the Unionists. O'Neill, in his autobiography, recorded his satisfaction with the events of 1965 thus, "the election at the end of 1965 proved that my policies were acceptable to the vast majority of Protestants and a growing number of Catholics." Yet the storm clouds were already gathering. O'Neill was to call 1966 "the most difficult period I had encountered."

1966 - Year of Anniversaries

The golden jubilee celebration of the events of 1916 revealed the yawning gulf which still separated Northern Unionists and Southern Republicans despite the goodwill gestures of the previous year. Whilst Irishmen everywhere prepared to celebrate the fiftieth anniversary of the Easter Rising and commemorate the dead of 1916, Ulster Unionists prepared to remember those who had died not fighting against but for Britain at the Battle of the Somme in July 1916.

Significantly, the first tensions of 1966 arose within the Protestant community not over a Republican issue, but over the naming of a new bridge over the River

Lagan. O'Neill hoped that the "Somme Bridge" would be acceptable to both Catholics and Protestants as thousands of French Catholics as well as Ulster Volunteers had given their lives at the Somme in 1916. Extreme Unionists preferred "Carson Bridge" after the great Unionist leader Carson. As a compromise the name Queen Elizabeth II Bridge was decided upon and the Queen was invited in July 1966 to officially open the bridge.

Militant Protestants, led by the forceful and outspoken Paisley, had vehemently opposed all of O'Neill's new departures. Paisley, founder of a break-away sect in 1951, the Free Presbyterian Church of Ulster, had already achieved notoriety by demonstrating against the lowering of the Union Jack in tribute to the memory of Pope John XXIII who died in June 1963 and by causing the Special Powers Act to be invoked for the first time ever against Loyalists. Deeming "Romanism and Republicanism" to be the twin evils of the age, Paisley opposed the "mongrelism of ecumenism" as "the curse of the country." To Paisley and his uncompromising followers, the drawing together of the Churches was a religious betrayal. O'Neill's overtures to Catholics and rapprochement with Southern Ireland were seen as political betrayals to those whose view of Unionism and Protestantism was equally unyielding.

Paisley and his small but vocal minority decided to turn the naming of the bridge into an election issue at the Westminster general election in March 1965. Paisley also used the Westminster election to intensify an "O'Neill must go" campaign. Fielding four Protestant Unionist candidates in the election campaign, among them Carson's son who was a reluctant candidate, Paisley hoped to break the Official Unionist monopoly of power at Westminster. It was not, however, Paisley who won the only non-Unionist seat but rather Catholic-Labour representative Gerry Fitt whose commitment to the working classes both Protestant and Catholic in West Belfast secured for his Republican Labour Party the West Belfast seat at Westminster. Electoral disappointment incensed Paisley's supporters who organised themselves into quasi-militant fringe movements ready to take to the streets in opposition to Republican celebrations at Easter 1966 or to any signs of "weakness" by either government or Protestant religious body appearing to favour ecumenism. By May, Paisley's followers had formed a formidable paramilitary force, the Ulster Protestant Volunteers, and had close links with another paramilitary force, the U.V.F., which modelled itself on the U.V.F. of 1913. Paisley had launched a newspaper in February 1965, the "Protestant Telegraph". In April 1965 he set up a twelve-man Ulster Constitution Defence Committee to safeguard the Protestant constitution of Northern Ireland under attack in his opinion from O'Neillism and the current move towards ecumenism.

By mid-1966, Paisley had therefore in place the machinery necessary to wage an unconstitutional campaign in defence of the constitution. The real violence of 1966 came from militant Protestant extremists. The Republican celebrations at Easter, although unnecessarily protracted in O'Neill's opinion, were confined largely to Nationalist Catholic areas and passed off relatively quietly. In June militant Protestantism threatened again. A demonstration against the General Assembly of the Presbyterian Church in Ireland for passing a resolution opposing "all forms of unfair religious discrimination" provided Protestant paramilitary forces with an opportunity to hold a provocative loyalist march through a Catholic area of Belfast. The subsequent rioting and noisy demonstration outside the Presbyterian General Assembly led to Paisley's arrest and eventual imprisonment. Short prison martyrdom (for three months in 1966 and in 1969 for an ever shorter period) only enhanced Paisley's position among Protestants and Unionists just as martyrdom and imprisonment of 1916 rebels had ensured the lasting popularity of the "1916 cause" fifty years before.

In June also paramilitary violence turned to murder. The gunning down of a young unarmed Catholic by a branch of the reformed U.V.F. forced Prime Minister O'Neill to cut short a trip to France ironically to honour the dead U.V.F. who fell in their thousands at the Battle of the Somme 1916. Upon his return, O'Neill used the Civil Authorities (Special Powers) Act of 1922, hitherto used only against the IRA and Republican organisations, to declare illegal the U.V.F. of the day, "an organisation which has misappropriated the title 'Ulster Volunteer Force', O'Neill told the N.I. House of Commons on 28th June 1966.

The visit of Queen Elizabeth in July 1966 to open the Queen Elizabeth Bridge over the Lagan did little to cool inflamed Protestant tempers. The Queen narrowly escaped injury when a brick was dropped from a "Loyalist" building site onto the bonnet of the Royal car.

The Orange marching season passed off relatively quietly although the Orange parades provided an opportunity for government ministers, who were also prominent Orangemen, to voice their opposition to O'Neillism. Although the Unionist newspaper the "Belfast News Letter" wrote in August 1966, "the stature of the Ulster Premier both at home and abroad has never been higher" O'Neill faced in September 1966 the first serious leadership crisis with senior government ministers, among them Faulkner, Minister of Commerce and Deputy Prime Minister, forming a "'66 Committee" to scrutinise more closely the actions of their leader. Although O'Neill survived this leadership challenge and managed to rid himself of unrepentant "rebel" ministers, West in 1967 and Craig in December 1968 who, as Minister of Home Affairs from autumn 1966, had proved totally unsympathetic to civil rights demonstrators, the '66 Committee remained in being. It was the timely resignation of Faulkner in January 1969 and the emergence of the so-called "Portadown Parliament" with over a dozen hardline Unionist M.P.s calling publicly for O'Neill's resignation which prompted the Prime Minister to call a February 1969 election in which for the first time he was forced to fight for his political life against the formidable adversary Paisley. Although the new parliament contained forty Unionist M.P.s, Prime Minister O'Neill could count on the support of only 27 of them. Less than two months later, on April 28th 1969, O'Neill resigned leaving a divided Unionist Party and an even more divided state behind him.

The real significance of the events of 1966 was that the paramilitary violence of chiefly Protestant extremists sowed the seeds of the street politics of the Civil Rights movement from 1968 which in the words of O'Neill was to "shake Northern Ireland to its foundations, split the ruling Unionist Party and initiate more reforms in two years" than he had thought possible in ten. The Northern Ireland Civil Rights movement undoubtedly owed much to the international civil rights movement of the Sixties and was much influenced by the American civil rights campaign and in particular by the television coverage thereof. Student anger in Belfast which found political expression in 1968 in People's Democracy can be seen as part of the

European student protest movement which was sweeping Europe from Prague in Czechoslovakia to Paris in France. The tactics of mass demonstration, protest marches and sit-ins, used so effectively by Paisley and Protestant militants, were copied, however, by the protest movements from 1968 who also benefited from the predictable Protestant backlash to the Civil Rights movement. Ironically, it was not civil rights disturbances but rather Protestant bombs in March-April 1969, threatening to paralyse the economic life of the capital Belfast, which literally blew him out of office on April 28th 1969, O'Neill recalled in his autobiography. The February 1969 election which preceded Prime Minister O'Neill's departure was known as the "Crossroads election". Yet, as early as 1966, O'Neill told the N.I. House of Commons on the day on which the U.V.F. was proscribed, "We stand at the crossroads. One way is the road to progress . . . . the other way is a return to the pointless violence and civil strife of earlier years." O'Neill's six years premiership represented a watershed in Northern Ireland's history. Before his premiership ended, Northern Ireland had already chosen the road to civil strife which meant not only the end of O'Neill's premiership but also, within three years, the end of the Northern Ireland state.

Although O'Neill attributed his downfall to the escalation of Protestant violence in the weeks before his resignation, in his autobiography, he claimed that as early as 1966, he intended to retire in autumn 1969 when he would be fifty-five years, "an appropriate age to start a new life", in his opinion. O'Neill's departure from Northern Ireland politics came in January 1970 when he received his reward and release from the political scene in Northern Ireland by being offered a peerage in the House of Lords as Lord O'Neill of the Maine. Thereafter, apart from writing his memoirs in the form of an autobiography largely written before the introduction of direct rule from Westminster in March 1972, O'Neill has taken little active part in the political development of the region. One of his final political observations about Northern Ireland in his autobiography sums up the tragedy of the Unionist position in Northern Ireland, "So far as Northern Ireland is concerned, she could have continued to enjoy her privileged position of being the only part of Ireland to enjoy a British standard of living. Instead she chose to put all this at risk in the interests of maintaining a Protestant ascendancy that had ceased to have any meaning anywhere else in the United Kingdom. "

Appraisal

English born, and with an English accent which sometimes sounded strangely out of place in provincial Northern Ireland, O'Neill was perhaps the most misunderstood of Northern Ireland's Prime Ministers. Although maligned as a traitor whom Paisley averred in 1966, "will sell the province down South unless he is removed from office" O'Neill's Unionism was never in question. The most courageous of his new policies, rapprochement with the Irish Republic through meetings with Irish government leaders Lemass and his successor Lynch, afforded O'Neill the opportunity to define publicly his Unionism. In one of his final electoral appeals before his last general election in February 1969 he stated bluntly, "As a Unionist, I believe passionately that Northern Ireland must remain an integral part of the United Kingdom". Immediately after, he called the "long-distance arguments about Partition, meaningless", because partition was "an issue which is not open to negotiation." Indeed it was fidelity to the British connection which prompted O'Neill to extend the hand of friendship to the Nationalist minority. O'Neill knew that as long as Nationalists withheld full allegiance from the state, Northern Ireland was under threat. Relations with both the Conservative Unionist government of Douglas-Home (1963-64) and with the Labour government of his successor, Wilson, were always cordial. O'Neill's close affinity to fellow Englishmen made it easy for him to co-operate with successive British governments in endeavouring to bring about what he deemed to be best for the N.I. state.

It was, however, O'Neill's misfortune that his bridge-building efforts within Northern Ireland and between the two states in Ireland unleashed forces both conservative and radical which neither O'Neill nor any succeeding government in Northern Ireland was able to control. O'Neill's talk of change and reform during his six-year premiership alarmed and alienated Right-wing Unionists and extreme Protestants for whom Unionism meant Protestant ascendancy, but failed to win the support of the Catholic minority who saw that real reform such as "one man one vote" in local elections, conceded in principle only days before Prime Minister O'Neill's resignation in April 1969, was won by the bloody civil rights campaign of 1968-69 rather than by an official willingness to introduce meaningful reform. The real lesson of the O'Neill Years was that extremism worked in Northern Ireland. O'Neill's failure to reconcile Catholics to the Northern Ireland state, to reconcile Catholics with Protestants and the Northern Ireland state with its neighbouring Irish state meant the failure of the state as constituted by the Government of Ireland Act 1920. Within three years, the Unionist regime in Northern Ireland was ended. Although not generally realised at the time, the O'Neill administration 1963-69 was N.I. Unionists' last chance to survive in a changing world in which Northern Ireland's sectarian unionism had no place.

Landmarks in O'Neill's Life (b. 1914)

1914	*September 10th* — Born in London.
1940-45	Captain O'Neill served with the Irish Guards during World War II.
1946	*November* — Returned unopposed as Unionist M.P. for Bannside constituency.
1956-63	Minister of Finance and most senior government minister.
1963	*March - April 1969* Premiership.
1964	*April* — First visit of a N.I. Prime Minister to a Catholic voluntary school.
1965	*January* — Historic O'Neill-Lemass meeting. *February* — Unfolding of six-year economic plan.
1966	Year of Anniversaries.
1968	Civil Rights Campaign forces O'Neill administration to introduce a reform package which included the civil rights demand of "one man one vote."
1969	*February 3rd* — Disaffected Unionists formed the "Portadown Parliament" and called for O'Neill's resignation. *February* — "Crossroads election" returned 40 official Unionists of whom only 27 supported O'Neill. *March-April* — Series of Protestant explosions forced O'Neill to resign.
1970	*January* — Retired from Northern Ireland political scene when offered a peerage in House of Lords.

9. Lemass

Early Influences

Sean Lemass, 1916 Rising, War of Independence and Civil war veteran, founding father of Fianna Fáil and, as successor to de Valera in 1959 architect of modern Ireland, was born on 15th July 1899 in Dublin. Of French Huguenot origins his father ran a drapery shop in Dublin's Capel Street. Neither Sean nor his older brother Noel were satisfied with their father's support for Redmond and the Irish Parliamentary Party's Home Rule campaign. Educated at the C.B.S. O'Connell School renowned for "the four Rs - reading, 'riting, 'rithmetic and revolution" the two brothers cut short their education to taken part in the Easter Rising 1916 and thereafter in the Irish War of Independence. Sean Lemass was drawn into the Volunteers at the age of fifteen and a half. His company commandant was de Valera with whom he was to develop a lifelong working relationship.

Sean Lemass 1899-1971 - the economic architect of modern Ireland.

Although an eager Volunteer, Lemass almost missed the Easter Rising. Unaware of the last-minute plans for Easter Monday the two brothers decided after the cancellation of the Easter Sunday military manoeuvres to go hiking through Wicklow on Bank Holiday Easter Monday. Ironically their first knowledge of an Easter Monday insurrection came from Eoin MacNeill Commander-in-Chief of the Irish Volunteers who opposed a Rising doomed to failure and had cancelled all Volunteer orders for Easter Sunday upon hearing on the Saturday of the arrest of Casement and the loss of the "Aud" shipment of arms from Germany. MacNeill failed to dissuade the Lemass brothers who next morning offered their services at the G.P.O. rebel H.Q. Armed with a shotgun and home-made bombs Lemass spent the time until evacuation of the G.P.O. on Friday on the roof preparing for the offensive by the British troops which did not materialise. Shelling from the British gun boat, the "Helga", was a far more effective means of reducing both the G.P.O. and its garrison to ruin. Lemass was arrested after the surrender on Saturday 29th April 1916 and was eventually imprisoned in Richmond Barracks. There his youth plus the good offices of a Dublin Metropolitan policeman who knew the family and vouched for the boy's good behaviour secured his early release.

Attempts to get young Lemass to continue his studies at Rosse College failed. Both Lemass brothers were fully committed to the Republican cause. By late 1917 he was a Lieutenant in C company second battalion of the Dublin Brigade. Although working by day in his father's shop he frequently held all-night training exercises for his men in the North Dublin area in preparation for the War of Independence.

Throughout his life Lemass was reticent about the part he played in the War of Independence and in the Civil War in which he took the anti-Treaty side. Promoted to captain in 1920 after a number of successfully executed arms raids he was captured when he attempted to return home in December 1920. He was interned at Ballykinlar until after the signing of the Treaty in December 1921. For a time Lemass appeared to support the Treaty. He served as a training officer to the new Garda Siochana, the new unarmed police force of the Free State. When, however, his first pay cheque revealed that his employer was the British-inspired and approved Provisional Government rather than the Irish-elected Dáil Eireann, Lemass resigned and joined the anti-Treaty Irregulars. When Rory O'Connor seized the Four Courts in April 1922 Lemass joined the Four Courts garrison as adjutant to the Commandant. Remembered by comrade-in-arms Ernie O'Malley in the Four Courts as "an efficient busy officer", Lemass surrendered with the garrison but succeeded in escaping from custody before he could be taken with the others to Mountjoy.

Lemass joined a Tipperary contingent of Irregulars and assisted in the capture of Ferns and Enniscorthy as the Irregulars, beaten in Dublin fell back on the Southern Counties and attempted to establish a Munster Republic in July 1922. In October Lemass became Minister of Defence and de Valera President of the Republican government proclaimed by the Irregulars but not recognised by anyone else. Lemass shared de Valera's pessimism about a successful military outcome and was critical of what he called "a great deal of misdirection and a lack of firm leadership" among the Irregulars. In December 1922 he was arrested and not released until October 1923 when news that the body of his older brother Noel had been discovered in the Dublin mountains secured his release on compassionate grounds. Noel, also an anti-Treaty Irregular, had disappeared during the early stages of the war. His murder gave his surviving brother Sean added stature among anti-Treaty sympathisers and ensured his election as Sinn Féin representative for South Dublin in a by-election in November 1924.

Lemass's ten-months imprisonment during the latter stages of the Civil War marked a turning-point in his life. Disillusioned with military initiatives which had yielded only limited success over a six-year period Lemass turned to political solutions. Although not a member of the old Sinn Féin political organisation before the Civil War, he was appointed to the Standing Committee of Sinn Féin by the S.F. Ard Fheis of 1923 without seeking election. Upon election to parliament in 1924, like other anti-Treaty T.D.s he abstained from the Free State Dáil, and became Minister for Defence, in de Valera's Republican "shadow" government. As titular Minister of Defence Lemass knew that he had no real power. When the I.R.A. repudiated the authority of the shadow government in November 1924 Lemass supported cutting all connections with the I.R.A. In February 1926 before the special Árd Fheis of March 1926 at which de Valera resigned his presidency of Sinn Féin over the issue of recognition of existing political institutions, Lemass, through the Sinn Féin newspaper, "An Phoblacht" called upon "any group, or section, or party, that finds it has outlived its utility... to quit." On the day of the fateful decision to leave Sinn Féin de Valera recalled how Lemass insisted, "We must form a new organisation along the policy lines you suggested at the Ard Fheis. It is the only way forward."

Lemass and the Formation of Fianna Fáil

Lemass played a key role in the formation of the new party and in its organisation at every level. It was he who convened the meeting at the old Sinn Féin H.Q. in Suffolk St. on Good Friday 1926 at which the new party was launched. At Lemass's instigation the new party was named not just Fianna Fáil but Fianna Fail (the Republican party). De Valera had already noticed Lemass's dynamism and organisational skills. Lemass was an obvious choice for membership of the organising committee. Shortly afterwards he became honorary secretary and, as "the driving genius" of the party literally driving around Ireland drumming up support among sometimes old I.R.A. and Sinn Fein contacts, he was able to report that 'within a year of the first Fianna Fáil executive being set up we had a nationwide organisation, the strongest in the country, fully geared for action with cumainn and county executives everywhere."

Electoral success in 1927, with Fianna Fáil winning 26% of the first preference vote and 44 seats in the first election and an increased first preference vote resulting in 57 seats in the second election in September 1927 was a triumph for Lemass, chief organiser. At both elections Lemass topped the poll in his own South Dublin constituency. When Lemass took his seat in the Dáil in August 1927 along with the other Fianna Fáil deputies he became for the first time a full-time paid politician. Lemass's comment in 1928 that "Fianna Fáil is a slightly constitutional party", drew the retort from the government benches that there were two Lemasses in the Dáil, the responsible economist and the irreconcilable militant. His first speech in the Dáil attacking the government's stringent Public Safety Act passed in the wake of O'Higgins' assassination in July 1927, included a plea for an end to "the bitterness and the jealousies that were created in this country after the Civil War." Reconciliation became a constant theme of Lemass's speeches during his long political life. He did more than any of his contemporaries to move away from the Civil war politics which bedevilled Irish political life.

Although Lemass remained chief organiser of the Fianna Fáil party and subsequently recalled the five years 1927-32 as the most exhausting phase of his career he rapidly emerged as chief Fianna Fáil spokesman on economic issues. Lemass's education in economics began during his internment in the Civil War. As early as 1924 Lemass was a member of Sinn Féin's economics sub-committee. In 1928 Fianna Fáil published its economic policy which Lemass as Minister of Industry and Commerce from 1932 was to implement. Lemass knew that a policy of economic self-sufficiency such as that envisaged by Griffith in Sinn Féin's Economic Policy of 1905 and that demanded by the Great Depression and the world-wide swing to protection during the Thirties could not be achieved without state intervention and economic planning on a scale never before attempted.

The 1932 election victory enabling Fianna Fáil to embark upon sixteen years in government was master-minded by Lemass who was rewarded with a ministerial post in the first Fianna Fáil government.

Minister of Industry and Commerce
Lemass while in opposition had frequently berated the Department of Industry and Commerce for what he called its "laziness". As Minister of Industry and Commerce he appointed as Department Secretary an outsider John Leydon from the Department of Finance. Lemass and Leydon proved a dynamic force for change and economic development in Ireland during the Thirties and the difficult war-years. Economic policy between 1932-39 has been summed up as "a full-blooded policy of protection with the stated object of relieving unemployment and of developing the resources of the country". The "economic war" with Britain 1932-38 enabled Lemass to present a policy of protectionism under patriotic guise. A biographer of Lemass, Brian Farrell observed, "the weapon of protection, barely invoked previously, became a blunderbuss in the hands of Lemass." By 1937, nearly 2,000 items were subject to restriction or control. Behind the protective walls thus erected, exclusively Irish industry was fostered. The Control of Manufacturers Acts 1932 - 1934, Lemass's first major legislative initiative, enabled the Department of Industry and Commerce to refuse manufacturing licences, required for new industry from 1932, to non-nationals. Lemass's plan however for "national reorganisation", submitted to the government in November 1932 as his solution to unemployment which then stood at 100,000 was rejected by the government. He himself described it as "revolutionary in character" and admitted that the level of state intervention envisaged in both agriculture and industry would "certainly require dictatorial powers for their execution". Nonetheless his desire to alleviate unemployment which, in his maiden speech in the Dáil in 1927, he called " a greater problem than subversion" led to the creation of state-sponsored bodies such as the Industrial Credit Company (in effect a state merchant bank providing for Irish industry commercial loans at attractive rates in the same way as the A.C.C. had provided to Irish agriculture). The Irish Sugar Company, another state enterprise by 1938, was producing four-fifths of domestic requirements and therefore coming close to the goal of economic self-sufficiency so desperately sought after during the pre-war years. The Turf Development Board set up in 1934 envisaged turf as a substitute for imported coal and paved the way for the state-sponsored Bord na Móna which from 1946 undertook the commercial exploitation of turf. Other semi-state successes of these years were Bord Fáilte and Aer Lingus the national airline. Lemass however was singularly unsuccessful in securing approval for an oil refinery, an essential prerequisite to self-sufficiency in motor fuels. Although Lemass proposed a large-scale refinery as early as 1935 government approval did not come until 5th September 1939 when World War II was already two days old and crude oil had already become precious and unobtainable.

The creation of a new all-embracing Department of Supplies on 2nd September 1939 indicated that the government believed that the supply and distribution of agricultural and manufacturing products would be the most-critical problem of the war years. It amounted almost to a government admission that protectionism had failed to achieve economic self-sufficiency. The appointment of Lemass to the new post of Minister of Supplies was an indication of the high esteem in which Lemass was held. De Valera's trust and confidence in Lemass was evident from the outset of the war. In the debate on the Emergency Powers Bill introduced by the Taoiseach on 2nd September 1939 demanding sweeping war-time powers for the government, de Valera told the Dáil that Lemass "will take charge of the bill... he will give you answer and reason as to why those powers are necessary".

Minister of Supplies

The worsening European situation meant that from the mid-1930s the Irish government was preparing for the emergency of major war in which the Irish state was determined to remain neutral. Since 1935 civil servants had been studying the difficulties of maintaining supplies of mainly imported essential goods such as fuel, foodstuffs and fertilisers. In September 1938 one year before the outbreak of war, Lemass's Department of Industry and Commerce had set up a separate emergency supplies branch. On September 2nd 1939 on day before World War II officially started the Department of Supplies was set up, with Lemass, the Minister responsible for ensuring economic survival during the war. As Minister of Supplies Lemass wielded inordinate influence. By June 1940 his department was responsible for the "regulation of the treatment, keeping, storage, movement, distribution, sale, purchase, use and consumption of articles of all kinds" in accordance with the terms of new powers allocated as the Emergency worsened with the fall of France. Described by Ronan Fanning, Lecturer in Modern Irish History at U.C.D. as an "economic overlord" Lemass, between 1939 and 1943, issued 602 orders rationing and regulating the supply and distribution of essential goods. Nick-named the "Minister for Shortages" and "Half-Ounce Lemass" a direct reference to the 1/2 ounce tea ration from April 1941, Lemass set an example to the nation by cycling rather than using his state car. Lemass made six separate ministerial radio broadcasts in which he depicted the supply situation as extremely grave. The people were thus psychologically prepared to accept even worse conditions than currently prevailed. The worst never did quite come to the worst. One contemporary commentator put it thus, "By a combination of care and fearlessness, foresight and drive, he sheltered the Irish people from the worst shortages, and where imported goods could not be got, a native substitute was developed and used in its place."

The creation of an Irish Shipping Line in March 1941 under the chairmanship of Leydon whom Lemass had brought with him to the Department of Supplies from Industry and Commerce was perhaps the boldest economic decision of the war years. The failure however to provide a merchant marine service in the pre-war years was an alarming omission by a government pledged to securing economic self-sufficiency. As late as September 1939 Ireland transferred Irish ships to Britain under informal charter arrangements. The bitter experience of 1940/'41 effectively deprived Eire almost entirely of space in ships bringing goods to the U.K., reduced fertiliser imports from 89,000 tonnes in 1939 to zero in 1942 and left Ireland without petrol supplies at Christmas 1940. By the end of the war Irish Shipping had carried over one million tons of cargo to Ireland. The Irish state had broken its total dependence on British merchant shipping.

Economic Planning

The most important economic development of the war years was the change in economic thinking. Protectionism had patently failed to bring economic self-sufficiency. During the war when international trade was disrupted, it was totally irrelevant. Both de Valera and Lemass realised that long-term economic planning was necessary for real economic progress. De Valera saw the Department of Supplies as "the central planning department for our economic life". By 1942 the threat of invasion had receded and it was possible for Ireland as well as Britain and the allies to begin "systematic planning not merely to end the pressing problems of the moment but also to provide for the situation ... when the Emergency comes to an end". This was the subject of a government discussion "Planning for post-war situation" held on June 30th 1942. To de Valera the most critical post-war problem would be the provision of jobs for the thousands of war-time emigrants whose return was expected after the war. Lemass's proposed solution to the problem of chronic unemployment, standing at 71,000 in 1944 was contained in a seven-page memorandum entitled "Labour Policy". Among other recommendations was the setting up a Department of Labour. It was not however until 1966, Lemass's last year as Taoiseach, that a Department of Labour dealing primarily with job creation actually materialised. In November 1942 a Cabinet Committee on Economic Planning was set up with the government's most senior ministers, de Valera, Taoiseach, O'Kelly, Tánaiste and Minister for Finance, and Lemass, leading an interdepartmental committee which invited proposals from all sectors of the economy and which from time to time included members from other government departments. The economic committee met for the first time on 2nd December 1942 and thereafter weekly until June 1945 when the exigencies of immediate post-war requirements and the devastation of the European economy made long-term planning impractical.

The weekly meetings of senior cabinet members provoked unprecedented discussion and debate on social and economic theory being expounded at the time by "modern" economist J.M. Keynes who, as early as 1933, had pointed out in Dublin that Ireland was too small a geographic unit ever to achieve more than "a very modest measure of national self-sufficiency". Publication in 1942 of the Beveridge Report in Britain promising the creation of a welfare state in Britain and N.I. provided cogent political and economic reasons for consideration of similar long-term projects. Both de Valera and Lemass knew that if the Irish government could not offer to N.I. citizens the same range and scale of social welfare benefits as that to be provided by Britain the Irish case for reunification would be considerably weakened. In addition, the level of social and economic discontent within Eire would rise as the gulf between living standards in both states became apparent. Lemass used a British White paper on Employment as inspiration for his own paper on full employment which he said could be achieved but only by complete reorganisation of agriculture and industry and by a degree of state intervention which government critics of the Lemass plan said "would involve a control of all economic processes so complete and detailed that it probably could not be realised without... the suppression of freedoms which no western people would sacrifice without a bitter struggle". Not surprisingly the Lemass plan of 1944 described by historian R. J. Raymond as "the most significant development arising out of the 'Emergency' was rejected, in the same way, as his plan for national reorganisation in 1932 was rejected. Nonetheless Lemass's contribution to the Cabinet Committee on Economic Planning was considerable. The war years saw the conversion of Lemass away from the "old" policies of protectionism and economic nationalism to the "new" Keynesian doctrine of government spending and government intervention in order to achieve full employment and a planned development of the economy. Although Lemass was unable to have his revolutionary plans implemented until he himself became

Taoiseach in 1959, he emerged during the war as "a decisive force in Irish economic development" according to one commentator. Membership of the Committee on Economic Planning gave Lemass valuable experience of interdepartmental activity and brought him into contact with leading young Irish economists such as Whitaker whose views coincided with Lemass's and whose "Economic Development" of 1958 provided the blueprint of the Programmes for Economic Expansion of the Sixties.

Recognition of and reward for Lemass's war-time services came in 1945 when upon O'Kelly's elevation to the Presidency, Lemass was chosen to succeed him as Tánaiste and therefore heir-apparent to de Valera. The post-war years were for Lemass, however, years of frustration. Associated with the continued rationing of essential supplies the war-time Minister for Shortages became the Minister for Hardship and his popularity suffered accordingly. Notwithstanding ongoing food shortages Lemass was anxious to improve Ireland's international image. One of the last actions of the Department of Supplies, which was wound up in July 1945 was to arrange for the sending of food, including 20,000 head of cattle and 10m pounds of canned meat, to war-torn Western Europe within forty-eight hours of the ending of the war in April 1945.

Lemass welcomed Ireland's inclusion in the Marshall Plan for European post-war recovery. Lemass who as Taoiseach made Ireland's application to join the E.E.C. in 1961, recognised that Ireland's economic future lay with Europe. In 1947 he said "Anything that promotes the creation of a workable European economy is of direct benefit to ourselves". Although he did not live to see Ireland become a member of the E.E.C. in January 1973 Lemass in 1947 was advocating Irish participation in a European customs union, prompting the "Irish Times" to comment optimistically, "The dream of self-sufficiency has been dispelled once and for all."

Lemass's main preoccupation during the post-war years was, however, with the ongoing economic crisis. In particular he was concerned with the growing industrial discontent which manifested itself in a series of strikes involving national teachers and bank officials as well as busmen and industrial workers. Lemass had always valued good labour relations. He was not responsible for the Trade Union Act of 1941 curbing the power of trade unions during the war which had been introduced by the Department of Industry and Commerce before Lemass's return to Industry and Commerce. When the supreme court in 1946 ruled that the Trade Union Act of 1941 was unconstitutional, Lemass used the opportunity to draw up a new Industrial Relations Act which made provision for a Labour Court, an independent body with equal representation from unions and employers, which quickly won the confidence of both sides and was in the opinion of one of the leading Irish trade unionists, "the first significant development in this area of affairs since the establishment of the state". Thus Lemass was placing in position the machinery necessary to ensure his economic revolution of the Sixties.

Awaiting Power

Defeat in the general election in February 1948 left Lemass, used to office for sixteen years, chief opposition spokesman in the Dáil. Lemass opposed inter-party government measures such as the setting up of the I.D.A. in 1949 which in principle he supported but which as Opposition spokesman he felt he must oppose. Return in 1951 to a minority Fianna Fáil government dependent upon the support of

Independents did not appeal to Lemass who in opposition had pursued private business interests including the launching of the "Sunday Press" newspaper in 1949. He told journalist and future ombudsman Michael Mills, "I did not welcome the prospect of coming back into government in the conditions of 1951". His verdict on the three-year minority government 1951-'54 was "It was not our most successful period in office." Lemass was annoyed by the reappointment of MacEntee as Minister for Finance. His conservatism had led him to oppose many of Lemass's revolutionary plans. Lemass knew that the economic climate for change was not right. Apart from encouraging the investment of foreign capital in Ireland there was no obvious new policy departure between 1951 and 1954. By 1945 Lemass had shed his opposition to foreign capital expressed in the 1929 Lemass document on economic policy. In May 1953 he went publicly on record as saying "We welcome foreign capital coming into Irish industrial development."

Lemass fully understood the weakness of the Fianna Fáil position. As a weak minority government dependent on the support of Independents, Fianna Fáil had been unable to introduce new policies. In July 1953 he admitted gloomily during a confidence motion, "The outstanding problem still is unemployment... We accept that the work we have done has not been wide enough in its scope or pushed ahead as vigorously as it should have been." Although Lemass was appointed national director of elections in March 1954 he was unable to prevent Fianna Fáil securing the lowest number of seats (65) since 1932. Lemass who became director of organisation in July 1954 after Fianna Fáil's worst electoral defeat since 1932 was determined not just to reorganise the party nation-wide but also to give it a positive programme for "National-Recovery". Once again Lemass set out around the country as he had done in the early days back in the Twenties revitalising Fianna Fáil at grass roots level in the constituencies. To help him in this demanding task Lemass appointed young dynamic men e.g. future Taoiseach C.J. Haughey and Brian Lenihan, on to his organisation committee.

Lemass knew however that dynamic new policies were also needed in order to woo the electorate in sufficient numbers to secure an overall majority. In October 1955 almost two years before the March 1957 election which was to sweep Fianna Fáil back to power with its biggest ever number of seats (78), Lemass made his most momentous speech to the party faithful in Cleary's ballroom in Dublin. Advertised in the Fianna Fáil newspaper, the Irish Press, as "a discussion on national development" Lemass in his "Proposals for a Full Employment Policy" held out the exciting possibility of providing full employment within five years by a "Keynesian" programme of increased public investment calculated to generate 100,000 new jobs. Lemass's plan for "National Recovery" published in January 1957 was almost the Fianna Fáil election manifesto for the March 1957 election. The Fianna Fáil election slogan "let's get cracking" suggested to the electorate that Fianna Fáil would waste no more time about putting into effect the dynamic new policies of Lemass. The election results gave Fianna Fáil a nine seat majority, its first overall majority since the war. Lemass, however, had to wait two more years before he attained the supreme office of Taoiseach and could begin the full implementation of his economic policies.

The Lemass Years

Lemass's domination, however, of the Fianna Fáil government led by the elderly ailing de Valera was evident from the start. De Valera acceded to Lemass's request not to reappoint the conservative MacEntee to the Department of Finance. Lemass, as Minister of Industry and Commerce was fortunate to have in the Department of Finance, which until then had opposed change, economic reformers whose ideas coincided with his. Lemass was lucky that before Fianna Fáil returned to power in 1957 the groundwork for economic change had already been laid. It was the weak unstable coalition government of Costello 1954-57 which, having led the country into one of the worst recessions in the history of the state, took the decisions which made possible the economic revolution of the Sixties. In 1956 the Coalition Minister for Finance, Sweetman appointed T.K. Whitaker as Secretary of the Department of Finance. Whitaker's economic views accorded with Lemass's. Encouraged by Lemass he prepared a report on the economy "Economic Development" published in 1958 and acclaimed as a landmark in modern Irish history. Sweetman also negotiated successfully Irish admission to the International Monetary Fund in 1957 thereby making it possible for the Irish government to negotiate loans drawn on the World Bank. The setting up of a Capital Investment Advisory Committee in 1957 which urged the directing of public investment into productive channels was also the brainchild of Sweetman whose government fell from office before, as Whitaker put it, the "ideas which he implemented could bear fruit." It was Lemass's good fortune that even before he became Taoiseach he was appointed chairman of the government committee set up to examine the conclusions of the Whitaker Report and to draw up the first Programme for Economic Expansion which Lemass outlined to the party in October 1958 and which was adopted by the government in November 1958.

Economic Development under Lemass

In 1957 the year in which Whitaker began his report "Economic Development" unemployment stood at 78,000 and emigration at 54,000. Between 1951 and 1961 the total loss due to emigration was 400,000. By 1961 the population had fallen to 2.8m. more than 5% below the level at the foundation of the state. Shattered was the dream of Pearse that the population of a free Ireland would expand rapidly and surpass pre-Famine levels. Far from being halted, the post-Famine emigration drain had continued apace apart from a few years during the 1930s when world industrial depression reduced the attractiveness of emigration. A government commission on emigration set up in 1948 and reporting in 1954 showed that government was aware of the gravity of the emigration crisis. The problem of the "vanishing Irish" was so acute that in the mid-1950s some commentators pondered the possibility of the disappearance of the Irish race. Whitaker cited the Bishop of Clonfert's indictment in 1957 "our greatest neglect of all - the capital sin of our young Irish state - is our failure to provide for our young people an acceptable alternative to emigration" as the inspiration for his "Economic Development". Whitaker's blunt statement "After 35 years of native government people are asking whether we can achieve an acceptable degree of economic progress" was the spur for the five-year development plan, the First Programme for Economic Expansion.

Whitaker's recommendation in the "Economic Development" for an integrated programme of national development for the next five or ten years" led directly to the First Programme for Economic Expansion which earmarked £220.4m. state money for productive investment over a Five-Year period. Although unemployment and emigration still continued unchecked with over 60,000 leaving during the first twelve months of Fianna Fáil rule, the austerity measures of both Fianna Fáil and the Inter-Party Coalition governments of the Fifties, had reduced the deficit on current account and had actually produced a surplus in 1957. In the opinion of the Central Bank which controlled the supply and circulation of money this presented an opportunity to do "some fresh thinking on economic policy." There was little innovation however until 1959 when with the election of de Valera as President, Lemass finally became Taoiseach at the age of sixty on June 23rd 1959. The first Five-Year Programme for Economic Expansion dated from 1959-60 to 1963-'64.

The investment programme concentrated on the agricultural and industrial sectors of the economy. The respective allocations of money, £20m per annum to agriculture and the rest to productive sectors of industry showed a marked preference for productive industry. City-bred Lemass, for long regarded as the enemy of the small farmer, approved of the replacement of general agricultural subsidies by selective subsidies to productive sectors of agriculture only. Grassland farming was encouraged. Farmers were encouraged to raise more cattle and sheep for export. Marketing boards such as An Bord Bainne made Kerry Gold Butter a household name throughout the U.K. A bovine tuberculosis scheme designed to eradicate TB in cattle was, however, only partly successful. Projected targets in agriculture were not reached. The number of cows fell short of the 1964 projected target of $1^1/2$m. Despite state subsidies on fertilisers the $2/3$ increase in fertiliser consumption was no greater a rate of increase than that of the period 1948-'57. The biggest disappointment however was that net agricultural output was only one per cent higher in 1963 than in 1957 and failed to reach the conservative 2% p.a. growth rate projected by the Plan. The resignation of Smith, Minister for Agriculture in October 1964, was interpreted by farming interests as a protest against the anti-agricultural bias in government policy. Smith had threatened to resign on many occasions and although his resignation was in protest against what he saw as government surrender to union demands in the settlement of a dispute in the building trade, at least one publication, the "Round Table", put it thus, "His action reflects the natural and growing resentment of the farmers, who alone among the community have seen their remuneration decrease in recent years." Farmers in 1966 were described by one Opposition T.D. as being worse off then than at any time since the Famine.

By contrast industrial output in 1963 was forty-seven per cent above its 1957 level. The emphasis on industrial development was unmistakable. In preparation for massive capital investment in industry, the resources of the Industrial Credit Corporation were more than doubled in 1958 from £2m. to £5m. Lemass, however, did not expect an economic miracle from small Irish industries. For too long small family industries had sheltered behind protective barriers, had not become competitive and had not attempted to produce for export or create employment. Twelve new state-sponsored bodies showed a commitment to the continuation of state investment in productive state enterprises. Expansion of existing semi-state bodies such as Bord na Móna and the Irish Sugar Company both of whom were producing for export as well as the home market, continued apace. The work and the budget of the I.D.A. (set up in 1949 to encourage industrial development) was increased. In 1958 thirty-eight new industrial enterprises were started. A survey of 3,106 Irish firms in 1961 revealed however that 50% employed less than 15 persons.

Only 31 companies or 1% of the total employed over 500. Irish-owned industries in the main remained small and uncompetitive.

Lemass looked to foreign investment and foreign-based companies to provide large-scale export-oriented industries which would create the desired employment. He knew that the Control of Manufacturers Acts 1932-34 cornerstones of his protectionist policy in the 1930s, had to be amended. They were not repealed altogether, however, as the Opposition Parties, Fine Gael and Labour advocated. The Industrial Development (Encouragement of External Investment) Act of 1958 provided tax and rates concessions to foreign companies and attractive financial incentives to foreign capital investment. Between 1960-69 more than 350 new foreign-owned companies were established, producing mainly for export. Although anxious to attract foreign investment, Lemass wanted to discourage the practice, increasingly popular in N.I., of foreign parent companies setting up branches in Ireland. Trouble with the parent company might mean the closure of the subsidiary branch in Ireland first. Lemass preferred "joint ventures" between Irish and foreign capital. Of 38 new enterprises started in 1958, 18 were joint-owned. Only three were wholly foreign.

One of the successes of the First Programme was the creation of industrial estates, in particular the Shannon Industrial Estate whose rapid growth from 1961 led to the first new town, Shannon, since the foundation of the state. From 1937 Lemass had encouraged the development of Shannon as the first airport of Aer Lingus. In 1959 Shannon became a transatlantic airport with the first Irish-American flights taking place. Shannon became an ideal location for the development of an industrial growth centre concentrating on manufacturing for export. The establishment of industrial estates outside of Dublin and away from major centres of population, in particular the location of Shannon Industrial Estate, west of the Shannon, traditionally an area of high unemployment, assisted in the attainment of another objective; the redistribution of industrial development and the provision of industrial employment in areas of unemployment. The Nationalist leader in N.I., Eddie Mc Ateer, saw this as Lemass's greatest achievement. In 1966 he said he would "remember him as a realist who blew away the mist on the bogs and brought welcome factory smoke in their place."

The achievements of the First Programme for Economic Expansion were impressive. The two per cent growth per annum forecasted in the Programme was more than doubled over the five year period which happily coincided with what has been described as an "unprecedented world economic boom" in the early Sixties. Economic growth slowed up during the Second Programme (a projected Seven-Year Period from 1963-1970), which was abandoned in 1967, mainly because over-optimistic targets set could not be realised in adverse international trading circumstances from the mid-Sixties. Economic growth, however, throughout the 1960s was faster and more sustained than during any other decade since 1922. The twin goals, reduction of unemployment and emigration were achieved especially during the period of the First Programme. The stemming of the emigration flow meant that by 1971 the population had risen by over 100,000 from the all-time low of 2.8m. in 1961 to the highest recorded since 1922.

By the mid-Sixties there was a reversal of the emigration trend. In August 1963 the Irish embassy in London recorded sixty/seventy enquires a month from Irish emigrants wanting to return home. The Ireland that they returned to was very different from the land they had left. It has been said that, while Ireland changed little during the de Valera era, social and economic change in the Sixites transformed life at every level. High-rise office and apartment blocks were rapidly changing the face of Dublin and major cities. In 1965 Dublin Corporation's planned new housing scheme at Ballymun was the largest corporation housing scheme in the history of the state and brought apartment-block living to Ireland. The first supermarkets were appearing in Dublin suburbs and threatening the corner-grocery shop. In 1965 Ireland's first shopping centre opened at Stillorgan Co. Dublin.

Living standards rose by 50% during the Sixties. The visible signs of affluence were everywhere. Private car ownership jumped from 143,000 in 1958 to 330,000 in 1968. The visit of U.S. President Kennedy in 1963 and the reduction of the transatlantic flight to New York from fourteen hours to six hours in the same year boosted the Irish-American tourist trade. Tourism became a major industry. In 1965 tourist revenue rose to £77m. The importance of the British tourist as well as the American tourist was recognised when the government bought the B & I shipping company in order to compete with British Rail car ferries. In 1965 the number of tourist cars in Ireland had increased by 53%.

The most powerful force for change in Irish life during the Sixties was the introduction of a national television service in 1962. Radio Telefis Eireann, established by the Broadcasting Act of 1960 began transmission at 7 p.m. on New Year's Eve 1962 and was welcomed by Lemass who said that the Irish people were citizens of the world as well as of Ireland. Rural electrification, largely completed during the Fifties meant that by the mid-Sixties one in two families had a television set. More and more families were acquiring labour-saving devices such as electric cookers, fridges, washing machines which liberated the house-wife from the home.

Education

The great "Leap forward" to an industrial economy necessitated sweeping changes in education, an area which resisted state control. The old British examination system was replaced in 1923 by the Intermediate and Leaving Certificate Examinations set up by the Department of Education whose first Minister for Education was Eoin MacNeill, a founder member of the Gaelic League. Although Irish was made a compulsory subject in both national and secondary schools, little had changed in Irish education since the nineteenth century.

The 1916 Proclamation of the Irish Republic had declared its resolve to cherish "all the children of the nation equally". Yet the first scientific study of Irish education "Investment in Education" published in 1965 showed that 75% of secondary students attended fee-paying secondary schools. The report showed that only 2% of manual workers who accounted for 25% of the work-force had third-level education. By 1962 only 1/2 of primary school children completed their primary education despite the School Attendance Act 1926 making school attendance compulsory between the ages of six and fourteen years. Only 1/4 of secondary school students sat the Leaving Certificate exam. Despite the Vocational Education Act of 1930 setting up 38 Vocation Education Committees which by 1964 provided 250 schools catering for 29,000 students, some 25% of the secondary school population, only one secondary school in six taught science to Leaving Certificate level. On the eve of Ireland's entry into the E.E.C. only 21% of boys in secondary schools took French. Eighty per cent however took Latin according to a survey done in 1962-'63. Even the teaching of Irish, compulsory in both national and secondary schools since March 17th 1922 had met with only limited success. Many national schools could not fulfill the one hour's prescribed Irish tuition per day in national school simply because of 12,000 national teachers surveyed in 1922 only 1,107 were competent to teach Irish. Financial inducements to teachers who taught through Irish and to all-Irish schools meant that by 1961 96% of national teachers were qualified to teach Irish. Despite this there was only a 10% increase in Irish speakers between 1911 and 1961. Even in its stated objective, the restoration of the Irish language, the Irish system was having only limited success. In 1964 a government Commission on the Restoration of the Irish Language under the chairmanship of Irish scholar and future Primate of all Ireland Cardinal O'Fiaich made 288 separate recommendations designed to popularise the Irish language. In 1965 the government announced a ten-year plan aimed at restoring Irish "as a general medium of communication in a bilingual Ireland".

Lemass, who never fully mastered the Irish language, was more concerned that Irish education should keep pace with the technological development needed in order to sustain the economic revolution of the Sixties. From 1957 Ministers of Education had been drawn from the ranks of dynamic ambitious younger men in the party. Lynch, a future Taoiseach, was followed by Hillery, a future President of Ireland. Both Ministers attempted to modernise Irish education. Attempts to close uneconomic one-teacher national schools in remote rural areas met with determined opposition from Catholic managers of such schools who opposed state interference. Opponents of educational change found an able spokesman in Dr. Browne, Bishop of Galway. Opposition from the Catholic hierarchy, however, did not prevent radical changes. In 1963 Education Minister Hillery announced the setting up of comprehensive schools offering both grammar and vocational courses in areas where there was no secondary school. The most sweeping change came with Donough O'Malley, Minister for Education from July 1966 until his death in March 1968. In September 1966 with Lemass's approval he announced the introduction of free post-primary education to be effective from the next year. In addition free transport would be provided to all who lived three miles or more from the school. Enrolment into non-fee-paying secondary schools increased immediately. By 1970 200,000 students attended secondary schools more than double the 88,000 who attended state-aided secondary schools in 1964. More than any other measure, free secondary education revolutionised Irish education and led to the creation of third level Regional Technical Colleges and the expansion of existing universities. In 1972 over 20,000 students attended university, a three-fold increase on 1949 numbers. By 1976 a further 6,000 were attending the new Regional Colleges, evidence of the growing importance being attached to technological education.

The best barometer of economic success is Lemass's electoral fortunes 1959-'66. Lemass called his first election in 1961, before the First Programme for Economic Expansion had run its course and at a time when emigration and unemployment were still rising. It was the first election campaign that Fianna Fáil fought without de Valera and resulted in Fianna Fáil losing 8 seats. The unwillingness of Fine Gael and Labour to join together in opposition ("the coalition mentality (of the Fifties) had all but disappeared" according to one political commentator) enabled Lemass to form a minority government with the support of 2 Independents. He thus had a mandate to continue his policies.

Lemass's spectacular success in 1965 when, with 75 seats, Fianna Fáil won an overall majority of five seats, was the first time since 1922 that any government increased its vote after the normal four and a half years in office. (Dail elections must be held every five years). The "electoral ghost of de Valera" was truly laid. Despite the introduction of controversial measures such as a turnover tax in 1963, an indirect tax on goods and services carried by only one vote and a national wages agreement in 1964 linking future wage increases to productivity, the 1965 election results were a personal mandate for Lemass and his Programmes for Economic Expansion. The economic benefits of the First programme were beginning to bear fruit. Unemployment had dropped by over 30% and emigration rates had slowed dramatically to the point where its cessation could be confidently contemplated. Fianna Fáil fought the 1965 election on the slogan "Let Lemass Lead On." Just over one year later in November 1966 Lemass, aged 67 years, resigned, stating bluntly, "It is time I moved on. I don't want to became a national monument around the place."

International Relations

The late 1950s saw a move away not just from the economic isolationism of self-sufficiency but also from the diplomatic isolation of the post-war period. Membership of the Council of Europe from its foundation in 1949 and of the world peace-keeping organisation, the United Nations in December 1955, brought Irish government representatives to the international conference tables. As in the League of Nations when, on his very first attendance at Geneva in 1932 de Valera found himself President of the Council of the League, the Irish Republic made an early and significant impact in the U.N. In 1960 Irish troops joined UNIFIL forces abroad on the first of a series of international peace-keeping missions which have brought Irish soldiers as far afield as the Congo, Cyprus, the Middle East and Namibia in South Africa. Tragedy, with the massacre of nine Irish soldiers at the Niemba ambush in the Congo in November 1960, did not deter the Irish Republic from its new role of international peace-keeper. In the same year the Irish ambassador to the U.N. became president of the General Assembly and presided over the historic session when Khrushchev, the Soviet leader was ruled out of order for conduct unbecoming to a member when he banged on the table with his shoe.

Lemass visited New York and the U.N. in 1963, the year in which the American bond of friendship was cemented by the visit of U.S. President Kennedy to Ireland just months before his assassination in November 1963. In his address to the U.N. Lemass saluted the international peace-keeping organisation as the guardian of the "free-world". Yet his main interests lay in Europe. Although Aiken remained Minister of External Affairs throughout the Lemass years, Lemass took an active interest and directed foreign policy especially relations with Europe and with Britain and Northern Ireland.

Lemass was the first senior Fianna Fáil member to declare openly for closer relations with Western Europe. In 1959 the choice for Lemass seemed to be either to join the non-aligned British-inspired and dominated European Free Trade Association (E.F.T.A.) or to seek membership of the European Economic Community the (E.E.C.). Either way protectionism had to go. One commentator has spoken of

1958/'59 as marking a turning point when the "orientation of the economy towards the world market became declared government policy and the radical departure from the protectionist development strategy of the 1930s official". Flirtation with E.F.T.A. (in November 1957 Lemass attended a free trade conference in Paris and expressed the hope that "other members will allow us a time lag of a few years in which to develop our young industries before facing the full blast of Free Trade area competition") showed Ireland's willingness to co-operate with Britain and other European countries and made it easy for the Lemass government to formally apply for membership of the European Community in July 1961. The rejection of the British and Irish application (the Irish application depended upon acceptance of the British application which was vetoed twice by the French President, de Gaulle during the 1960s) gave Ireland time in which to make necessary economic adjustments before becoming a member of the E.E.C. along with Britain and Denmark on January 1st 1973.

Relations with Britain
The history of Ireland's entry into the E.E.C. demonstrated the degree to which the Irish economy depended upon Britain. Lemass's stated aim was "to secure the economic foundation of independence." He helped Ireland to move towards economic independence by entering freely into international trade agreements such as GATT (General Agreement on Tariffs and Trade) negotiated in Geneva in 1947 but not signed by Ireland until 1960. In the same year the Lemass government entered into the first of two trade agreements with Britain. The 1960 trade agreement provided for reviews of tariffs on manufactured imports from Britain and led to the Anglo-Irish Trade Agreement of December 1965 after protracted talks in London involving both government leaders Lemass and Wilson, reminiscent of the discussions preceding the Anglo-Irish agreements of 1938 in which Lemass had played a part. The Anglo-Irish Trade agreement of 1938 has been described as a "one-way free trade agreement in Ireland's favour". The 1965 Agreement was prompted by the decision of the Labour government of Wilson to introduce a 15% levy on all imports excluding foodstuffs and raw materials. Twenty-one per cent of Irish exports were affected. Lemass immediately announced supportive measures of grants and loans to affected industries and requested Anglo-Irish negotiations to restore the preferential treatment afforded to Irish imports under the terms of the 1938 and 1948 agreements. The compromise agreement in 1965 removed all import duties on Irish goods entering Britain by July 1966. Ireland on the other hand undertook to reduce by 10% import tariffs on British imports until they were duty-free by 1975. This was in accord with a gradual shift from protection to free-trade which envisaged the removal of tariffs gradually over a twelve-fifteen year period. The real significance of both the GATT and Anglo-Irish Trade Agreements were explained by Lemass thus, "These two steps will give Irish industry better prospects of exports beyond the UK to Europe. Ultimately the aim of becoming a member of an enlarged Common Market remains."

Relations with Northern Ireland
While the emphasis in international relations was primarily economic, relations with Northern Ireland were conducted at both economic and political levels. Co-

operation was the key note both of international relations and relations with the Northern Irish state. The success of the welfare state in N.I. coupled with the failure of the Irish government's anti-partition campaign of the late 1940s early 1950s had convinced Lemass that reunification of Ireland was not a practical possibility in the foreseeable future. Lemass's views on Irish unity "unity means first... bringing the people together. It is not a matter of territorial acquisition" were a welcome departure from the republican rhetoric associated with other members of his party. Lemass's desire to break down what he called in 1959 "the barriers of suspicion, antagonism, prejudice and misunderstanding which now divide a minority in the north-east from their fellow countrymen" led to friendly gestures such as the replacement of the offensive term "Six Counties" by the inoffensive description" Northern Ireland" and eventually to the series of historic meetings between the two leaders Lemass and O'Neill in 1965. Lemass's "willingness to meet at any level and without any preconditions" led to the first ever official visit by a Southern leader to the Northern capital, Belfast, in January 1965. The return visit by the Northern leader O'Neill to Dublin in February 1965 was another first. Although Lemass expected "trouble" over his alleged recognition of the jurisdiction of the N.I. state by visiting the Northern P.M. at Stormont Castle, seat of the N.I. government, it was not Lemass but O'Neill the Northern leader, who suffered. O'Neill had not prepared public opinion as well as Lemass. Lemass predicted as much when, calling the January 1965 meeting "a breakthrough" he added "I knew at the time that O'Neill was going to have a problem".

As with every other aspect of Lemass's policy the stated motive behind the Lemass - O'Neill meetings of 1965 was economic. Both Lemass and O'Neill needed no convincing of the economic benefit accruing from joint cross-border economic projects and from closer economic co-operation between the two states. As Minister for Industry and Commerce Lemass had concluded an agreement on the joint operation of the Great Northern Railway, the Dublin-Belfast railway link. In an interview to the Northern newspaper the "Belfast Telegraph" he commented, "the economic problems of both parts of the country derive from the same sources... they will yield more readily to action on a nation-wide basis". Above all Lemass was anxious to point out that the success of economic planning in Southern Ireland held out the promise of prosperity which was bound to make the concept of self-reliance and ultimately of unity more attractive to Northerners. "Freedom is not a barrier but an aid to economic advancement," Lemass stressed, as he urged co-operation on a range of projects from promoting cross-border tourism to a national hydro-electric system.

The future of mutually beneficial economic projects was jeopardised by the events of the difficult year 1966, the fiftieth anniversary of the Easter Rising 1916. The blowing-up of Nelson's Pillar in Dublin centre just before the golden jubilee celebrations demonstrated to Northern Unionists that, despite the new mood of moderation and reconciliation, anti-British and therefore anti-Unionist terrorist sentiment was not dead. The Easter celebrations themselves, although provoking objective reappraisal of the whole War of Independence period, were regarded by Unionist extremists as provocative and an excuse for the resurgence of militant republicanism in both parts of Ireland.

It was particularly appropriate that de Valera should be President and Lemass

Taoiseach in the Year of the Golden Jubilee. De Valera was popularly perceived as having been the architect of political independence. His dismantling of the Treaty and his drawing up of the Constitution in 1937 laid the political foundations of the state. Lemass declared in 1959, "The historic task of this generation is to secure the economic development". The success of the First Programme for Economic Expansion meant that in 1966 citizens of the Irish Republic could celebrate not just political independence but also a greater degree of prosperity and economic stability than at any other time since the foundation of the state and could look forward with confidence and optimism to the future. It was also fitting that Lemass should choose to resign in 1966. In the knowledge that the economic foundations of the state had been laid by the First Programme for Economic Expansion and, having drawn up the Second Programme and introduced it in 1963, Lemass felt that his task was finished. In 1969 Lemass resigned from the Dáil, ending over forty years in public life. On May 11th, 1971 Lemass died. The "Irish Times " obituary included the finest tribute perhaps could that be paid to a government leader, "he came to power too late - he left power too early."

Appraisal

Lemass, a founder member of Fianna Fáil and party organiser since its foundation, ensured the survival of Fianna Fáil as the national party in modern Ireland. Lemass lived in the shadow of de Valera. He had to wait almost fifteen years after becoming Tánaiste and heir apparent to the Taoiseach before assuming leadership in 1959 and was regarded by some as a stopgap Taoiseach. Lemass, however, was the first Irish leader to have come to power because of his proven track record as a minister, firstly in Industry and Commerce and, during the war, in Supplies. Far from being a care-taker leader, Lemass brought about political and economic change which transformed and has influenced the development of Ireland ever since.

Political change was expected when Lemass became Taoiseach but understanding fully the adage, "hasten slowly", Lemass was content, until after his first election in 1961, to appoint young men to junior positions only. Thus Charles J. Haughey, Lemass's son-in-law and future Taoiseach became parliamentary secretary to the Minister for Justice in May 1960. The composition of his own first government in 1961 demonstrated Lemass's astuteness as a politician. While key positions went to relative newcomers such as Lynch, Lemass's successor in 1966, who moved from Education to Industry and Commerce, Lemass retained three members of de Valera's first administration Ryan, Aiken, and MacEntee who, during the Thirties and Forties, had opposed Lemass's policy of increased state intervention. It was only in 1965 that Lemass, by retaining only one of the founder members of Fianna Fail, Aiken, at Foreign Affairs, made the complete transition to post-de Valera politics and created "the youngest cabinet in Europe". The two other main political parties, Fine Gael and Labour had both acquired new leaders. Corish replaced Norton as Labour leader in 1960. Cosgrave, son of W. T. Cosgrave, became leader of Fine Gael in 1965. The 1960s can thus be regarded as a period of political rejuvenation and renewal.

Lemass acted as a bridge between Ireland's past, the War of Independence and the Civil War, and its future as a viable economic unit with a role to play in Europe and the greater world and in which the divisive issues of the War of Independence and the Civil War have no part.

"A mould breaker and a mould maker", Lemass was the architect of protectionism in the Thirties but was realist and pragmatist enough to break with traditional policies which were no longer in Ireland's interests. Of Lemass Professor Lee has said, "Lemass set out on the first stage of a long hard slog to change mentalities". This was particularly true in relation to Northern Ireland, Britain and the economy. Lemass had little time for the romantic patriots of yester-year. His preference for realities rather than pious aspirations dictated a bold and imaginative policy towards Northern Ireland culminating in the historic Lemass-O'Neill meetings in 1965, Lemass's greatest diplomatic achievement. Co-operation was the keynote in international relations and was to lead to improved relations with Britain and Europe.

Tragically Lemass, the great European, died before Ireland voted in 1972 to accept membership of the European Community.

Lemass's greatest legacy was the adoption of new ideas which made possible the development of modern Ireland and what has been called its transformation from frustrated idealism to dynamic realism. Lemass's economic philosophy can be summed up in his oft-repeated phrase, "A rising tide lifts all boats". His optimism about Ireland's economic future provided a welcome contrast in the Sixties to the "gloom and doom" prophecies of the Fifties. The economic transformation which took place during the Sixties under Lemass's leadership is his best monument. John A. Murphy Professor of Irish History has said, "When Eamon de Valera departed from active politics in 1959 he left Irish society very much as he found it". Change and development over the next seven years under Lemass surpassed that at any other time in the history of the state. While de Valera can be called the political architect of modern Ireland it is equally fair to regard Lemass as the economic architect of modern Ireland.

Landmarks in Lemass's Life 1899 - 1971

1899   *15th July*   Birth in Dublin.

1916   *April*   Minor role in the G.P.O. during Easter Week.

1919-21   Guerilla activist during War of Independence.

1922   As anti-Treaty Irregular joined the Four Courts garrison under Rory O'Connor.

1922   *December - October 1923*   Imprisoned by the Free State government.

1924   As Sinn-Féin Anti-Treaty T.D. abstained from the Dáil, acted as Minister for Defence in Republican "shadow" government.

1926   *March*   Welcomed de Valera's break with Sinn Féin.

1926-32   Lemass a founder member and party organiser of Fianna Fáil.

1932-39   Minister for Industry and Commerce and architect of protectionism in 1930s.

1939-45   Minister for Supplies during the Emergency.

1945-59   Tánaiste.

1959-66	The Lemass Era.
1959-63	First Programme for Economic Expansion.
1965	Lemass-O'Neill historic meetings.
1965	Anglo-Irish Free Trade Agreement.
1966	Golden Jubilee Celebrations of Easter 1916.
1966	*November* Resignation as Taoiseach.
1971	*11th May* Death of Lemass.

Sean Lemass (1899 - 1971)

10. MacBride

Early Influences

Sean MacBride, the only person ever to be awarded both the Nobel and Lenin Peace Prizes, started life as a revolutionary and was, for a brief period during the Thirties, Chief-of-Staff of the IRA. He was born in Paris on 26th January 1904 to parents both of whom were legends in their own life-time. His mother Maud Gonne, daughter of a British Army officer, was an ardent Irish nationalist and romantic figure of the Irish Literary Renaissance of the last quarter of the 19th century. Described by W.B. Yeats as "the most dazzling woman I have ever seen", Maud Gonne was the inspiration for some of his finest love poems. His strong-willed mother became the most important influence in MacBride's life. At her insistence the baby Sean was brought to Ireland to be christened. John O'Leary the old Fenian was his godfather. Sean MacBride was destined, however, not to live in Ireland until after the execution of his father, Major John MacBride in 1916. His mother feared to bring him to Ireland as a child in case he fell under the influence of his father, her estranged husband after 1905. In Paris Maud Gonne never lost sight of the Irish revolutionary cause and ran a republican publication "Irlande Libre" during the mid 1900s.

Sean MacBride (1904-88)

MacBride's father was equally famous and has earned a place in Irish history, firstly, as the colourful leader in the Irish Brigade who fought for the Boers against the British in the Boer War in South Africa 1899-1902. Although his part in the Easter Rising was small, Major MacBride was executed following court-martial on 5th May 1916, mainly, it was felt, because the British had never forgiven him for his role in the Boer War. Sean MacBride learned of his father's death from priests at the Gonzaga College in Paris which he attended. Returning to live in Ireland was not as easy as Maud Gonne had hoped. The British War Office informed her the day before they were due to leave that she would be allowed to live in Britain but not in Ireland. Eventually in February 1918 they entered Ireland unobtrusively in disguise and stayed in Dublin at a secret location in the St. Stephen's Green area.

It was almost inevitable that Sean MacBride, whose mother was passionately involved in the independence struggle, should be drawn into revolutionary circles. In May 1918 he witnessed his mother being arrested, one of the 73 Sinn Féin victims of the so-called "German Plot". Although only 14 years of age he joined Fianna Eireann. Not content, however, with being a youth member of the IRA MacBride made himself out to be more than his sixteen years and joined B Company Active Service Unit in Dublin 1920. In September 1920 MacBride was arrested while driving Countess Markievicz, Dáil Minister for Labour. MacBride was also enrolled at U.C.D. as a student of agriculture and law. Although Kevin Barry was an eighteen-year-old medical student who paid the supreme price for involvement in IRA activities, being hanged in Mountjoy jail on 1st November 1920, MacBride was struck by the lack of support generally among the student body for the revolutionary cause.

MacBride himself had some difficulty in gaining acceptance in IRA circles. His French back-ground and his French accent which remained with him throughout life set him apart from the Irish revolutionaries. One of the greatest problems that MacBride encountered during his brief period as IRA Chief-of Staff in 1936 was the language barrier between himself and subordinate officers which meant that frequently his orders were misinterpreted. Daring exploits, however, such as the "rescue" of a wounded comrade from hospital on Bloody Sunday 1920 before he could be apprehended, enhanced the reputation of the youthful IRA leader. Collins, Director of Intelligence during the War of Independence, appreciated MacBride's potential as a continental contact. Under cover of returning to France MacBride undertook assignments abroad including the negotiation of arms purchases in Germany. MacBride was furious at the announcement of the truce ending the War of Independence on 11th July 1921. Over sixty years later MacBride was still convinced that the truce was ill-timed. At the time he wanted to negotiate an arms deal on the continent. He also felt that, despite serious losses of men and arms by the failure of large-scale operations such as the Customs House attack of May 1921, the IRA could have carried on military operations for at least two to three months. Despite MacBride's youth he was chosen to accompany the Irish delegation to London as Collins's aide-de-camp and dispatch carrier between London and Dublin. He was, therefore, during the Treaty negotiations close to the centre of power and decision-making, commuting regularly with dispatches between de Valera in Dublin and the Treaty delegates in London. In his opinion the first mistake the Irish delegation made was not to return to Ireland each week-end. Later misunderstandings might not have arisen if regular contact with home had been maintained. MacBride was always an outspoken opponent of the Treaty. To him it was "a sorry mistake". MacBride quickly found himself in the anti-Treaty camp. He supported the Anti-Treaty decision to set up a rival junta government in the Four Courts. On June 22nd 1922 he joined Rory O'Connor and the Four Courts garrison. He took part in the spirited defence of the Four Courts at the end of June 1922 and was among the hundred prisoners taken after the two days bombardment by the National Forces. He shared a jail-cell with Rory O'Connor, the Commander-in-Chief of the Anti-Treaty IRA. The memory of the awful night when, almost six months after their capture, all were awakened about three o'clock in the morning and told to dress, never left him during his long life. As he was dressing he was asked his name and told to return to bed. His name was not on the list. Later that morning, 8th December 1922, he heard the shots when his cell-mate O'Connor and comrades Mellows, McKelvey and Barrett were executed as a reprisal for the assassination of T.D. Sean Hales on his way to Dáil Eireann the previous day. MacBride knew that, like other prisoners taken since the start of the Civil War and not charged with any offence, he was also under sentence of death.

MacBride languished in prison for sixteen months. In October 1923 almost six months after the end of the Civil War 400 prisoners, among them MacBride, went on hunger strike in protest at their long confinement. On the fifth day of his hunger strike MacBride was transferred to Kilmainham jail when an escape tunnel was discovered. En route to Kilmainham MacBride escaped from a prison convoy. Two months later, after the death of two hunger strikers, the Cosgrave government granted a Christmas amnesty to 3,000 prisoners.

After the Civil War MacBride, like so many other Anti-Treaty supporters, found it safer to live outside of Ireland. Unlike many other political emigrants he did not join the Irish-American community in the U.S. He returned instead to his native France and became an international journalist working at intervals in Paris, London and Dublin, throughout the Twenties. In 1926 he married fellow revolutionary Kid Bulfin who had been arrested with him after the fall of the Four Courts and was one of over 300 women prisoners held during the Civil War. His mother Maud Gonne MacBride had bought Roebuck House in Dublin in 1923. Roebuck House became the MacBride family home and one of the few centres of occupation for ex-Republican prisoners. The intrepid and resourceful Maud Gonne started a range of activities including "Roebuck Brand jam" for the unemployed ex-prisoners and their families.

Although married and intermittently pursuing legal studies, MacBride retained close links with the illegal IRA movement. Arrested in July 1931 with seven other IRA leaders he was described in official police reports as the "principal travelling organiser of the Irish Republican Army". The discovery of a pamphlet entitled "Saor Eire" on MacBride who was a member of the IRA Executive was taken as "proof" of the links between Communist-oriented movements and the IRA. (The aims of Saor Eire, according to its literature, were "to turn the Free State into a Soviet republic, in which manual workers only will have any rights"). Sean MacBride was said to have contacted Russians during stays in Paris. MacBride's arrest gave "substance" to the "Red Scare" of 1931. A charge of high treason however failed. The release of the IRA leaders demonstrated the inadequacy of existing legislation. The draconian Public Safety Act of October 1931 setting up a Military Tribunal with sweeping powers to convict on suspicion was rushed through parliament just one month after Saor Eire went public. Fianna Fáil victory in February 1932 meant that MacBride and the IRA could breathe freely again.

The hope expressed by MacBride on the day in March 1932 on which 17 IRA prisoners were released that, "all the national forces in the country would unite in marching forward achieving a free Irish Republic for the whole of Ireland", was rudely shattered. To his dismay the IRA found themselves fighting an internal enemy - ideological disputes and divisions which rent the movement in the Thirties - and an external enemy - an unsympathetic Fianna Fáil government as determined as the Cosgrave government to crush a rebel private army. In 1934 Socialists within the IRA led by Saor Eire founder Peadar O'Donnell broke away from the main Republican body and formed the Marxist Republican Congress. Although Secretary of Saor Eire in 1931 MacBride was never a Communist nor even a social revolutionary. He sided with the Republican IRA and became joint leader with Maurice Twomey of the Republican IRA whose primary objective was the attainment of an all-Ireland Republic. The arrest of Twomey in 1936, following the banning of the IRA by de Valera in June 1936, left MacBride Chief-of Staff of a demoralised depleted IRA, suffering from the split with Socialist Saor Eire elements and the defection of large numbers of the IRA. These were being attracted by offers of military pensions for ex-IRA men who fought for the Anti-Treaty IRA during the Civil War and commissions in the Army and positions in the Broy Harriers, an armed auxiliary police force manned chiefly by former IRA men. MacBride questioned the wisdom of continued armed resistance and welcomed the 1937 Consitution which declared Eire to be a republic in everything but name. MacBride had already been toying with political alternatives to violence. In 1929 he had been a founder member of the short-lived Comhairle na Poblachta. In 1936 he had founded with his mother Cumann Poblachta na hEireann as a Republican alternative to Fianna Fáil. His mother at the age of seventy had stood for election in 1937. Her defeat did not deter him from choosing the constitutional path. In 1937 he resigned from the IRA, the organisation in which he had spent almost half his life. Called to the Irish Bar in 1937 and to the Inner Bar a record six years later, MacBride spent the war years pleading the cause of former IRA colleagues on trial for their lives before the military tribunals set up by the de Valera government during the Emergency to deal with the special threat posed by possible joint German IRA action. He successfully challenged the Offences against the State Act of June 1939 and caused it to be amended in 1940. MacBride's identification with the IRA cause meant that he was frequently chosen by the families of IRA men who had died on hunger-strike in 1940 and 1946 to represent them at inquests. When MacBride decided to enter the political arena in 1946 his first and staunchest supporters were IRA sympathisers. Historian John A. Murphy said that the well-spring of the new party Clann na Poblachta was the "republican university", the jails and internment camps of the 1940s. Its first organising committees were the committees formed to help republican prisoners.

Clann na Poblachta - A Republican Alternative to Fianna Fáil

Clann na Poblachta was formally launched in July 1946 as a radical republican party dedicated "to work for the achievement of republican ideals by purely political means". "By purely political means" was important because it meant that its founder, MacBride, who just ten years before had been the IRA Chief-of-Staff, was formally and publicly renouncing violence as a means to bring about the republican ideals which he and the IRA equally cherished. The "Irish Times" of 8th July 1946 commented thus "a large section of what you might call the IRA were taking constitutional action".

From the outset MacBride was determined that Clann na Poblachta would play a full role in the political life of the state. Parliamentary abstention which had rendered Sinn Féin and other non-Fianna Fáil Republican parties impotent was not Clann na Poblachta Party policy. Clann na Poblachta recognised the institutions of state and was determined to use the constitutional process to bring about a republic and the unity of Ireland - the twin political objectives of the new party. Unlike de Valera who put the ending of partition before a republic, MacBride was a doctrinaire republican and made the securing of a republic his first political priority. The repeal of the External Relations Act passed by the de Valera government in 1936 and the last tenuous link with the British Commonwealth became the cornerstone of the party's political programme. An active campaign against partition was also urged as a means of achieving the ultimate objective of a united thirty-two county republic. MacBride also wanted Dáil Eireann to become what it had originally set out to be in 1919, the national parliament of all Ireland, by admitting elected representatives from Northern Ireland. In 1948 MacBride was instrumental in having the first Northerner a Protestant nationalist, Denis Ireland, appointed to the Senate. As Nationalists had finally agreed to enter the N.I. Parliament and had adopted the role of parliamentary Opposition only in 1946, the political climate for Northern participation in Southern politics was not favourable.

Clann na Poblachta also had a radical programme of social reform. Anxious to capitalise on the economic and social discontent caused by the indefinite continuation of war-time emergency rationing and restrictions, MacBride's able and informed spokesman on health and social issues, Dr. Noel Browne, attacked the government's appalling record on health and social services. Departments of Health and Social Welfare had only been created, in response to public pressure, on Christmas Eve 1946. Browne called for a complete reform of public health and the setting in place of a public health service comparable to that being provided in the post-war British welfare state. Victory in two of three by-elections held on October 30th 1947 brought MacBride into the Dáil as a deputy for Dublin South West and encouraged the infant party to organise on national lines in order to fight the snap general election called by an alarmed de Valera. For de Valera, however, there was to be no repeat of the snap election victories of 1933, 1938 and 1944. Disillusioned and discontented voters were attracted by the heavy emphasis on social issues in Clann na Poblachta's nine-point election manifesto. Workers were attracted by the promise to implement a comprehensive Social Insurance scheme along the lines recommended by Bishop Dignan, bishop of Clonfert and chairman of the National Health Insurance Society. All welcomed the commitment to eradicate tuberculosis as a killer disease. Teachers, attracted into the ranks of Clann na Poblachta by the long, bitter and inconclusive national teachers' strike of 1946, welcomed the pledge to raise the school leaving age to 16 and to provide free primary, secondary and university education for all, even though this was an unrealistic target not to be attempted for another twenty years. Farmers welcomed the promise to subsidise the production of essential foodstuffs while all looked forward to the consequent reduction in the cost of living. Republicans, disappointed with de Valera's failure to declare a republic, were wooed by the last point of the manifesto "Freedom and Independence for all Ireland as a Democratic Republic." Fielding two candidates in every constituency in the February 1948 general election was a tactical error for the young Clann na Poblachta party with slender resources. Of ninety candidates nominated only 10 Clann na Poblachta TDs were elected. Six of the ten won Dublin seats. Yet, Clann na Poblachta's ten votes were needed to form a government as the election results showed Fianna Fáil 68 seats, Fine Gael 31, Clann na Poblachta 10, Clann na Talmhan (the small farmers' party founded in 1938) 7, Independents 12. The Labour Party, split by the power-struggle which had weakened it since the return of Larkin in 1923, had finally divided into two Labour parties of which the original Labour Party formed in 1912 returned 14 TDs, the break-away National Labour party 5 TDs. Fianna Fáil, however, remained the largest party. The union of all the other parties plus the support of the Independents was needed to prevent them from taking office.

Formation of the First Inter-Party Government

MacBride played a key role in bringing together the Opposition parties in a series of meetings over a long St. Valentine's Day Weekend. Fine Gael was the largest of the Opposition Parties but MacBride was determined not to serve under the then Fine Gael leader, the former General Mulcahy who, as successor to Collins as Commander-in-chief and as Minister for Defence in the first Cosgrave government, was held by MacBride to have been responsible for some of the worst excesses in the Civil War. Norton, the Labour Party leader was determined not to accept any party leader as government leader. This led to MacBride on Saturday 14th February asking Costello, a lesser figure in the Fine Gael party and untainted by Civil War hatred, to lead an inter-party government. Costello, a fifty-seven year old barrister, who like MacBride had been involved in IRA trials during the war-period, at first refused. When it became clear that Norton also wanted Costello as Taoiseach, Fine Gael issued a short statement on the Sunday night saying that Costello would accept nomination as Taoiseach when the Dáil met on Wednesday 18th February 1948 in response to a unanimous request made by the leaders and representatives of all opposition parties (other than National Labour which was to pledge their support only on the eve of the Dáil vote) and announced that "all parties have agreed to co-operate in the formation of an inter-party government".

In practice this meant that even before the Dáil met and Costello was elected Taoiseach by 75 votes to 68, not only allocation of departments between the parties but also the government ministers, had been decided by the party leaders. Of the thirteen government ministers six were to be from Fine Gael, two each from Clann na Poblachta and Labour and one from Clann na Talmhan, National Labour and the Independents. Historian Ronan Fanning asserts that MacBride's "influence on the shape of the government was peculiarly decisive". To MacBride the two most important departments in a government, which he was determined would declare a republic and would bring about social and economic reform, were the department of external affairs and the relatively new department of health. MacBride was determined to hold External Affairs himself. Mulcahy who had already surrendered the leadership at MacBrides's insistence allowed MacBride to take External Affairs, his second choice, and accepted without demur the less-important portfolio of Education, having failed to get Finance which went to MacBride's choice McGilligan, Minister for Industry and Commerce under Cosgrave from 1924 until 1931. Not only therefore did MacBride take exactly what he wanted for Clann na Poblachta but he also influenced the choice of Fine Gael Ministers as well. Although MacBride later paid tribute to Mulcahy's "constructive and magnanimous selflessness" in 1948 and although relations were generally cordial between the barristers in the Coalition government, Costello, MacBride, McGilligan, and the Taoiseach's parliamentary secretary Liam Cosgrave, son of W.T. Cosgrave and a future Taoiseach, the first inter-party government (1948-1951) was generally regarded as an ill-assortment of unlikely bedfellows. MacBride's protegé Noel Browne was at Health. A barrister colleague McGilligan was at Finance and at Agriculture was MacBride's school-mate for a brief period in 1918-19 James Dillon, who had left Fine Gael in 1941 because of its support for war-time neutrality and was then an Independent. The key positions of Defence and Justice were however held by Fine Gael stalwarts T. F. O'Higgins, brother of the assassinated Kevin O'Higgins and a founder member of the Blueshirts and the Civil War veteran General Sean MacEoin respectively. Fianna Fáil propagandist Frank Gallagher derisively referred to the first inter-party coalition government as an "alliance between a dog and its fleas." The wonder at the time was not that it collapsed within three years but that it lasted so long and achieved so much both at home and abroad.

As well as influencing the composition of the coalition cabinet MacBride also endeavoured to influence the conduct of government business. Convinced that civil servants who had transferred from the British civil service in Ireland in 1922 were "mainly British secret service agents," MacBride insisted upon the exclusion of the government secretary and any civil servant from cabinet meetings. Government records and minutes were kept instead by the parliamentary secretary to the Taoiseach, Liam Cosgrave who had not the experience of senior civil servants in secretarial matters. Brian Farrell, political analyst and broadcaster, judged "that this departure from established procedure weakened both Taoiseach and cabinet". It is noteworthy that during the second inter-party government of 1954-1957 of which MacBride was not a member, the government secretary attended cabinet meetings.

MacBride and Foreign Policy: The Declaration of the Irish Republic
The Declaration of the Irish Republic

Although MacBride did not make repeal of the External Relations Act a condition of his entering government, his commitment to a republic was such that his first concern as Minister for External Affairs was to create the climate both at home and abroad for breaking the last link with Britain. The choice of Costello as Taoiseach was no mere accident. Costello had been the most outspoken Fine Gael critic of the External Relations Act in the Dáil in 1936 saying that the provisions conferring "authority on the new king and his successors to act in international affairs on behalf of this country... are completely and absolutely unnecessary."

In the first six months after taking office the inter party government generally, and MacBride in particular, were preparing the way for repeal. In the Dáil debate on the estimates for the Department of External Affairs in July 1948 MacBride remarked, "The Crown and outworn forms that belong to British constitutional history are merely reminders of an unhappy past that we want to bury... We are clearly a sovereign and independent state." Two weeks later MacBride found a repeal ally in Norton, the Labour leader and Tánaiste and Minister for Social Welfare in the Costello government who declared that immediate abolition of the External Relations Act "would do our national self-respect good both at home and abroad." Costello found himself in the difficult position of representing in an inter-party government a party which since its formation in 1934 had been known as the "Commonwealth" party standing for a united Ireland within the British Commonwealth. He knew that the government must adopt a common policy on the issue. Otherwise, as Costello pointed out in a letter to historian F. S. L. Lyons in 1969, a private member's motion by "some person not well-disposed to the government" might have forced a division on an issue on which Fine Gael and Clann na Poblachta might have taken different sides and consequently have brought down the government.

Fianna Fáil who had been drafting their own repeal of the External Relations Act before they went out of office in February 1948 made it known in early August that they would not oppose repeal. Health Minister Browne's subsequent denial that this was so may have been because he did not attend all cabinet meetings. In the same month a cabinet decision to repeal the External Relations Act was taken. No decision on the timing or manner of such an announcement was taken, however, before Taoiseach Costello left on an official visit to Canada in early September. As a guest of the Canadian Bar Association he delivered a speech on "Ireland in international affairs". The text had been approved by the cabinet before he left Ireland. In the course of a speech on how the constitutional relations of Ireland with the Commonwealth had changed since the Treaty, Costello referred to the "inaccuracies and infirmities" of those sections of the External Relations Act which dealt with the position of the Crown. It was clear especially to newspaper journalists that Costello wanted the External Relations Act repealed. The "Sunday Independent" newspaper headline of 5th September 1948 "External Relations Act to go" came the very morning after Costello felt he had been insulted twice at a dinner given in his honour by the Canadian government in Ottawa. Costello regarded the placing before him at the Governor General's table of a replica of "Roaring Meg", the cannon used in the defence of Protestant Derry in 1689 and thereafter a sacred symbol to Ulster Unionists, as an affront. The refusal, however, to propose a toast to both the King and the Irish President, even though such a double toast had been agreed beforehand, was considered a calculated insult.

At a press conference in Ottawa two days after the "Sunday Independent's " sensational lead story, Costello knew that he would be questioned closely as to his government's intention and, bearing in mind the cabinet decision to repeal, he announced that it was his government's intention to repeal the External Relations Act. Upon his return Costello made it his first concern to introduce and pilot the Republic of Ireland Bill through the Dáil.

The Republic of Ireland Act did not, in the opinion of de Valera leader of the Opposition, declare a republic but declared rather that "the state that exists under the 1937 constitution is a republic".

MacBride played only a behind-the-scenes role in securing what Costello called the greatest achievement of the inter-party government. Speculation that he or another informed source had leaked confidential information to the "Sunday Independent" has been denied by the pro-Fine Gael newspaper. Fourteen years later the "Sunday Independent" still maintained that its headline had derived from "an intelligent reading" of events. There is evidence to show that MacBride was disconcerted by the newspaper headline as he sent a telegram to Costello next day urging him to make no comment on the provocative headline.

The most important role that MacBride played in the whole affair was to act as intermediary, with Britain. MacBride who, during the last years of British rule in Ireland, was a subversive, wanted and harassed by the British, set about the task of fostering good relations with the British Labour government of Attlee. MacBride, cosmopolition and urbane, started practising the diplomatic skills which were to make him in later years one of the United Nations most skilled peace ambassadors. On the evening of Costello's announcement at the press conference in Canada, MacBride was dining with the U.K. representative to Eire, Lord Rugby. In 1962 Lord Rugby recalled MacBride's surprise on hearing the news from his secretary. MacBride claimed, however, that if he did seem surprised it was because he was astonished that such an announcement should be seen to be sensational. MacBride took little part in the drafting of the Republic of Ireland Bill (two repeal drafts prepared by MacBride were rejected in favour of the unambiguous title Republic of Ireland). MacBride as Minister for External Affairs, however, had the task of explaining and justifying the action to both Britain and the Commonwealth member states.

Although the British government may have been surprised and annoyed at the manner in which the Irish government in another Commonwealth country announced its intention to repeal the External Relations Act and thereby to leave the Commonwealth, the decision to repeal came as no surprise to the British. Since the war the de Valera government had been in negotiation with the British about repealing the External Relations Act. De Valera's only reason for retaining the last link with the Commonwealth was the faint hope that external association might bring eventual unity of Ireland. Costello's Canadian announcement may have been controversial but it did have the effect of winning Canadian support for Irish secession from the Commonwealth. At the next commonwealth conference held in London in October 1948 i.e. after the Costello's announcement but before the introduction of the Republic of Ireland Act in November 1948, Britain was determined to take a hard line upon the proposed secession. A formal British warning of possible retaliatory measures against Irish trade and against Irish nationals living in Britain led to feverish diplomatic activity by MacBride and McGilligan among the Commonwealth delegates. Although excluded from some of the Commonwealth meetings, they were particularly successful in securing the support of the Canadian and Australian prime ministers for the Irish case. In meetings at Chequers, the country home of the British Prime Minister, and in Paris on 16th November 1948, the eve of the introduction of the Republic of Ireland Bill in the Dáil, Canadian and Australian delegates impressed upon the British the desirability of having the Irish state friendly disposed to both Britain and the Commonwealth. The Attlee Labour Government was reluctantly forced to admit "that, if they insisted on treating Èire as a foreign state... the practical difficulties would be greater for the United Kingdom than for Èire, and, furthermore, that they would thereby forfeit the sympathy and support of Canada, Australia and New Zealand."

Consequently, the British Nationality Act passed just before the repeal crisis broke, remained unchanged. British reaction to the declaration of the Republic, the Ireland Act of 5th June 1949, left unchanged the status of Irish people resident in the U.K. Citizens of Eire were no longer British subjects but while resident in Britain would be treated as British subjects. Article 1 of the Ireland Act recognised that, as from Easter Monday 1949, and the day on which the Irish Republic was officially proclaimed, "Eire ceased ...to be part of His Majesty's dominions". Article 2 stated that "notwithstanding that the Republic of Ireland is not part of His Majesty's dominions, the Republic of Ireland is not a foreign country."

Fianna Fáil fears that the declaration of a republic would emphasise "the yawning gulf which exists between Eire and Northern Ireland", as the N.I. Prime Minister Brooke asserted, were well-founded. In November 1948 while the Dáil was debating the Republic of Ireland Bill, Sir Basil Brooke the N.I. Prime Minister was meeting the British P.M. Attlee and receiving assurances that "in no event will Northern Ireland or any part thereof cease to be part of... the United Kingdom without the consent of the parliament of Northern Ireland." Article 1 Clause 2 of the Ireland Act gave this statutory guarantee to the Northern Ireland parliament. The leader of the British Liberal party summed up the situation thus, "It would seem that the purpose of Eire in deciding to become an independent Republic was to secure the reunion of Ireland... but they had now taken the one step most calculated to defeat that purpose." In 1949 as in 1922 considerations of political independence took precedence over aspirations to eventual national unity. A parody of the 19th century

unofficial national anthem "God save Ireland" ran thus,
> "God save the Southern part of Ireland.
> Three quarters of a nation once again"

and summed up the feelings of critics, most notable of whom were de Valera and the Fianna Fail party who, although they did not oppose the Republic of Ireland Bill, refused to take part in the Easter Monday celebrations accompanying the proclamation of an Irish Republic on April 18th 1949 just 33 years after it was first proclaimed on Easter Monday 1916.

Notwithstanding, the declaration of the Irish Republic has been hailed as one of the most successful acts of statesmanship achieved by an Irish Government. Costello spoke of taking the gun out of Irish politics. The last chapter in the long saga of the Treaty had been written by the political heirs of those who had fought for the Treaty. The old political divisions and animosities of the Treaty and Civil War were no longer relevant. Both main parties, Fine Gael as well as Fianna Fáil, could portray themselves as republican. For Ireland, declaring a republic also meant leaving the Commonwealth. Significantly nobody seriously considered the alternative which was made available to India at the same time as the Irish Republic was leaving the Commonwealth, i.e. remaining as a republic within the Commonwealth. Interestingly the decision to allow the Republic of India to remain within the Commonwealth came just two days after the Irish Republic was proclaimed but Britain did nothing to appraise the Irish government of its decision regarding India. The independence issue was finally settled. Britain and the Irish Republic could look forward to a new era of goodwill such as was aspired to in the closing words of the Republic of Ireland Act of December 1948 which stated "The whole basis... of this Bill is founded on goodwill,... on the end of bitterness." Among messages of congratulations received by the Irish Republic were goodwill messages from King George VI and British P.M. Attlee.

Partition

Partition remained the only outstanding issue between Britain and Ireland after the declaration of the Republic. As the second of his political objectives MacBride was determined to use his position as Minister for External Affairs to mobilise "world opinion in such a manner as to ensure that the maintenance of partition constitutes a real inconvenience to her (i.e. Britain) and is an actual hindrance to her own policies." This was how MacBride represented "the policy of the sore thumb", the deliberate raising of the partition issue at every international conference with the double aim of embarrassing Britain and enlisting foreign support and sympathy for the Irish case. To that end MacBride expanded the Foreign Service which included among its members journalist and writer Conor Cruise O'Brien who as well as being a Counsellor in charge of the Information Section of the Department was also placed in charge of the Irish News Agency set up by MacBride, a former journalist, in 1950 to release Irish newspapers from their dependence upon British news media for their world news and to provide an Irish "window" on the world.

Partition like neutrality united the Irish people. Even before the reaffirmation of partition in the Ireland Act of June 1949 an all-party anti-partitionist group, the Mansion House Committee was set up in January 1949. Church-gate collections raised £50,000 and demonstrated the depth of popular support for the cause. MacBride and Opposition Leader de Valera, who embarked on a world-wide crusade against partition in 1948, were at one in seeking to put "an anti-partition girdle round the earth".

Partition however was being seen as a means of solving post-war problems, e.g. the partition of defeated Germany. It was hardly the most favourable time for Ireland to attempt to persuade the international community of the woes of partition. Nonetheless MacBride insisted on an anti-partition policy about which in later years Dr. Conor Cruise O'Brien was to say, "The only positive result of this activity, so far as I was concerned was that it led me to discover the cavernous inanities of 'anti-partition' and of government propaganda generally."

The ending of diplomatic isolation, a by-product of war-time neutrality, however, became an objective of MacBride's foreign policy. The Irish republic sought and secured membership of international movements such as the Council of Europe where Ireland became a founder member in 1949. By 1950 MacBride was President of the Council of Foreign Ministers of the Council of Europe and helped draft the European Convention on Human Rights. Ireland became the first country to accept the jurisdiction of the European Court of Human Rights at Strasbourg following the tradition established by the Cosgrave government which accepted the jurisdiction of the International Court of Justice at the Hague in 1929. The first Irishman to take proceedings at the European Court of Human Rights against the Irish state was an IRA detainee who, in 1956, counselled by MacBride S.C. protested at his unlawful detention without trial.

Neutrality, however, still remained Ireland's defence policy. Neutrality in the post-war period and especially under MacBride became an expression not of national sovereignty as it had been during the war but of anti-partitionism. The strategic importance of Ireland's geographic position on the western seaboard in the military defence of western Europe was fully appreciated. When Ireland formally received an invitation from the U.S. on January 7th 1949 to join the North Atlantic Treaty Organisation, a military defence alliance proposed by the U.S. to join the countries of western Europe in an alliance with the U.S. and Canada against the Communist Soviet-led states of Eastern Europe, MacBride decided to play the anti-partitionist card. In what has become a policy statement on Irish neutrality MacBride declared categorically, "Any military alliance with or commitment involving military action jointly with the state that is responsible for the unnatural division of Ireland, which occupies a portion of our country with its armed forces, and which supports undemocratic institutions in the north-eastern corner of Ireland, (i.e. Britain) would be entirely repugnant and unacceptable to the Irish people. No Irish government, whatever its political views, could participate with Britain in a military alliance while this situation continues."

To show that it was Britain and not the U.S. which was the obstacle to Irish participation, two years later the Irish government endeavoured to negotiate a bilateral treaty of defence with the U.S. To this end MacBride went to the U.S. in March 1951 but hopes that, in return for the promise of U.S. defence facilities in Ireland, the U.S. might be persuaded to bring pressure on their military partner in N.A.T.O. , Britain, to end partition, were cruelly dashed when president Truman informed MacBride that "partition was an issue between two countries with which the United States was equally friendly." The Irish Republic has remained a non-aligned neutral country in a Europe divided by N.A.T.O. and the Warsaw Pact into two opposing military blocks.

Ireland's refusal to join military alliances did not deter MacBride from seeking to secure for Ireland the economic aid being offered to the West European community of states then being assisted to recover from the ravages of World War II. While de Valera had staked Ireland's claim to Marshall Aid in 1947, MacBride's fluent French and European background enabled him to become Vice-President of the Organisation for European Economic Co-operation (OEEC) of which Ireland was a founder member and to participate actively in the European Recovery Programme, undertaken by the OEEC. By 1950 Ireland had received nearly 150m. dollars in U.S. loans and was in a position to undertake new economic initiatives in order to get the stagnant post-war economy moving.

Economic Policy

The 1948 election was the first election in which social and economic issues dominated. Although the declaration of the Republic has been the most enduring achievement of the inter-Party period, the Coalition governments 1948-'51 and 1954-1957 have been judged on their handling of the social and economic problems of the post-war period. MacBride and the other Coalition ministers knew that it was the failure of the de Valera government to offer a comprehensive recovery programme after the war, which cost Fianna Fáil the 1948 election and ended de Valera's sixteen-year rule. At the second meeting of the inter-party government on 27th February 1948, at MacBride's suggestion, an inter-departmental economic committee was set up, not unlike the economic sub-committee of cabinet set up by de Valera during the war. Costello, Norton, Dillon, McGilligan and Morrissey, the Minister for Industry and Commerce, were MacBride's nominees on the economic committee of which MacBride was also a member. Costello added the names of Mulcahy and Cosgrave but MacBride's domination of the economic committee ensured that the Minister for External Affairs exercised an undue influence on economic policy.

MacBride was lucky that economic and foreign policy were closely interlinked at this period. The Marshall Aid loans secured by MacBride through participation in the OEEC encouraged him to draw up a Long Term Economic Recovery Programme in 1949. Although its ambitious aims and objectives were not realised during the three short years in office, the need for economic planning was appreciated. A large-scale afforestation programme plan to plant 25,000 trees each year was begun. In retrospect, Dillon, Minister for Agriculture, lists the preservation of the inland waterways and the initiation of a serious programme of afforestation, recommended by Griffith as part of his programme of economic nationalism, as MacBride's lasting achievements. Agriculture also benefited enormously from prudent spending of U.S. loans made available through the European Recovery Programme. Dillon, a dynamic Minister for Agriculture, was able to embark upon an ambitious Land Rehabilitation Project which proposed spending £40m. state money over a ten-year land reclamation programme aimed at turning some 4m. acres previously uncultivated land into farm land. The costly project was immediately popular as it provided employment in the most deprived areas of rural Ireland, and attempted to continue in a small way the work begun by the Congested Districts Board in 1891. One Irish economist put it thus, "Removing the rocks from Connemara... was the best news since the activities of the Congested Districts Board" at the turn of the century. Extension of the rural electrification scheme, already well advanced when the government took office, plus an intensive programme of house-building throughout the country were evidence of the government's concern to improve living standards, especially in rural Ireland. As in Northern Ireland a massive programme of house-building was needed after the war. By 1950 12,000 houses were being built each year providing a much-needed boost to the construction industry. Local Government's record in providing houses was better than anything achieved in pre-war years.

The biggest boost of all to the rural sector came from a favourable trade agreement with Britain signed on June 23rd 1948, after six days of negotiation in which MacBride as well as Costello played a key role. The Anglo-Irish trade agreement 1948 reviewed the 1938 Trade Agreement and offered more favourable terms for Irish agricultural exports to Britain. A four-year trade agreement promised to raise within two years store cattle exports to Britain from 300,000 to 400,000 per annum and fat cattle exports from 50,000 to 100,000 per annum.

Economic independence, however, was important to MacBride. He welcomed the setting up of the Industrial Development Authority (I.D.A.) in 1949 to plan and assist industrial development. MacBride endorsed the policy of state investment and state spending which, according to a leading Irish economist, became "the conspicuous feature of inter-party economic policies". Similarly he welcomed the setting up of An Coras Trachtála, the Irish Export Board which from the early Fifties endeavoured to find new markets for Irish goods mainly in the U.S. and Canada.

Although MacBride strongly influenced economic policy, especially during 1948-'49, not all of his economic ideas were adopted by the cabinet. Once political independence was achieved with the declaration of the Republic, MacBride was anxious to secure economic and financial independence from Britain. The devaluation crisis of September 1949 when Britain was forced to devalue the pound sterling against the U.S. dollar seemed, to MacBride, the opportune moment for breaking with sterling and declaring an independent Irish currency. Costello and cabinet colleagues disagreed and, despite MacBride's protests devalued the Irish pound in line with the British. The Irish Republic had to wait thirty years before finally breaking with sterling in March 1979 when Ireland joined the European Monetary System (EMS) and Britain remained outside. After the devaluation crisis MacBride's judgement on economic issues was not so readily accepted. In March 1950 he was excluded from an economic sub-committee set up to decide upon "a programme of capital works to be undertaken by the state" and to prepare the first "capital budget" in May 1950. Notwithstanding, MacBride made an important contribution to the ongoing economic debate of the post-war years which was to result in the Programmes for Economic Expansion of the Lemass Years.

The Mother and Child Scheme:
The last year of the Inter-Party Coalition government was dominated by the controversy surrounding MacBride's fellow Clann na Poblachta minister Noel Browne, Minister for Health. Born in 1914 Browne was one of the few Irish politicians at the time with no clear memory of the events of 1916-22. His boyhood memories were of his family's losing battle against an even greater scourge, the killer disease TB, which claimed the lives of his father, his mother, a brother and sister and threatened Browne's own life after he qualified as a young doctor. The eradication of TB which was killing 3,000/4,000 people per year became Browne's immediate target

on becoming Minister for Health in February 1948 on his very first day in the Dáil.

Browne was lucky that his campaign against TB coincided with some of the century's most exciting medical discoveries which made possible not only cure but also prevention of what had been one of the worst killer diseases of impoverished young people in Ireland. Mass radiography had already been introduced by the Department of Health as an early detection scheme. The recent discovery of BCG vaccination made possible the protection of the nation's children against the killer disease. The war-time discovery of antibiotics made available powerful new drugs for the effective treatment of those stricken with the disease. Browne is usually credited with providing free treatment in TB sanatoria set up for TB sufferers irrespective of means. The Health Act of 1947, however, one of the last measures of the Fianna Fáil administration, provided free treatment in TB sanatoria in Dublin, Cork and Galway set up under the Tuberculosis (Establishment of Sanatoria) Act 1945. Browne, however was the dynamic person needed in order to utilise all the means at his disposal including the channelling of large amounts of Hospital Sweepstakes money, previously used by private hospitals, into a national campaign against TB. The Hospital Sweepstakes had been started in 1930 by ex-Cumann na nGaedheal Minister Joe McGrath who had resigned from the Cosgrave government as a result of the Army Mutiny of 1924 and had been enormously successful in raising money for a much-needed hospital-building programme. Until 1948 most of the money had been used by voluntary hospitals many of which were run by church bodies, but Browne was determined to change all that. Between 1948 and 1958 a record £27.4m. was spent on public hospital construction and modernisation, £9.3m of which was spent on TB hospitals. The Hospital Sweepstakes Fund provided £17m. The dramatic drop in the number of deaths from TB (3,101 in 1948, 581 in 1958) was attributed to the impetus given to a national programme of TB eradication and public health awareness by the indefatigable Browne.

Browne's successful campaign against TB encouraged him to attempt a much more ambitious and controversial project viz. a "Free Mother and Child Welfare Service" described by the "Sunday Independent" which broke the story to the public on 3rd September 1950 as "revolutionary plans". The Fianna Fáil Health Act of 1947, however, had proposed within a reorganised health service the establishment of a scheme for maternity and child welfare to be available to all mothers and children up to the age of 16 years. A letter from the bishops expressing the disquiet of the Catholic hierarchy was enough to make de Valera quietly shelve the controversial aspects of the Act and leave his successor to deal with the combined opposition of doctors and the Catholic Church to the introduction of free medical care for mothers and children to 16 years. Browne, a junior house doctor in a TB sanatorium before becoming Minister for Health, had ill-concealed contempt for doctors in private practice who opposed free medical care because it would affect lucrative private medicine. Browne, whose political apprenticeship before becoming a minister was less than six months, made no effort to secure the support of the doctors. On the contrary he seemed to antagonise all whose support was necessary for the smooth implementation of the scheme. Department of Health personnel resented his refusal to use the proposals drawn up by the Department of Health for the 1947 Act and his insistence upon appointing his own advisory committee whose draft "Mother and Child Scheme" differed little from the 1947 recommendations. Browne used every opportunity including an address to medical students at the Royal College of Surgeons to attack the doctors. Dr. Deeny Chief Medical Adviser to the Department of Health, whose inability to work with Browne forced his resignation from the Department in 1950, said of Browne's public attacks upon the medical profession, "Up till then Dr. Browne had the general support of the Irish doctors; he threw it away and for his own reasons antagonised them".

The real opposition to the "Mother and Child Scheme" came not from the doctors but from the Catholic Hierarchy. Browne by his own account did not believe there would be effective opposition from the Church. Reaction from the Catholic bishops was swift and resolute. One week after the sensational "Sunday Independent" disclosure, in a letter to Costello the Catholic hierarchy made known its objections, "The powers taken by the state in the proposed Mother and Child Health Service are in direct opposition to the rights of the family and of the individual . . . If adopted . . . they would constitute a ready-made instrument for future totalitarian aggression." The memory of the horror of medical experiments carried out in the name of state medicine by Nazi Germany was still very vivid while anything which smacked of socialist or communist control of the individual was equally unacceptable. "The right to provide for the health of children belongs to parents, not to the state" the bishops pointed out. While admitting that the state may help indigent or neglectful parents the bishops' letter continued, "it may not deprive 90% of parents of their rights because of 10% necessitous or negligent parents. It is not sound social policy to impose a state medical service on the whole community on the pretext of relieving the necessitous 10% from the so-called indignity of the means test." Browne was urged to meet the bishops with a view to resolving differences. After meetings with Dublin Archbishop McQuaid in October 1950 Browne claimed that he had satisfied the bishops. In March 1951, having failed to win the support of either the Irish Medical Association or the Catholic Hierarchy, Browne published the Mother and Child Scheme to a storm of protest not least from government colleagues and Taoiseach Costello who rejected Browne's assertion that the Mother and Child Scheme was agreed government policy. Costello who was later to say,"I am an Irishman second; I am a Catholic first" and "I accept without qualification in all respects the teachings of the Hierarchy and the church to which I belong" insisted on dropping the scheme on April 6th 1951 following receipt of another letter from the Archbishop of Dublin on April 5th. Four days later MacBride, who had been summoned from the U.S., demanded the resignation of Browne as Minister of Health. MacBride made no effort to save his party colleague. For long he had been dissatisfied with Browne's alleged failure to attend cabinet meetings and reported habit of walking out of meetings. The developments of March/April 1951 revealed deep divisions within, not just the Coalition government but also within Clann na Poblachta, which had already lost one of its founder members, Noel Hartnett, who had resigned from the party in February 1951 alleging that the party, and MacBride in particular, "had become obsessed with power". Historian Ronan Fanning points out that "the decisive breach was between government colleagues rather than between government and hierarchy" who were at one in resisting the introduction of a no-means test health and welfare service.

The Mother and Child Controversy dealt the deathblow to the inter-party government beset by both internal divisions and an inability to deal with continuing problems of inflation and unchecked emigration. A Commission on Emigration had been established in 1948, evidence that the inter-party government appreciated that emigration was a national, social and economic problem. The Commission's report was not ready, however, until 1954. It was Costello's second inter-party government 1954-'57 which had the task of trying to respond to the Commission's findings. The first inter-party government was dissolved in May 1951. At the ensuing general election known as the "pork barrel" election because of the overriding importance of economic issues, Clann na Poblachta and MacBride realised just how damaging the Mother and Child Crisis and the resignations from the party had been for the whole party. Clann na Poblachta representation in the new Dáil fell from 10 to 2 seats. Fianna Fáil with 69 seats had just one more seat than in 1948 but yet were able to form a government. Browne elected as an Independent had sweet revenge on his Coalition colleagues by voting for Fianna Fáil and enabling them to hold power as a minority government supported by Independents for three years.

Political Eclipse

Although elected in 1951 and again in 1954 MacBride was never again to hold a position of political dominance. He declined a government post in the second coalition government 1954-'57 and indeed was instrumental in bringing it down in January 1957 when MacBride moved a vote of no confidence in the government because of its poor economic performance, its failure to deal with the twin problems, unemployment and emigration, and the government's determination to take tough action against the IRA who had launched a "border war" in 1956. MacBride boasted that the period of the first Inter-Party government, one of whose first actions was to release remaining war-time political prisoners, was the only time since the foundation of the state when no political prisoners were held by the state. Critics however attributed the resurgence of the IRA to the relaxation of restrictions on republican activities and the encouragement given to the IRA by having MacBride, a former Chief-of-Staff of the IRA, in a position of prominence in the government between 1948 and 1951. In 1957 Clann na Poblachta polled only 22,000 votes and MacBride failed to get elected. Thus, ten years after making his dramatic entry unto the Irish political scene, MacBride was gone. He made a valiant effort to re-enter the Dáil in a by-election in 1959, and made his last unsuccessful bid in the 1961 general election. By 1965, Clann na Poblachta, the party which had shown such promise in 1948, had disappeared. Ironically MacBride's greatest political achievement was to raise political opponents, Fine Gael, to a position of real power and influence. Fine Gael representation jumped from a low of 31 seats in 1948 to 40 in 1951 and to 50 in 1957 a record for Fine Gael during the period 1934-1965, Fine Gael awareness of their increased political strength was evident in the formation of Costello's second coalition in which Costello was no longer content with being chairman of an inter-party government of equals but assumed the position of "chief" in a coalition government dominated by Fine Gael. The biggest political casualties of the inter-party coalition governments of the Fifties were the small political parties representing minority political interest. By 1961 both Clann na Poblachta and Clann na Talmhan were no longer represented in the Dáil and were on the point of political extinction.

International Ambassador of Peace

The fame and success which eluded MacBride in the field of domestic politics awaited him on the international scene. His cosmopolitan outlook, fluency in French, the international language of diplomacy, and the valuable experience in the world of international diplomacy gained as Minister of External Affairs made him ideally suited for work as a U.N. roving ambassador for peace. By 1961 he was a respected international diplomat and founder of Amnesty International, a world-wide organisation to highlight the plight of political prisoners of conscience throughout the world. An esteemed member of the International Commission of Jurists between 1963 and 1970, MacBride was chosen as U.N. Commissioner for Namibia in South West Africa and supervised that country's first tentative moves towards full independence. His unceasing work for international peace and world nuclear disarmament brought him to the top of the U.N. He eventually held the number two post in the United Nations, Assistant Secretary-General. In 1974 he became the first Irishman to receive the Nobel Peace Prize. Three years later when he received the Lenin Peace Prize he became the world's first recipient of the double peace award. In 1983, in his eightieth year, MacBride was made President of the U.N. Committee on world nuclear disarmament.

In the 1980s MacBride resumed practice at the Irish Bar and spent his last years as he had spent his first years in civilian life defending political prisoners in the Irish law courts. The driving force behind all MacBride's actions during a long and eventful life was a desire to expose injustice in all its forms and to help political prisoners whom he perceived to be victims of political oppression.

Appraisal

Described as a "child of the revolution", MacBride's transition from revolutionary activist to man of peace has been compared to the evolution of the Irish state born in bloodshed and developing into a fully fledged democracy within MacBride's life-time. The year 1937 was the first big turning-point in MacBride's life. For MacBride, the goal of a united thirty-two county Irish Republic remained unchanged. From 1937 MacBride resolved to use the institutions of state to work towards the republican ideal and to help those striving towards the same ideal who refused to give up unconstitutional methods. The constitutional path led MacBride into politics. As in his revolutionary career MacBride's rise in politics was meteoric. In the lead up to the 1948 general election he was being projected as a second and more glamorous de Valera. His eclipse in Irish politics was as sudden as his rise.

The recognition that eluded him on the domestic scene awaited him in the field of international diplomacy. Described by contemporary and U.N. colleague Proinsias Mac Aonghusa as a "visionary but an outsider" MacBride was always more at home on the international scene than he was in Ireland, whether as an international gun-smuggler for the IRA or as Minister for External Affairs between 1948 and 1951 or as internationally acclaimed champion of world peace. Yet MacBride, born and raised outside of Ireland, remained true to the patriotic ideals instilled by an English mother and the memory of a Fenian father. Although not an Irish native, MacBride became one of Ireland's finest representatives abroad, an ambassador of peace and justice everywhere in the world.

Landmarks in MacBride's Life (1904-88)

1904   *26th January*   Birth in Paris.

1918   *February*   Secret return to Ireland with his mother Maud Gonne MacBride after the execution of his father Major John MacBride.

1919-21   IRA activist during the War of Independence.

1921   *October - December*   Collins's aide-de-camp and courier during Treaty talks in London.

1922   *June 22nd*   Joined anti-Treaty forces in Four Courts, imprisoned after fall of the Four Courts and shared prison cell with anti-Treaty leader Rory O'Connor.

1923   *October*   Escaped from prison convoy transferring him to Kilmainham Jail.

1924-31   International journalist and principal travelling organiser of the IRA.

1936   Chief-of-Staff of the Republican wing of the IRA.

1937   Resigned from the IRA and commenced practice at the Irish Bar.

1946   *July*   Launched new Republican party Clann na Poblachta.

1947   *October 30th*   Entered Dáil as Deputy for Dublin South-West.

1948   *February*   Clann na Poblachta electoral success in by-elections during 1947 forced snap election on Fianna Fáil. 10 Clann na Poblachta seats essential for formation of anti-Fianna Fáil Coalition government.

1948   *February 14-18th*   MacBride took leading part in inter-party negotiations resulting in inter-party government.

1948-51   *February/May*   Minister for External Affairs - Republic of Ireland Act. Anti-Partition Campaign. Refusal to join N.A.T.O.

1951   *April*   Supported Costello in Mother and Child controversy and demanded resignation of Browne, Clann colleague and Minister for Health.

1951   *May*   Collapse of First Inter-Party Government.

1954   Refused to join Second Inter-Party Government.

1957   Lost his Dáil seat.

1961   Founder of Amnesty International.

1974   Received Nobel Peace Prize.

1977   Awarded Lenin Peace Prize.

1988   *January 15th*   Death in Dublin.